HI   TES

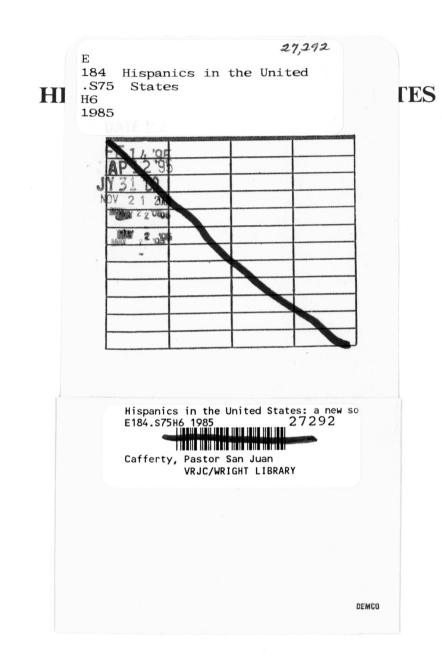

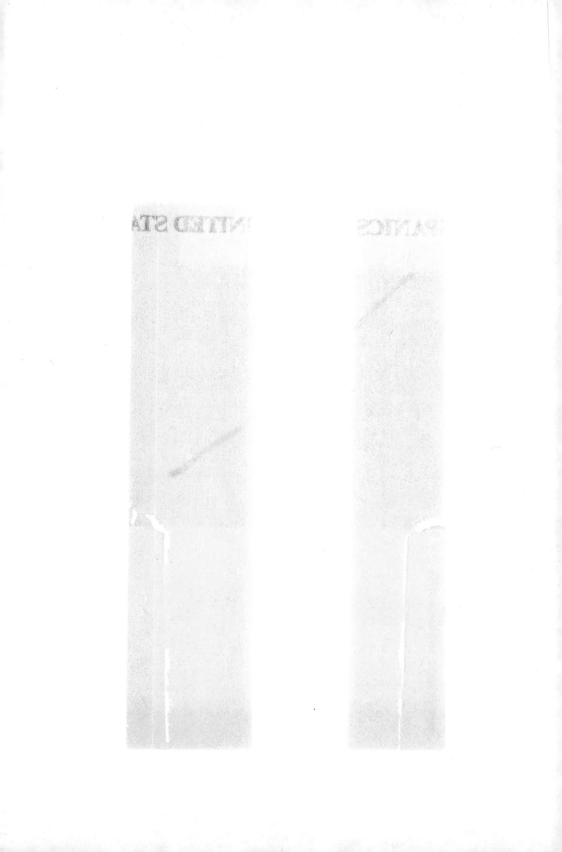

HISPANICS IN
THE UNITED STATES

A New Social Agenda

Edited by

Pastora San Juan Cafferty
and William C. McCready

Transaction Publishers
New Brunswick (U.S.A.) and London (U.K.)

Third Printing, 1992
Copyright © 1985 by Transaction Publishers,
New Brunswick, New Jersey 08903

Library of Congress Catalog Number: 84-23943
ISBN: 0-88738-018-2 (cloth) 0-87855-975-2 (paper)
Printed in the United States of America

Library of Congress Cataloging in Publication Data
Main entry under title:

Hispanics in the United States

1. Hispanic Americans—Addresses, essays, lectures.   I. Cafferty, Pastora
San Juan.   II. McCready, William C., 1941-
E184.S75H6 1985   973'.0468   84-23943
ISBN 0-88738-018-2
ISBN-0-87855-975-2 (pbk.)

Contents

Acknowledgments   vi

Introduction   1
     Pastora San Juan Cafferty and *William C. McCready*

1. A Demographic Portrait   7
     Teresa A. Sullivan
2. The "New" Immigration   33
     Pastora San Juan Cafferty
3. Culture and Religion   49
     William C. McCready
4. Toward a Model of Socialization for Hispanic Identity:
     The Case of Mexican-Americans   63
     Marco A. Martínez
5. Language and Social Assimilation   87
     Pastora San Juan Cafferty
6. Hispanics and Education   113
     Neil Fligstein and *Roberto M. Fernández*
7. Jobs and Employment for Hispanics   147
     George J. Borjas
8. Hispanics and Health Care   159
     Aida L. Giachello
9. Hispanics and the Social Service System   195
     Carmen Rivera-Martínez
10. Hispanics and the Criminal Justice System   215
     Leo M. Romero and *Luis G. Stelzner*
11. Political Participation   235
     Ricardo Tostado

Conclusion   253
     Pastora San Juan Cafferty and *William C. McCready*

Acknowledgments

We are deeply grateful to our many colleagues who have taken the time to discuss issues concerning Hispanics in American society with us over the years. We are particularly grateful to those of our colleagues who agreed to contribute the essays which constitute this book. They made this book possible.

The outstanding support of staff at the National Opinion Research Center and in particular its director, Norman Bradburn, facilitated our work. Susan Campbell and Suzanne Erfurth provided valuable editorial advice and assistance and the Word Processing Department (Cassandra Britton, Karla Maze, Irene Edwards, and Art Landeros) handled revisions and copy production most professionally. Peggy Osberger-Wilder provided research assistance early in the project and David Engstrom provided valuable assistance at every step. His collegial research and analysis contributed, not only to every chapter, but more importantly to designing and implementing a social agenda for Hispanics. We are in his debt.

Finally, without the encouragement of Irving Louis Horowitz and the fine staff at Transaction Books, this would not be a book at all, just an idea. The translation into reality is largely due to his constant support.

Introduction

Pastora San Juan Cafferty and *William C. McCready*

The essays in this book are meant to raise important questions concerning the social agenda for our country in the coming years. The United States began as a place of refuge and opportunity for those fleeing from oppression and persecution. Over the course of our history we have continued to be that place for peoples from many lands. However, as our country has developed, due in large part to the contributions of those many peoples, our very success has made it difficult for us to continue to see ourselves as a place of refuge and opportunity. We are entering an era of scarce resources and limited solutions. Many problems have proven to be less easily solved than we once thought they would be. Energy, full employment, access to equal opportunity, safety and security—all these and more are challenges we face which we are not fully confident of solving.

New migrants coming to this country are faced with a different society than that which faced forerunners. They have to deal simultaneously with a bureaucracy meant to improve their welfare and with diminishing resources in the society at large. They are viewed by many as unwelcome and threatening. Many whose families have been here for several generations are no longer in touch with their own immigrant roots. Still many others of those who come here not as strangers but either as citizens, although from another culture and place, or as people joining family who have already been here for many years—yet they are indistinguishable in the public's mind from those who are migrating here as true strangers.

Because of the changed social context within which immigrants find themselves and because of the changing nature of the immigrant populations themselves, new questions must be asked and new agendas for social policies must be established. Because of the numbers of Hispanic immigrants and the geography we share, those from Hispanic cultures are the subject of special concern.

Any serious attempt to understand the diverse complexity of Hispanics in the United States is an enormous challenge to research, theory, and social policy. It demands an understanding of the history of Hispanics in the United States, and of the United States as a nation of immigrants, as well as its ambivalence toward every "new" migration. It demands an

1

understanding of the institutional structures of American society, as well as of the importance of the traditions, experiences, and cultures that are the woof and warp of the Hispanic communities. More importantly, it demands an understanding of the socialization processes both within the ethnic community and in interaction with the majority society.

Hispanics share a common heritage, in that all the nations which constitute what is now Latin America were at one time or another colonized by Spain. The Spanish conquistador left his mark not only over all of South and Central America, but over vast portions of North America as well, including the Southeastern and the Southwestern United States. The mark of the conquistador also exists in the geopolitical sense in that all Hispanics come from nations to the south of the United States, nations which have shared a history of interaction with the English speaking country to the north. Hispanics lived in what is now the United States long before the thirteen colonies declared their independence from Great Britain, and Hispanics also constitute the largest number of the most recent immigrants to this country. They do not all share common ethnic memories or common symbols, or even speak the Spanish language, but the majority of them are identified both by themselves and by majority society as Hispanics. They are further identified not only as an ethnic group but as a racial minority. Demographers tell us Hispanics may be the largest minority in the United States by the end of the century.

Identification as a Hispanic is thus more than the condition of common racial or historical origins or of shared language, traditions, sentiments, or cultural networks. It is also a form of self-conceptualization that others assign or force upon the individual. It is important to understand this, for there is no guarantee that a shared ethnic and cultural heritage produces homogeneity of thought, feeling, behavior, or even group loyalty. The same Hispanic identity may have different meanings to its different bearers. There is evidence that certain features of ethnic identity are deeply imbedded and persist even after experience has shown them to be dysfunctional; other aspects of ethnic identity may be easily shed or subject to change over time. The strength of a person's identification with his ethnic origins is influenced by situational factors: during periods of cultural stress or political threat, individuals may return to familiar sources of comfort and help available within an ethnic group. These voluntary and involuntary aspects of ethnicity make it difficult to discuss the reality of Hispanics in the United States.

Part of the reality can be summarized in numbers and demographic descriptions. Between 1970 and 1980 the Hispanic population in the United States increased from 4.5 percent of the total to 6.4 percent. Eleven states account for nearly 90 percent of the Hispanic population, which is heavily metropolitan, despite stereotypes to the contrary. The median age of the Hispanic population is about 6 or 7 years younger than for the United States as a whole, with almost one-third of Hispanics in the United States under age 15. These numbers cannot adequately describe the nature of the differences between Hispanics and the majority society, nor do they describe the considerable differentiation among the various Hispanic subgroups; but they do offer some insight into the scope of the differences between Hispanics and the general U.S. population.

We also know that Hispanics in the United States have experienced prejudice, discrimination, and exploitation. The treatment of an ethnic group by the majority society is often dependent on the group's social and economic position. Although Mexican Americans inhabited the Southwest long before it was annexed by the United States, they have been segregated socially and economically for over a century. Puerto Ricans who became American citizens are seen (and see themselves) as strangers in a strange land. Cubans have been coming into the United States as political refugees since the nineteenth century, yet they are viewed as a recent large refugee migration from an unwelcome Communist stronghold in the Caribbean. Growing migration from Central and South America as well as from other Caribbean countries may be part of the continuing migration stream that has existed among the Spanish-speaking nations in Latin America for hundreds of years.

The influence of culture on behavioral patterns is a complex issue which continues to be debated by sociologists and anthropologists. Behavior may be interpreted as cast by ethnic culture and group identity, or as a reaction to poverty and feelings of alienation and discrimination. The relationship between ethnicity and social class is difficult to establish. Each ethnic group may contain within it several or all of the social classes found in American society. Members of the same ethnic group but of different social classes may share peoplehood, that is historical identification, but do not necessarily have similar values or behavior. While America is a nation of immigrants and thus a nation of ethnic groups, historically the pressure has been toward conformity to an Anglo-Saxon ideal. Theories of asssimilation for over two centuries resulted in policies which supported assimilation and conformity. In spite of these pressures, ethnic pluralism continues to be a reality in American society. In this context, Hispanics could be seen as yet another ethnic group, yet they are different.

First, the history of Hispanics in the United States antedates the reality of the United States as a nation. The Spanish had not only explored but had settled Florida, as well as parts of Alabama and Louisiana and large territories in what is now California, Texas, and New Mexico, in the sixteenth century. The Spanish conquistador took possession of land for God and the crown. His presence was perpetuated and assured by the presence of countless churches and schools which brought the Roman Catholic faith and allegiance to Spanish language and values to the native American tribes that populate the Southeast and Southwest United States. It was only in the nineteenth century after a brief war with Mexico that these territories became part of the United States. Even then the diversity of the Hispanic peoples inhabiting the territories was obvious even to their conquerors; bilingual schools flourished in California and in New Mexico while Texas banned the speaking of Spanish in public.

Later in that century when the United States fought a war with Spain, it found itself loath to give up the territories whose independence it had aided to win from Spain. Cuba finally established its political if not its economic independence from the United States in 1907. Puerto Rico became a commonwealth in 1952 and to this day its confusing political status is debated both at the United Nations and in the halls of Congress.

In a nation that has traditionally been preoccupied with questions of color and race, Hispanics pose a particular problem. The mixture of White (Spanish conquistador) and (American) Indian or Black (African slave) does not constitute a new race, yet both Hispanics and majority American society refer to a "brown" race and worry about a large non-White population and its possible inability to assimilate to majority White society.

Although native language retention has been a very real and continuing aspect of ethnic group life in America, Hispanic subgroups seem to have retained their language more than others. There are a number of explanations for this. One is that Hispanics were largely rural people until very recently, and retained their language because of ethnic and class isolation throughout the Southwestern states. Others argue that this isolation was not so much the result of geography and economic reality but discrimination (that continues in contemporary society). Others say that Hispanics have greater cultural and ethnic loyalty. Yet others point out that because of the continuing migration stream the language tradition in Hispanic communities renews itself. The reasons are many and complex; the facts are that Spanish language retention is seen as a threat to political and social cohesiveness in America. The fact that Spanish language retention and specifically bilingual education and bilingual provision of public services has become a civil rights issue in the Hispanic communities adds to the concern as well as the controversy.

A series of assumptions has long dominated formulation of the public policy agenda in this country. Public school systems were created to teach American democracy as well as the English language to the children of immigrants. Although educational policy may be the most clearly articulated statement of assimilation policy in the United States, it is not the only one. Public policies, the field of social welfare, criminal justice—all reflect assimilationist values. This disregard for the differences among us may create serious social problems.

While it is dangerous to ignore diversity, it is equally dangerous to assume certain behavioral characteristics based on group identity. The serious thinker expresses legitimate concern when he worries that any examination of Hispanics in the United States may result in negative stereotyping. Hispanics are individuals, and as such each is different. Hispanic identity may be a significant factor in individual identity, but it does not necessarily define it.

Sensitivity to ethnic identity in the formulation of public policy is difficult to achieve. To make a public health program responsive to the values of the ethnic community requires sensitivity. To create public health legislation flexible enough to address the diversity of need requires first an understanding of this diversity and then an understanding of its interpretation in policy and program formulation. It is difficult for the policymaker and the service provider to understand the needs of the poor and to meet these needs with a sensitivity that empowers the individual. This difficulty is only made more acute when the policymaker and the service provider are asked to address the needs of the Hispanic poor, for they are being expected to understand not only a class whose values are alien to them, but an ethnic group whose complexity and diversity they have not begun to understand.

To further complicate the issue, our knowledge about the Hispanics in the United States is scant. There is little data. Since most studies of Hispanics in the United States have used samples taken from communities densely populated by Hispanics, there is a legitimate concern that what we know about Hispanics may be typical only of those living in the barrio—an ethnic or class ghetto. Even when data is available, its interpretation is difficult. We know very little about the importance of group identity to the individual. We do not know how important it is for an individual to either belong to a particular ethnic group or to assimilate into a majority society. We know much less about how these processes take place.

The essays in this book have been designed with two goals in mind: first, to summarize and order what is known so that our understanding about specific social issues related to Hispanics can be increased; and second, to raise questions which need to be answered before our collective social agenda begins to adequately address the concerns of all Americans. We feel that the nature of the new migrations and their impact on the social context within which we all live is great enough and different enough to warrant these exploratory discussions. We are being forced to reexamine old conventions and design new models of social interaction to deal with this new phenomenon. We hope the essays contained within this book will be a starting point from which many other discussions and developments will follow.

1

A Demographic Portrait

Teresa A. Sullivan

Hispanics are cited as the fastest-growing minority in the United States. Seldom do such claims go beyond the intended shock effect and analyze what this means for the present and the future. Much of this vagueness results from various definitions of the term Hispanic. *Hispanics are referred to either as a minority group or as an ethnic group and then compared with other minority or ethnic groups, depending on the definition. Such comparisons result in different conclusions about the position of Hispanics in the United States. To cloud the issue further, Hispanics are often treated as a homogeneous group. When Hispanics are lumped into one group, important differences between Hispanic groups are missed. In this chapter, Teresa Sullivan argues that any conclusions about Hispanics must be "drawn from comparisons within Hispanic groups and from comparisons contrasting Hispanics to other groups." Comparisons must be made between comparable groups. A critical analysis is presented concerning the accuracy of the 1980 Census, the data base which will frame policy decisions for the next decade. Even though the 1980 Census is an improvement over the 1970 Census, Sullivan maintains that it still undercounted the number of Hispanics living in the United States. Sullivan describes the methodologies employed by the Census Bureau to report the size and composition of the Hispanic population and takes issue with the instruments developed for this task. After methodological questions are treated, the chapter proceeds with a demographic portrait of the Hispanic population and highlights the differences between Hispanic groups. Sullivan concludes by pointing out that the 1980 Census still leaves policymakers in the dark over such important issues as migration, mortality, and fertility of the Hispanic population. Recommendations for correcting deficiencies in the data are outlined.*

Contemporary issues in the demography of Hispanics are better understood in the framework of the population history of the Hispanic peoples in North America. The confrontation between English- and Spanish-speaking peoples was a dominant feature of the early European colonial period. Spain and England were combatants in the hostilities of the Old World and rivals in the conquest of the New World. Initially, however, their colonists had little contact with each other. There were relatively few Europeans in the vast areas of North America; the first population event of significance was the contact of Europeans with indigenous populations.

The indigenous populations fared poorly in both the English and Spanish colonies of North America. Contagious diseases brought by the conquerors largely accomplished the conquest. The word decimation passed into common usage in the European languages after the indigenous Mexican population came into contact with measles and smallpox. The devastating mortality brought about by European disease demoralized the native population, and superior European armaments completed their subjugation.

Later, as the colonial populations increased, their territory expanded. The English-speaking populations moved westward and southward from the eastern seaboard of what is now the United States. The Spanish-speaking population expanded eastward and northward from the Caribbean and from the present country of Mexico. Inevitably, the two migration patterns intersected and the two groups entered into open competition, and occasionally violent conflict, for land and other resources. The struggle for control in what is now the American Southwest resulted in a lengthy period of subjugation of the Spanish-speaking population (McLemore, 1973; Estrada et al., 1981).

Meanwhile, although retaining the languages of their European mother countries, the North American colonies became politically independent. Control over territorial borders became a test and proof of sovereignty. At least some armed conflict marked the establishment of control over many international borders during the 1800s. During the 1900s, control of the movement of persons across the borders also became a political issue. The United States, concerned about the increasing volume of immigration during the first two decades of this century, sharply limited immigration from the Eastern Hemisphere.

While Congress was debating immigration quotas, there was substantial public opinion in favor of curtailing immigration from Mexico and other countries of the Western Hemisphere. For a variety of political reasons, including the desire for friendly relations with other American nations and the influence of wealthy ranchers and railroad owners in the Southwest, no numerical limitations were placed on immigration from the Western Hemisphere. Not until 1965, with the passage of the amendments to the

Immigration and Nationality Act of 1952, were numerical limits placed on immigration from the Western Hemisphere. This quota took effect in 1968.

These political events meant that southward migration of the English-speaking population was defined as "internal migration," while the northward migration of the Spanish-speaking population was defined as "international migration" (and hence problematic). Well-established patterns of seasonal or cyclical migration across the U.S.-Mexico border became defined as "illegal" or "undocumented" immigration. Nevertheless, because social and economic networks already spanned the border, the immigration did not end.

The Hispanic Population

The term *Hispanic population* in the United States vastly oversimplifies the situation. The heterogeneity of the Hispanic population reduces the term to a merely heuristic device. As each element of this population's history indicates, there are many variables that divide the Hispanic population into distinctive and important subpopulations.

One variable is race. The original Spanish colonists—and many of their descendants—are Caucasians phenotypically indistinguishable from the English colonists. Some of the Hispanic population, especially if that term is defined by Spanish surname, are American Indians. Others are Black, the descendants of African slaves brought to the Caribbean islands or (in small numbers) to Mexico. The descendants of these groups are the Hispanics, some of whom consider themselves to be a separate "brown" race.

A second variable is language. While many Hispanics speak Spanish as their primary language, many do not. English speakers frequently do not distinguish among speakers of Spanish and speakers of Portuguese or French who also come from the Western Hemisphere, but the distinction is important.

A third variable is time of arrival in what is now the United States. Some Hispanics, notably those of the American Southwest, trace their origin to the Spanish colonists who had arrived before the United States had expanded beyond the Appalachians. Others are immigrants or their children—and the immigrants must also be subdivided into legal residents and undocumented persons.

The fourth variable is national origin, which interacts with time of arrival. The Hispanos arrived before there existed a Mexican nationality; other Hispanics have diverse national origins in the Western Hemisphere. Some still immigrate from Spain. The major national groups identified in the U.S. Census reports are Mexicans, Cubans, "Central and South Americans" (excluding Brazilians), and "other Spanish" (excluding Portuguese). Puerto Ricans are also identified separately, although since 1907 they have been U.S. citizens. It is believed that most Hispanos who identify themselves by Spanish origin report themselves as "other Spanish."

A fifth important variable is minority status. Because of the historic subjugation of Spanish-speaking people, especially in the Southwest, Hispanics share with Blacks and other racial minority groups a history of de jure and de facto segregation. Before the contemporary civil rights movement, some persons of Spanish origin attempted complete assimilation with the majority White population in an effort to avoid social and economic discrimination. More recently, with the rise of the Hispanic civil rights movement, there has been a strong reassertion of the values and dignity of the Hispanic community. But not all Hispanics agree that they themselves are part of a minority group, and some who claim minority status for themselves would reject it for certain others (for example, they might reject it for well-educated professionals who immigrate from South American countries).

Demographers have conducted quite different studies depending on the key variable chosen as defining "the" Hispanic population. Some tables published by the Census Bureau and the U.S. Commission for Civil Rights clearly indicate a conception of the Hispanic population as a minority group to be compared with Blacks, Asian-Americans, and other minorities. Studies done by demographers in substantive demography have viewed Hispanics as another ethnic group to be compared with previous ethnic groups. National origin is often the key defining variable for these studies; Mexican-Americans or Puerto Ricans are compared with ethnic groups of European origin. Migration studies, particularly of international immigration, tend to stress time of arrival in the United States. For these studies, "the" Hispanic population is an immigrant population or a population made up of immigrants and their children.

These considerations suggest an important caveat for those interested in the demography of Hispanics: comparisons of research results must be made from comparable populations. Apparently conflicting results may be explained by analyzing the definitions of the populations studied. More seriously, because of the "ethnic group" approach of many demographers, bits and pieces of information about Hispanics are scattered throughout the demographic literature without being brought together into a unified statement. Finally, in the absence of good historical data, the Hispanic population must always be studied in reference to, or in comparison with, another population to provide context. Ultimately, a demographic approach to the Hispanic population must be dialectic in that its conclusions must be based on data drawn both from comparisons within the Hispanic groups and from comparisons contrasting Hispanics to other groups. Without this dialectical approach, many of the conclusions of demographers will appear to be paradoxical or misleading.

Demographic Methods and Data

Demographers are especially sensitive to the quality of data available for their studies. For this reason, many of the most important studies on Hispanics have devoted a disproportionate number of pages to data issues. (For important examples see Siegel and Passel, 1979; Hernández et al., 1973.) Even so, assessment of data reliability and validity remains one of the most important incomplete tasks in the study of Hispanic demography.

The major data sources used in recent studies of Hispanics include the monthly Current Population Survey and its supplements (Featherman and Hauser, 1978); the Survey of Income and Education (Tienda, 1981); and the General Social Surveys (Sullivan and Pedraza-Bailey, 1980)). A number of important surveys have recently become available, including the new National Longitudinal Surveys of Labor Force Participation and Work Experience, which include an oversampling of Hispanics; the "High School and Beyond" study; and the National Chicano Survey. The Hispanic Health and Nutrition Survey (HHANES) will soon be available. It is the first large-scale survey of Hispanic health in the country. Several important surveys of particular segments of the Hispanic population have been reported in the literature (e.g. see the one described in Portes, 1979). The 1940 and 1950 censuses, while not "new," are being repackaged as machine-readable microdata sets. When available, they will provide a more versatile resource for historical research then the published tables for those censuses.

It seems likely that the key resource for the next five years will be the 1980 U.S. Census. This is true for many reasons. It is the most complete data source; only with the census are there sufficient cases to study small subgroups of the Hispanic population (e.g. Colombians; Hispanics living outside the eleven states that account for 89 percent of the Hispanic population; the elderly Hispanic population). The census forms the basis for the sampling frames used by government and private survey researchers during the subsequent ten years. Moreover, the U.S. census is used for a variety of public purposes, including Congressional reapportionment, federal revenue sharing, identification of target populations for social services, and population projections. Many states use the census for legislative redistricting, for state revenue sharing, and for projecting needed facilities. For all these reasons, the census is a critical data base that requires further discussion.

The Identification Problem

The Bureau of the Census has used a number of identifiers for the Hispanic population or its subgroups (Siegel and Passell, 1979; Hernández et al. 1973; Haub, 1981; Passel and Word, 1980). These include:

- Country of birth: Mexico, Cuba, Central or South America, other (1880-1980), Puerto Rico (1950-1980).
- Country of birth of parents (1880-1970).
- Mexican "race" (1930).
- Spanish surname (five Southwestern states,1950-1980).
- Spanish mother tongue (1940-1970).
- Language other than English (1980).
- Self-identification of Spanish origin: Mexican, Puerto Rican, Cuban, Central or South American, other (1970); (the terms *Mexican, Mexican-American,* and *Chicano* were all coded as "Mexican"), Puerto Rican, Cuban, other Spanish/Hispanic (1980).

The self-identification question was first asked in the March 1969 Current Population Survey, and experimentation with it continued throughout the 1970s. In the 1980 Census, two forms of the self-identification question were asked (U.S. Census, 1980, App. E). The first was asked on 100 percent of census forms: Is this person of Spanish/Hispanic origin or descent?

Fill one circle

○ No (not Spanish/Hispanic)
○ Yes, Mexican, Mexican-Amer., Chicano
○ Yes, Puerto Rican
○ Yes, Cuban
○ Yes, other Spanish/Hispanic

The second was asked on a 22 percent sample of questionnaires: "What is this person's ancestry?" A blank was provided for a hand-written answer. A version of the first question had been asked on the 1970 Census of a 15 percent sample of the population. The second question was new in 1980 and replaced the previously asked question about parents' birthplace.

As this abundance of identifiers suggests, the size of the Hispanic population depends on the identifier used. Table 1.1 shows that the number of Hispanics in the United States in 1970 ranged from 5.2 million to 10.1 million, depending on identifier. The Spanish origin (i.e. self-identification) figure of 9.1 million is usually reported now as "the" figure for 1970, partly because it is comparable to the measure asked of 100 percent of the

TABLE 1.1
Size of Hispanic Population According to Six Identifiers, United States and
Southwestern States, 1 April 1970

Identifier	United States	Southwestern States[1]
Spanish origin[2]	9,072,602	5,008, 556
Spanish surname	n/a	4,667,975
Spanish language[3]	9,589,216	5,662,700
Spanish heritage[4]	9,294,509	6,188, 362
Spanish language or surname	10,114,878	6,188,362
Spanish birth or parentage[5]	5,241,892	2,321,642

n/a = not applicable
1. Arizona, California, Colorado, New Mexico, and Texas.
2. Self-identification.
3. All persons of Spanish mother tongue and all other persons in families which the head or wife reported Spanish mother tongue.
4. An identifier which combined the following: persons of Spanish language or surname in the five Southwestern states, persons of Puerto Rican birth or parentage in the Three Middle Atlantic states, and persons of Spanish language in the remaining states and the District of Columbia.
5. An identifier that refers to country of birth of the person's parents.
Source: Siegel and Passel (1979).

population in 1980. (See, e.g. U.S. Census, 1981c:9.) At this writing, self-identification appears to be the identifier of choice.

But self-identification is by no means a problem-free identifier (see Sullivan et al., 1983). Individuals' responses as Hispanic or non-Hispanic may vary from one time to the next. Longitudinal matches of responses to the Current Population Survey showed response consistency of 91-95 percent for all Spanish origins. The consistency of "other Spanish" origins was lowest, 41-47 percent. The consistency of response was highest for Puerto Rican origin (92-95 percent), with Mexican and Cuban origins intermediate in consistency. In another study, 76 percent of those who reported ancestors from Hispanic countries also reported a Spanish origin for themselves; the percentage was highest for those with Spanish surnames, and it also varied directly with the time elapsed since the arrival of the ancestor (Siegel and Passel, 1979; U.S. Census, 1974). Two other studies by the Census Bureau have inquired into inconsistent responses.

A related problem is incorrect responses. The response "Central or South American" was dropped in 1980 because of the confusion about the expression in 1970. In 1970, many non-Hispanics confused "Central or South America" with the Midwestern and Southern portion of the United States. It appears that despite efforts to avoid this problem, the 1980 Census involves a similar error. Critics charged that non-Hispanics had to read through a whole list of Hispanic identities before finding a suitable response. Pretests showed that non-Hispanics would circle the word *American* and cross out the word *Mexican* in *Mexican-American*, apparently to indicate native birth or American identity. In response, the Census Bureau made the option "No (not Spanish/Hispanic)" first in this list and abbreviated "American."

Census Bureau officials now privately concede that this question still had high rates of error. So far unpublished data indicate that 30-40 percent of the "Mexicans" in some Southern states are Black—a likely indication of response error. Critics hypothesize that poor readers or persons wishing to identify themselves as "Americans" (even in the abbreviated term "Mexican-Amer."), checked off the "Mexican" response.

A different and unanticipated response error was a massive reporting of Hispanic identity as a "race." The race question read: "Is this person _____?" and was followed by fourteen classifications (none Hispanic) and a category marked "other" followed by a space to fill in. Persons who wrote in "French," "German," and similar designations were recoded as "White." Persons who wrote in "Cambodian" or "Vietnamese" were recoded as Asian. Persons who wrote in "Spanish," "Mexican," or other Hispanic designations were designated as "other." As a result, the racial classification of Hispanics will appear to change dramatically between 1970 and 1980. In 1970, only 1 percent of Spanish-origin persons classified themselves as being of "other" race; in 1980, 40 percent reported their race as "other."

In Texas, where there were 45,026 persons of "other races" in 1970, there were 1,160,090 in 1980—an increase of over 2,400 percent—while the Spanish-origin population increased 62.2 percent! Some 114,000 of these "others"—people who were neither White, Black, Asian, nor American Indian, Eskimo, or Aleut—lived in Bexar County (San Antonio), which is heavily Hispanic. Other states with large Hispanic populations reported similar increases in persons of "other" races, from 843 percent in New York to 1,412 percent in Florida. It is possible that these loci of heavy immigration from all areas may truly have experienced increased racial heterogeneity. The Texas data, however, make it likely that Hispanics are choosing new expressions of identity, at least in terms of race. This analysis is based on data taken from the U.S. Census (1973a,b, 1981a,d).

Demographers normally report demographic change in terms of a balancing equation: population at time 2 is equal to the population at time 1, plus births and immigrants, minus deaths and emigrants. This discussion suggests that the Hispanic population may also grow (or shrink) through changes in the identification process, a possibility that could contaminate many demographic conclusions.

The possibility of "recruitment" into the Hispanic population is most dramatically posed in terms of third-party identification. In the 1970 Census, parents were allowed to report the Hispanic identity of their children. Later, Census Bureau personnel changed their procedures, and children under 14 were classified as Hispanic if either parent was Hispanic, with the result that the Hispanic population took a 1-year leap of 300,000 persons. In most censuses and surveys, one person reports data for an entire household. This poses the possibility that many Hispanics are not self-identified as they would identify themselves.

Finally, self-identification cannot be used in the "balancing equation" presented above because one cannot self-identify background on birth and death certificates. By definition, this must be done by someone else. This point will be developed further in the following section.

Size and Coverage of the Population

The estimated size of the Hispanic population, according to Census Bureau reports, is as follows:

TABLE 1.2
Estimated Size of Hispanic Population (U.S. Census Data)

Year	Size
1 April 1970	9.1 million
March 1977	11.3 million
March 1978	12.0 million
March 1979	12.1 million
March 1980	13.2 million
1 April 1980	14.6 million

These figures indicate an intercensal growth rate of 3.8 percent a year, a growth rate that would cause the Hispanic population to double in about eighteen years if it continued. By comparison, the population growth of the United States during 1970-80 was 1.1 percent and the Black population grew at an annual average rate of 1.7 percent. The 1980 Census figures make the United States the seventh largest "Hispanic" country in the world, exceeded only by Mexico, Spain, Argentina, Colombia, Peru, and Venezuela.

The 61 percent growth in the Hispanic population was not anticipated by the Census Bureau. This is indicated by the intercensal estimates; one month before the census, the Hispanic population was estimated to be 1.4 million persons smaller than the subsequent enumeration. The other intercensal estimates also suffer from inaccuracies and changes in procedure. For example, a processing problem in the March 1979 Current Population

Survey led to published estimates that were too small by about 0.3 million (U.S. Census, 1981c).

The initial response to the 1980 data by the Census Bureau was that there had been an "overcount," and indeed the enumeration was larger than the expected figure. But the expected figure, especially for Hispanics, was probably much too low. The expected figure is based on the balancing equation previously mentioned.

$$\text{Population}_{1980} = \text{Population}_{1970} + \text{Births}_{1970\text{-}80} - \text{Deaths}_{1970\text{-}80}$$
$$+ \text{Immigrants}_{1970\text{-}80} - \text{Emigrants}_{1970\text{-}80}$$

Every element on the right side of this equation is problematic. The population in 1970 was probably undernumerated by an unknown percentage (Siegel and Passel, 1979). Vital statistics data on Hispanics are sadly lacking. During 1970-80, births and deaths were classified by Hispanic background in only four states, and each of these states uses slightly different coding procedures. The inadequacy of immigration and emigration data is well known. Because many of the undocumented aliens are undoubtedly Hispanic—and their numbers are unknown—it seems likely that Hispanic immigration data are especially poor. Finally, changes in census procedures, patterns of identification, and other unknown factors affected the left side of the equation but not the right side. For example, Spanish-language census publicity and census forms probably improved the coverage (and therefore the size) of the Hispanic population in 1980.

Demographers have developed a number of techniques for determining the coverage of the population in such situations. Unfortunately—and this is a fact little understood—none of these techniques appears to work satisfactorily for Hispanics. The methodology underlying most demographic techniques rests on one of two assumptions: (1) the population is closed—that is, there is virtually no international migration; (2) there are multiple records kept on individuals in the population. The former assumption is used in developing countries, where inadequate data are nevertheless transformed into usable statistics. This assumption, however, does not seem reasonable for the U.S. Hispanic population.

The second assumption is used in economically advanced countries, where vital statistics data, social security or tax records, and other data sources can be used to cross-check facts. Unfortunately, none of these auxiliary records provides an adequate identifier of Hispanics. Recording Hispanic surnames, while possible, is reported only for five states (see Table 1.1). The most important result of these inadequate auxiliary data is that the error of coverage (i.e., undercount or overcount) cannot be established. As Judge Gilmore wrote in his opinion in *Young v. Klutznick,* a court case in which the City of Detroit challenged the accuracy of the 1980 Census:

> All of the experts agree that in deriving an estimate of the undercount for Hispanics, novel problems are presented arising from the fact that accurate birth, death, immigration and emigration statistics are not available. Thus, a demographic analysis, comparable to the demographic analysis for white people and Black people, which can adjust the actual count . . . cannot be completed for Hispanics [*Young v. Klutznick*, 497 F. Supp. 1318, 1328].

It seems likely that there was an undercount of Hispanics in 1980. U.S. experience suggests that undercounts will be higher in low-income, poorly educated populations, especially those that are rural or geographically mobile. Historically, the South has had especially high rates of under-enumeration. Language barriers and motivations to avoid the government are additional obstacles to a complete count. To a greater or lesser extent, these variables tend to be more characteristic of minority groups than of the White majority.

All these characteristics apply with particular force to the Hispanic population that has been enumerated. The most recent data indicate that Hispanic-origin families reported a mean household income of $17,168, $6,120 less per year than majority Whites (U.S. Census, 1981b: 22). Over one-fifth (21.6 percent) were below the poverty level in 1980, compared with 26.6 percent of all Blacks and 8 percent of all Whites (U.S. Census, 1981d: 56). Median schooling of Hispanic-origin males and females over age 14 lags 1.9 years behind that of majority Whites; for those aged 25 and over, the lag is 2.2 years for males and 2.3 years for females (U.S. Census, 1980a: 8-10). Although not as rural as many people believe, 16.8 percent of the Hispanic population lives in nonmetropolitan areas (U.S. Census, 1981d: 55). About 73 percent of the Hispanic-origin population lives in the Southern or Western states. Hispanics include large numbers of persons who are recent immigrants or their children, as well as many who have recently moved to the United States (U.S. Census, 1980a: 6). Native Spanish speakers are among the most likely of all Americans to retain their mother tongue. Approximately 18 percent of Mexican-American men in the civilian labor force are believed to be Spanish monolinguals (Tienda and Neidert, 1981: 266). There is no direct evidence of motivation to avoid the government, but there are indicators that Hispanic-origin citizens are less likely to register to vote and to vote (see, e.g., U.S. Census 1981d: 27). But in addition, there is a population of undocumented aliens—a population of undetermined size—whose members have an incentive to avoid all contact with the federal government.

An underenumeration of Hispanics would have important ramifications for political representation, social services, projections for school enrollment, revenue sharing, accuracy of future sample surveys, and a host of other areas. For these reasons, research on errors of coverage is badly needed. Two research efforts have recently been undertaken. The Census Bureau has undertaken an ambitious program to match census records with other government data. Their preliminary, unpublished estimate of Hispanic undercount appears to be in the range of 4-5 percent. Unfortunately, this procedure cannot accurately detect persons who have avoided *all* contact with government agencies.

The second effort is an independent estimate of the size of the Hispanic population in Texas, Arizona, and New Mexico. This study is based upon a matching of Catholic burial records with state death certificates; the data are then recorded by Spanish surname using Census Bureau procedures. The advantage of this procedure is that it generates a new set of data independent of the census, but a set that persons cannot avoid: the records of their own deaths (Sullivan et al., 1981).

Data Quality

Most data sources are subject to sampling error; all data sources are subject to response error. Sampling error can be estimated (although as noted above, this does become somewhat more problematic for Hispanics). Response error, however, is difficult to estimate and yet it may be far more important than sampling error. The same variables that make a population susceptible to underenumeration may also affect the quality of responses.

The one type of response "error" for Hispanics that has been extensively studied is variation in Hispanic identity (Fernández, 1975). A little work has been done on errors of age reporting. Siegel and Passel (1979) find little evidence of age heaping, although there is evidence of age misreporting. Other researchers have found evidence of age exaggeration among older Hispanics (Sullivan et. al., 1981). (This finding is commonly made in Latin American populations and in the U.S. Black population.) But other aspects of response error have been ignored.

The type of response error or variation that is most important is one that for religious, cultural, social, or economic reasons distinguishes Hispanics from other Americans (or distinguishes among Hispanic groups). For example, Sullivan and Pedraza-Bailey (1980) matched Hispanic and majority White respondents in the General Social Surveys on objective indicators of social class. At equivalent socioeconomic levels, Hispanics were significantly less likely than majority Whites to report themselves as "middle-class." For Hispanics as a group, self-reported class ranking was downwardly biased. Whether such response variation applied to many variables is not yet known.

An important aspect of response error is nonresponse. The majority of the recent research studies on Hispanics have been done with a data set that has been processed by the U.S. Census Bureau (e.g. the Survey of Income and Education, the Current Population Survey, the Census itself). The Census Bureau uses a procedure called "hot-deck editing" to supply any data missing for a respondent. These "allocated" data, as they are called, account for up to 20 percent of the responses on some variables in the 1970 Census. To our knowledge, no researcher has yet analyzed edited data to see whether there are nonresponse patterns unique to Hispanics. Instead, allocated data have been used without question by most researchers. This is an issue that deserves prompt attention.

Demographic data and techniques are not yet adequate for studies of the Hispanic population. A good deal of unglamorous and painstaking work is required before demographers can place full confidence in their substantive conclusions about Hispanics. Nevertheless, some of these substantive conclusions seem to hold despite data defects. It is to these issues—fertility, mortality, migration, and related issues—that we now turn.

The following section will review the major substantive conclusions about Hispanics; the references cited provide detailed information. All these conclusions, however, should be considered in light of the preceding discussion. Unless otherwise noted, the term *Hispanic population* in the following sections is identical with the *Spanish-origin population* (i.e., the self-identified population). All conclusions are based upon the author's analysis of Census Bureau data, except where otherwise noted.

Population Composition and Distribution

The Hispanic population increased from 4.5 percent of the U.S. population in 1970 to 6.4 percent in 1980. By 1980, Mexican-origin persons accounted for about 60 percent of the Hispanic population. Between 1977 and 1980, the estimated proportion of Hispanics of Mexican origin fluctuated between 58.1 and 60.6 percent. Puerto Rican origin accounted for 13.8 percent of Hispanics in 1980. There have been small declines in the estimated proportion of Puerto Ricans for every year since 1977, when the estimated proportion was 15.5 percent. The proportion of Cuban origin has fluctuated between 5.7 and 6.6 percent, with 6.3 percent estimated in 1980. Central or South American origin accounted for 7.7 percent of the Hispanic population in 1980, the same percentage as in 1977. "Other Spanish origin" has fluctuated between 11.4 and 12.7 percent since 1977; the 1980 estimate was 12.3 percent. The pattern of small fluctuations suggests that there has been no major shift in national origin groups, although there may be a relative decline in the proportion of Puerto Rican origin. Some observers attribute this trend to return migration to the island.

Eleven states account for 89 percent of the Hispanic population. The majority of Hispanics still live in the five Southwestern states, with the largest concentration in California (3.5 million) and Texas (2.7 million). The proportion of the population that is Hispanic increased in 1970-79 in every Southwestern state except Colorado, where it declined slightly. In California, the Hispanic percentage increased from 11.9 to 15.8 percent; in Texas, it increased from 16.4 to 20.4 percent. Almost one-third of New Mexico's population was Hispanic in 1979. Outside the Southwest, 9 percent of Florida's population and 8 percent of New York's were composed of Hispanics in 1979. Illinois and Pennsylvania recorded substantial increases in the proportion of Hispanics. Other states with substantial Hispanic populations are New Jersey and Michigan.

The Hispanic population of the Southwest is 86 percent Mexican origin. The Puerto Rican-origin population, which is heavily urban, is concentrated in Northeastern cities, with growing concentrations in major Midwestern cities, especially Chicago. The Cuban-origin population is concentrated in Florida, with a secondary concentration in New York City and its New Jersey suburban area. Many of the "other Spanish" are found in New Mexico and Colorado, where it is believed that they are "Hispanos" (the descendants of Spanish colonists; see Jaffe et al., 1980).

Within states there are also distinctive patterns of Hispanic residence. In the Southwest, the concentration of Spanish surnames is greatest near the international border and diminishes toward the states' northern borders. Outside the Southwest, Hispanics are concentrated in major metropolitan areas.

Despite a hardy stereotype of Hispanics as rural farm workers, the Hispanic population is heavily concentrated in metropolitan areas, and the Hispanic metropolitan population is concentrated in central cities. However, trend data for 1977-80 reveal a slight deconcentration trend:

TABLE 1.3
Proportion of Hispanics in Metropolitan Areas and Central Cities

Year	Metropolitan %	Central Cities %
March 1977	85.0	51.3
March 1978	84.0	50.0
March 1979	84.0	49.0
March 1980	83.5	48.2

By comparison, in the non-Hispanic population the proportion in metro-politan areas hovered around 67 percent.

The Puerto Rican-origin population is most likely to live in central cities—75 percent, compared to 25 percent of the non-Hispanic popula-tion and 43 percent of the Mexican-origin population. The slight decline in the proportion of Puerto Ricans in the Hispanic population may help explain the decline in central city residence. The Cuban-origin population, while the most likely to live in metropolitan areas (96.7 percent compared with 79.3 percent for Mexican origin), are also the most suburbanized: 57.2 percent live outside the central cities of metropolitan areas. One-fifth of the Mexican-origin population live outside metropolitan areas, compared with only 3 percent of the Cuban-origin population.

Historically, although the Hispanic population has suffered from various forms of segregation, indices of residential segregation for Hispanics have been fairly low (Grebler et al., 1970; Massey, 1979). But segregation tends to be higher in central cities than in suburbs. (Three exceptions to this generalization are Miami, Minneapolis-St. Paul, and Portland.) The immi-grant Hispanic population is noticeably more segregated than the native-born.

Age and Sex Composition

Possibly the most significant demographic fact about the Hispanic popu-lation is its age. Although the median age of both the U.S. and Hispanic populations has been increasing slightly, the median age of the Hispanic population is still 6-7 years below that of the non-Hispanic population. It is almost 8 years below that of the White population, and almost 2 years below that of the Black population.

TABLE 1.4
Median Age of Hispanic and Non-Hispanic Populations

Year	Hispanic	Non-Hispanic
March 1977	21.7	29.2
March 1978	22.1	29.5
March 1979	22.0	29.8
March 1980	22.1	31.0
1 April 1980	23.2	30.0

For the U.S. population as a whole, there was a substantial decline in 1970-80 in number of children. But the Hispanic population remains young, with 11 percent under age 5 (compared with 7 percent in the general population) and almost one-third under age 15 (compared with 22.7 percent). On the other hand, only 4.8 percent of the Hispanic population was age 65 or over compared with 11.3 percent of the general population. Thus, the age dependency ratio for Hispanics is only a little larger than that for the country as a whole, but it is a result of a youthful age structure rather than a combination of dependent elders and children.

The age structure of subgroups within the Hispanic population varies substantially. The younger group, of Puerto Rican origin, has a median age of 20.7. The oldest group, of Cuban origin, has a median age of 33.5. Unlike the other groups, however, there has been a substantial decline in the median age of those of Cuban origin from its 1977 figure of 37.7 years. One simple explanation for this is sampling variability, given the small size of the Cuban-origin population. It is also possible that the most recent group of Cuban refugees was younger, on average, than the resident Cuban-origin population. Cuban fertility does not explain the lower median age. For other groups, the median age in March 1980 was: Mexican origin, 21.4 years; Central/South Americans, 25.1 years; other Spanish, 22.1 years.

The sex ratio for all Hispanics is approximately 100; that is, there are approximately 100 Hispanic males per 100 Hispanic females. This is a relatively greater number of males compared with the general population, which has a sex ratio of 94. The sex ratio varies by Hispanic subgroup.

TABLE 1.5
Sex Ratio of Hispanic Subgroups, 1980 Census

Subgroup	Ratio
Mexican origin	106
Puerto Rican origin	85
Cuban origin	99
Central/South American origin	82
Other Spanish origin	97

The surplus of males in the Mexican-origin population is characteristic of an immigrant population, although it is not nearly so lopsided as the sex ratios of European immigrants at the turn of the century. The sex ratios for Cuban origin and "other Spanish origin" are somewhat higher than for the general population; for the "other Spanish origin," a young age structure helps to account for this favorable sex ratio. (The sex ratio tends to be close to 100 after childhood and through the young adult years.) It is difficult to explain, especially in light of the young age structure, the female-dominated Puerto Rican-origin and Central/South American-origin sex ratios. A sex ratio this lopsided is often considered evidence of a social or economic problem; it may also alert researchers to a large differential under-count of young males.

Marital Status and Fertility

In March 1979, Hispanic-origin women were more likely than Hispanic-origin men to be widowed or divorced, and less likely to be single:

TABLE 1.6
Marital Status of Spanish-Origin Men and Women

Marital Status	Men %	Women %
Single	34.8	27.4
Married	60.2	60.2
Widowed	1.4	6.3
Divorced	3.5	6.1

These percentages were fairly stable during 1976-80. A longer time period (1970-80) shows that the divorce ratio for Spanish-origin persons has in-creased from 61 to 94—a sharp increase, but not so sharp as the 44 to 92 increase registered by Whites. The divorce ratio for Blacks in 1980 was 203. (The divorce ratio is the number of divorced persons per 1,000 mar-ried persons with spouse present.) There is now a small literature on His-panic marital instability (e.g. see Frisbie et al., 1978).

Looking at subgroups, "other Spanish" were less likely to be married; Puerto Ricans were the most likely to be divorced; and those of Cuban origin were the most likely to be married. Over 10 percent of Cuban-origin women are widows, a larger proportion than in the general population. (This fact is probably related to the older age structure of Cubans.)

It is commonly assumed that Hispanics marry at an early age. Recent data indicate, on the contrary, that Hispanic women are more likely to be single at age 20 than the general population. At age 20, 78.9 percent of all women and 83.6 percent of Spanish-origin women are still single. Over 94 percent of Spanish-origin men are still single at this age. Mexican-origin persons seem to marry at somewhat earlier ages than other Hispanics: 84.2 percent of Mexican-origin women and 92.1 percent of Mexican-origin men are single at age 20.

Several investigations indicate that Hispanic levels of exogamy may be rising (Fitzpatrick and Gurak, 1979; Grebler et al., 1970; Murgia and Frisbie, 1977). This will be an important phenomenon to monitor, not least of all because it affects the number of persons who identify themselves as Hispanic.

Hispanic fertility is high, but it is falling. Rindfuss and Sweet (1977), in their historical study of fertility rates, found that Mexican-American women had the highest rates, being superseded only by American Indian women during the 1960s. In 1970, Spanish-origin women aged 45-49 who were, or at one time had been married, had borne 3.8 children on average, compared with 2.8 for all women. But by 1979, Spanish-origin women expected only 2.4 children on average, compared with 2.1 for the general population. Actual numbers of Hispanic births, however, will remain high for two reasons: the population is relatively young, so that there are many Hispanic women entering the chilldbearing years, and Hispanic women tend to bear their children at younger ages. In 1979, Hispanic women aged 18-24 had completed 36.9 percent of births they expected in their lifetime, compared with 25.3 percent for the general population. Between June 1978 and June 1979, about 10 percent of all U.S births were born to Hispanic women, although they comprised only 6 percent of the women of childbearing age.

Bradshaw and Bean (1972) found a high rate of premarital conceptions, premarital births, and short birth intervals for Mexican-American women. Sabagh (1980) found that Mexican-American women desire larger families. Other studies (Marcum and Bean, 1976; Kritz and Gurak, 1976) have suggested that controlling for socioeconomic variables does not eliminate the fertility differential between majority White and Mexican-American women. While there are fewer studies on other Hispanic groups, these results seem sufficient to suggest that the cultural context of childbearing is an important issue for understanding Hispanic fertility levels. High fertility, in turn, is an important issue in terms of the size and growth of the Hispanic population.

Family Status

In 1980 there were 3.1 million Hispanic-origin families, of which 76.5 percent were husband-wife families and 19.2 percent were families headed by a female. The majority of Hispanics under age 18 were living in families. About three-quarters of them were living with both parents, and one-fifth lived with their mother only. Hispanic families were larger, on average, than non-Hispanic families. The average number of persons in a Hispanic family is 3.85 persons, compared with 3.28 persons for non-Hispanic families.

There are significant differences in family status by type of Hispanic origin. Mexican-origin familes are larger (4.07 persons) and less likely to be headed by a women. But 40 percent of Puerto Rican families are maintained by women; this proportion is comparable to that found in the Black community.

Angel and Tienda (1982) found that all Hispanic husband-wife households are more likely to be extended households than among majority Whites. Over one-fifth of households headed by Mexican or Central/South American women are extended; over one-fourth of households headed by "other Spanish" women are extended. Puerto Rican women are again an exception: only 12.3 percent of households headed by women are extended, less than the majority white proportion of 16.5 percent.

Migration

Between 1975 and 1978, 32 percent of all Hispanics had moved within the same SMSA (Standard Metropolitan Statistical Area), compared with 24 percent of all non-Hispanics. There was no difference between the proportion of Hispanic and non-Hispanic persons who moved from one SMSA to another. Thus, in terms of internal migration, Hispanics are notable for short-distance moves.

The more interesting fact about Hispanics is the percentage of international migrants among them. Among both male and female respondents, 5 percent of Hispanics reported they had moved from abroad to an SMSA during 1975-78. This compares with about 1 percent of the non-Hispanic population. Thus, not only does the Hispanic population contain a large number of immigrants—about 13 percent of them are not citizens—it also contains an exceptionally large number of recent immigrants.

While most demographers who have analyzed illegal immigration from Hispanic countries have concluded that the *stock* of illegal immigrants is not so large as the speculated estimates of 5-6 million, there is a large *flow* of undocumented immigrants (Siegel et al., 1980). The size and coverage of the undocumented immigrant population remains a critical issue (Massey, 1981). For a review of the many attempts to estimate this population, especially its Mexican and Central American component, see García y Griego (1981).

Morbidity and Mortality

Relatively little is known about Hispanic morbidity (the relative incidence of disease), although Public Law 94-311 has inspired the inclusion of Hispanics in national health surveys. Intriguing bits of epidemiological evidence are now being produced, such as the evidence that Hispanics have a lower incidence of some forms of cancer. But these isolated findings have not been incorporated into a demographic assessment.

Instead, two assumptions have prevailed in the literature. The first is that Hispanics are healthier than the population as a whole. Hispanics are younger, and younger persons have fewer health problems. Many Hispanics are immigrants, and immigrants are usually self-selected for good health. Moreover, it is argued that older Hispanics who become ill return to live with family members in Puerto Rico or foreign countries. Thus, survey data reflect a relatively healthy population. If the mortality rates do not support this view, it is because the census undercount has unrealistically deflated the denominator of the rates.

The contrary position argues that Hispanics have poorer health care and, like other disadvantaged groups, are more exposed to contagious diseases and the other diseases associated with poor nutrition, excessive childbearing, overcrowding, and poverty. If the morbidity statistics do not support this view, it is argued, it is because sick Hispanics do not report their symptoms to caregivers. These conflicting arguments about the health of the Hispanic population are also made about their longevity.

This controversy is of particular interest to demographers, for infant mortality rates and the expectation of life at birth are critical indicators that summarize a population's living conditions. Many of the obstetric indicators of high infant mortality (young mothers, premature delivery, lack of prenatal care, etc.) are more pronounced among the Hispanic population than the majority White population. Nevertheless, infant mortality rates for Hispanics remain low—for some years in the Southwest, even lower than those of Whites. Powell-Griner and Streck (1982) have explored a number of possible reasons for these low rates, but all the reasons may be summarized in one term: poor data. Rogers (1980) found discrepant ethnic codes between birth and infant death certificates, which accounts for differential reporting of ethnic infant mortality rates. Both the underreporting of infant deaths and the possible overreporting of births as having occurred in the United States have been alleged. Public health officials in Texas border counties believe that infant mortality rates are unreliably low. But convincing demographic studies are difficult to do because of the geographic mobility of Hispanics (including their infants) and because of inadequate vital statistics data (Palloni, 1978).

Studies done of mortality rates at older ages (Schoen and Nelson, 1981; Bradshaw and Fonner, 1978, 1980) find Hispanic mortality levels very similar to those of non-Hispanics, with one major exception: the death rates of young males are higher than would otherwise be expected. Analysis of the causes of death shows that the cause-specific death rates for violent deaths are much higher than for non-Hispanics. The "violent subculture" argument holds that Hispanic children are as healthy as young majority Whites, but as they move into their teen years, they enter a risky world of more dangerous blue-collar work, more abuse of alcohol and drugs, and more predation by street criminals.

A counter argument has been made by Robinson (1980), who has argued that the death rates for young Hispanic males have been inflated by under-enumeration. The problem is most pronounced for the prime immigration group: young males. And because young Hispanic immigrants are relatively healthy (and would return to their home countries if ill), violent death is almost the only mortality risk they would face while in the United States. From this perspective, the high violent death rates of young Hispanic men are an artifact of immigration and inadequate statistics, not a "fact."

Life tables for Hispanics are based on death rates, whose inaccuracies have just been discussed. Many demographers are skeptical about life table values for Hispanics. Nevertheless, the following data for Texas are helpful (Siegel and Passel, 1979).

TABLE 1.7
Expectation of Life at Birth in Texas, 1969-1971

	Male	Female
Spanish surname	67.2	73.4
White, non-Spanish surname	68.1	76.5

These life tables imply very little difference in the mortality experience of males, and a somewhat greater difference for females. Life expectation in Mexico in 1970 was 61.4 years, well below the 70.2 for Texas Hispanics of both sexes in 1970. While this seems to suggest that Hispanics are relatively well off, the data are so controversial that many demographers remain skeptical of this conclusion.

Public Policy Issues

No social or economic planning, no evaluation of polcy initiatives, and no reform of existing social programs can be intelligently undertaken without adequate data. Because of the youthfulness and mobility of the Hispanic population, accurate projections are both more necessary and more difficult to make. The 1980 Census will be extensively mined for data on Hispanics, but the data need to be assessed for accuracy first. A good deal of the evaluation for the nation as a whole will be done by the U.S. Census Bureau. What will be left to the states and localities is the assessment of data quality for their own areas. The scarcity of local data on Hispanics has become a major planning headache for many cities.

At a minimum, states and localities need to consider the following measures: (1) a careful evaluation of the extent to which data for Hispanics have been edited or allocated; (2) a cross-classification of the multiple indicators of Hispanic origin; and (3) a comparison of 1970 and 1980 data for patterns of migration. Areas with large numbers of Hispanics might consider the feasibility of recording their own records by Spanish surname, and of purchasing a special Spanish surname recode of their Census data from the U.S. Bureau of the Census. A pilot project to set forth sample procedures and outcomes for such studies would be useful.

More generally, much more needs to be known about response error or variation among Hispanics. Many of the major studies of Hispanics done during the past four years should be replicated with consideration of the data-editing process. It might be that conclusions based solely on unedited data would differ substantially if the nonresponse rates are high. An analysis of missing data in surveys on Hispanics would also be appropriate. These analyses should be coupled with sensitive field studies of Hispanics' interaction with statistical agencies (private and public) and interviewers.

Possibly the most important substantive area for further investigation is Hispanic mortality. Mortality indicators are important for health planning, but they are also key data for population projections, life tables, census evaluation techniques, and demographic accounting systems. Possibly the most important single study would be a matching of 1980 death certificates with 1980 Census returns, but this study would be prohibitively expensive and, because of Census confidentiality requirements, would require the Census Bureau to stretch its already inadequate budget to produce the tabulations. In lieu of this study, recoding and analysis of state death certificates would be a major advance.

Finally, there is a need for basic data sources that can be "spliced" with available government and private data but that will provide an avenue for collecting data uniquely salient to the Hispanic population. These issues are too specialized to be included in surveys of the general population. Such issues include: (1) the attitudes toward and practices of childrearing; (2) information on number of children now alive (as well as children ever born); (3) a demographic history that coordinates respondents' major life events (e.g. marriages, childbirth, migration history); and (4) relationships with family in another country, plans for return migration, contingencies under which one would return (e.g. terminal illness). A number of experiments of data reliability and validity could be built into the questionnaire. Such a study would shed light on the unresolved issues of fertility, mortality, and migration in the Hispanic population. Equally important, issues unique to one subgroup (age at marriage among Mexicans, sex ratio among Puerto Ricans, Cubans' suburbanization) could be studied in detail.

Bibliography

Angel, Ronald J., and Marta Tienda. 1982. "Determinants of Extended Household Structure: Cultural Pattern or Economic Need?" *American Journal of Sociology* 87 (May):1360-83.

Bean, Frank D., and Benjamin S. Bradshaw. 1970. "Intermarriage between Persons of Spanish and Non-Spanish Surname: Changes from the Mid-Nineteenth to the Mid-Twentieth Century." *Social Science Quarterly* 51 (September):389-95.

Bean, Frank D., and W. Parker Frisbie, eds. 1978. *The Demography of Racial and Ethnic Groups*. New York: Academic.

Bradshaw, Benjamin S., and Frank D. Bean. 1972. "Some Aspects of the Fertility of Mexican Americans." In C.F. Westoff and R. Parke, Jr., eds., *Demographic and Social Aspects of Population Growth: Research Reports*, vol. 1. Commission on Population Growth and the American Future. Washington: USGPO.

Bradshaw, Benjamin S., and Edwin Fonner, Jr. 1978. "The Mortality of Spanish-Surnamed Persons in Texas, 1969-1971." In F.D. Bean and W.P. Frisbie, eds., *The Demography of Racial and Ethnic Groups*. New York: Academic.

————. 1980. "Survivorship and Longevity of Spanish-Surnamed and Other White Persons: Texas, Border and Non-Border Regions, Bexar County, 1969-71, and San Antonio, 1950-1960." Report to the National Institute on Aging.

Estrada, Leo F., F.C. García, R.F. Macías, and L. Maldonado. 1981. "Chicanos in the United States: A History of Exploitation and Resistance." *Daedalus.* 110:103-31.

Featherman, David L., and Robert B. Hauser. 1978. *Opportunity and Change.* New York: Academic.

Fernández, Edward W. 1975. "Comparison of Persons of Spanish Surname and Persons of Spanish Origin in the United States." U.S. Bureau of the Census Technical Paper no. 38. Washington: USGPO.

Fitzpatrick, Joseph P., and Douglas T. Gurak. 1979. *Hispanic Intermarriage in New York City, 1975*. New York: Fordham University Hispanic Research Center Monograph No. 2.

Frisbie, W. Parker, Frank D. Bean, and Isaac W. Eberstein. 1978. "Patterns of Marital Instability among Mexican-Americans, Blacks, and Anglos." In F.D. Bean and W.P Frisbie, eds., *The Demography of Racial and Ethnic Groups.* New York: Academic.

Grebler, Leo, Joan W. Moore, and Ralph C. Guzman. 1970. *The Mexican-American People.* New York: Free Press.

García y Griego, Manuel. 1981. *The Importation of Mexican Contract Laborers to the United States, 1942-1964: Antecedents, Operation, and Legacy.* La Jolla: Program in United States-Mexican Studies, University of California, San Diego.

Haub, Carl. 1981. "The U.S. Hispanic Population: A Question of Definition." *Intercom* (November-December):8-11.

Hernández, José, Leo Estrada, and David Alvirez. 1973. "Census Data and the Problem of Conceptually Defining the Mexican-American Population." *Social Science Quarterly* 53 (March):671-87.

Jaffe, A.J.; Ruth M. Cullen; and Thomas D. Boswell. 1980. *The Changing Demography of Spanish Americans.* New York: Academic.

Kritz, Mary M., and Douglas T. Gurak. 1976. "Ethnicity and Fertility in the United States: Analysis of 1970 Public Use Sample Data." *Review of Public Data Use* 4(3):12-23.

Marcum, John P., and Frank D. Bean. 1976. "Minority Group Status as a Factor in the Relationship between Mobility and Fertility: The Mexican American Case." *Social Forces* 55 (September):135-48.

Massey, Douglas S. 1979. "Residential Segregation of Spanish-Americans in United States Urban Areas." *Demography* 16 (November):553-654.

———. 1981. "Dimensions of the New Immigration to the United States and the Prospects for Assimilation." *Annual Review of Sociology* 7:57-85.

McLemore, S. Dale. 1973. "The Origins of Mexican American Subordination in Texas." *Social Science Quarterly* 53 (March):656-70.

Murguia, Edward, and W. Parker Frisbie. 1977. "Trends in Mexican American Intermarriage." *Social Science Quarterly* 58 (December):374-89.

Palloni, Alberto. 1978. "Application of an Indirect Technique to Study Group Differentials in Infant Mortality." In F.D Bean and W.P. Frisbie, eds., *The Demography of Racial and Ethnic Groups.* New York: Academic.

Passel, Jeffrey, and David L. Word. 1980. "Constructing the List of Spanish Surnames for the 1980 Census: An Application of Bayes' Theorem." Paper presented at the 1980 Annual Meetings, Population Association of America.

Portes, Alejandro. 1979. "Illegal Immigration and the International System: Lessons from Recent Legal Mexican Immigrants to the United States." *Social Problems* 26:425-438.

Powell-Griner, Eve, and Dan Streck. 1982. "A Closer Examination of Neonatal Mortality Rates among the Texas Spanish Surname Population." *American Journal of Public Health* 72 (September):993-99.

Rindfuss, Ronald R., and James A. Sweet. 1977. *Postwar Fertility Trends and Differentials in the United States.* New York: Academic.

Robinson, J. Gregory. 1980. "Estimating the Approximate Size of the Illegal Alien Population in the United States by the Comparative Trend Analysis of Age-Specific Death Rates. *Demography* 17 (May):159-76.

Rogers, Richard G. 1980. "Reliability of Measuring Ethnic Codes on Birth and Infant Death Certificates." Paper presented at the 1980 Annual Meetings, Southern Regional Demographic Group.

Rogers, Richard G. 1984. "Infant Mortality among New Mexican Hispanics, Anglos, and Indians." *Social Science Quarterly* (forthcoming).

Sabagh, George. 1980. "Fertility Planning Status of Chicano Couples in Los Angeles." *American Journal of Public Health* 70:56-61.

Schoen, Robert, and Verne E. Nelson. 1981. "Mortality by Cause among Spanish Surnamed Californians, 1969-71." *Social Science Quarterly* 62 (June):259-174.

Siegel, Jacob S., and Jeffrey Passel. 1979. "Coverage of the Hispanic Population of the United States in the 1970 Census." *Current Population Reports*, series P-23, no. 82, Washington: USGPO.

Siegel, Jacob S., Jeffrey Passel, and J. Gregory Robinson. 1981. "Preliminary Review of Existing Studies of the Number of Illegal Residents in the United States." Working document of the research staff. Washington: U.S Select Commission on Immigration and Refugee Policy.

Social Science Quarterly. 1973. "The Chicano Experience in the United States." special issue 53 (March).

Sullivan, Teresa A., Francis P. Gillespie, Andrew M. Greeley, and Michael Hout, 1981. "Estimating Hispanic Undercount in the 1980 Census through the Use of Catholic Parish Records." Report to the Ford Foundation.

Sullivan, Teresa A., Francis P. Gillespie, S.J., Michael Hout, and Andrew M. Greeley. 1983. "Surname versus Self-Identification in the Analysis of Hispanic Data." Proceedings of the Social Statistics Section, 1983 Joint Statistical Meetings in Toronto (forthcoming).

Sullivan, Teresa A., and Silvia Pedraza-Bailey. 1980. "Differential Success among Cuban-American and Mexican-American Immigrants: The Role of Policy and Community." Report to U.S Department of Labor.

Tienda, Marta, ed. 1981. "Hispanic-Origin Workers in the U.S. Labor Market: Comparative Analyses of Employment and Earnings." Report to U.S. Department of Labor.

Tienda, Marta, and Lisa J. Neidert. 1981. "Language, Education, and the Socioeconomic Achievement of Hispanic-Origin Men." In Marta Tienda, ed., "Hispanic-Origin Workers in the U.S. Labor Market: Comparative Analyses of Employment and Earnings." Report to U.S. Department of Labor.

U.S. Bureau of the Census. 1973a. *Census of Population, 1970*. Vol. I: *Characteristics of the Population*. Pt. 1, sec. 1. Washington: USGPO.

_____. 1973b. *Census of Population, 1970*. Subject Report. Final Report PC (2) -1C. "Persons of Spanish Origin." Washington: USGPO.

_____. 1974. "Consistency of Reporting Ethnic Origin in the Current Population Survey." U.S. Bureau of the Census Technical Paper No. 31. Washington: USGPO.

_____. 1977 *Current Population Reports*. Advance Report. "Persons of Spanish Origin in the United States, March 1977. Series P-20, no. 317 (December). Washington: USGPO.

_____1979. *Current Population Reports*. "Population Profile of the United States, 1978." Series P-20, no. 336 (April). Washington: USGPO.

_____ 1980a. *Current Population Reports*. "Persons of Spanish Origin in the United States, March 1979." Series P-20, no. 354 (October). Washington: USGPO.

_____. 1980b. *Current Population Reports*. "Population Profile of the United States, 1979." Series P-20, no. 350 (May). Washington: USGPO.

———. 1981a. *Census of Population and Housing, 1980*. Advance Report. "Texas: Final Population and Housing Unit Count." PHC80-V-45 (March). Washington: USGPO.

———. 1981b. *Current Population Reports*. "Money Income of Families and Persons in the United States, 1979." Series P-60, no. 129 (November). Washington: USGPO.

———. 1981c. "Persons of Spanish Origin in the United States, March 1980." Advance Report. Series P-20, no. 361 (May). Washington: USGPO.

———. 1981d. *Current Population Reports*. "Population Profile of the United States, 1980." Series P-20, no. 363 (June). Washington: USGPO.

U.S. Statutes at Large. 1976. Public Law 94-311: Americans of Spanish Origin-Social Statistics. 90 stat. 688.

———. 1983. *Census of Population, 1980*. "General Population Characteristics," U.S. Summary. Washington: USGPO.

Young v. Klutznick. 1980. 49F. supp. 1318 (E.D. Mich. 1980), rev'd., 652 F. 2d. 617 (6th Cir. 1981).

2

The "New" Immigration

Pastora San Juan Cafferty

Each generation of Americans confronts the issue of what to do about immigration. There is good reason for this. Our attitudes and beliefs concerning what is "American" are implicitly intertwined with our attitudes and beliefs about immigration. The history of the United States is one of different waves of immigrants coming to its shores seeking a new life. Central as immigration is to our national identity, we have always been ambivalent about the "new immigrants." These newcomers threaten us because they bring with them foreign languages, dress, customs, and religions. The new immigrants represent diversity, which makes them the focal point for the ongoing debate over how much diversity is good for society. Ultimately, the issue of immigration is framed as one of whether these new immigrants make the United States a better country for all. This chapter discusses the Hispanic immigration in the historical context of how the United States has responded to newcomers. Using historical examples as a backdrop, Cafferty argues that the Hispanic immigration is not that different from previous ones. In contrast to the often-stated position, Hispanics are no less skilled or educated than were other immigrant groups. Furthermore, there is little empirical evidence supporting the claim that the labor market cannot absorb Hispanic immigrants. Cafferty points out that the close proximity of sending countries to the United States and the relative ease of transportation to and from countries of origin and the United States is a significant difference between the Hispanic immigration and earlier ones. The cyclical migration might contribute to the nurturing of Hispanic culture and language retention. However, it is still too early to determine the nature and extent of this process. Finally, Cafferty observes that both illegal aliens and refugees comprise a significant proportion of the Hispanic migration stream to the United States. Both illegal aliens and refugees create unique problems for the United States in terms of international and domestic policies. The chapter concludes with a set of policy implications which suggest areas for additional research and debate.

It is impossible to discuss issues concerning Hispanics in the United States without addressing the issues of immigration in contemporary American society. Not all Hispanics are immigrants; nor are all immigrants Hispanic. Discussion of contemporary immigration policy, however, has focused on Hispanics—often to the exclusion of all other groups. There is good reason for this. During the 1970s, 42 percent of all legal entrants were from Mexico; roughly an additional 10-15 percent came from other countries in Latin America. One could argue, then, that about half of all immigrants during the 1970s were Hispanic. To understand the Hispanic immigration, it is necessary, however, to put this relatively recent immigration in the context of previous emigration to America.

Immigration in the Nineteenth Century

America is a nation of immigrants. For over 200 years peoples from diverse nations have been coming to its shores, and with the passage of time, they became "Americans." It is equally true that throughout the years many of the new Americans looked with fear upon the foreigners who continued to come.

America has always been ambivalent about immigration: political oratory has extolled the "land of the free and the home of the brave" and congratulated those who wished to join this "best of all societies" for their wisdom of choice. Yet this oratory has been counterbalanced by those who would restrict immigration and those who feared "race suicide" or deterioration of the American political system and economy as more and more immigrants landed on the nation's shores. The reality was always somewhere between the welcoming words of Emma Lazarus and the fear expressed by the caricature of the "last American" surrounded by brutalized foreign gnomes in the Thomas Nast cartoon. The ambiguity of this reality was reflected in the laws passed by state legislatures and the Congress—some designed to ease immigration and recruit new immigrants, others designed to stem the flow. The fact is, however, that during most of the nineteenth century there were few restrictions placed on immigration in the United States. The country was in a period of rapid economic expansion. Workers were needed to supply the new industrial nation, which in less than fifty years managed to expand from thirteen small colonies hugging the eastern shoreline to a federation of states and territories spanning the continent. As these political entities became established, workers and farmers needed to settle the new territories came from the nations of Europe. All were welcome: the first naturalization laws denied White indentured servants and all non-White aliens the right to U.S. citizenship (ch. 3, 1, 1 stat. 103). Immigration from Asia was hotly debated. In 1868 the

Burlingame Treaty had specifically granted Chinese the right to enter the United States. In the following year, however, the Union Pacific Railroad was completed and the ensuing large floating labor supply tended to drift to California. There they competed for jobs with the Chinese who by 1890 accounted for 10 percent of the California population and racial hostility intensified. In the 1880s, Congress repeatedly voted to restrict the immigration of Chinese. It was not until 1904, however, that the Chinese were permanently excluded.

Immigration in the Twentieth Century

By the turn of the century American ambivalence about immigration had become an acrimonious debate. Those who employed immigrants—including the very vocal chambers of commerce—continued to fight the growing restrictionist sentiment; but their voices were drowned out by an uneasy coalition of conservatives and progressives. Intellectuals fascinated by theories of social Darwinism and a growing number of anthropological studies seeking to establish the importance of racial differences supported the restrictionists' demands. The publication in 1899 of Ripley's *The Races of Europe*, hailed as a seminal work by the new anthropologists, argued that racial lines conform not to national groups but to physical types, and these were determined by geography. The noted historian Frederick Jackson Turner argued his thesis that American democracy had been born in the councils of the German tribes and thus was a political system more congenial to Northern Europeans descended from those tribes. Social Darwinists encouraged the Anglo-Saxon theorists to think of nations—and national groups—as species in a desperate battle for survival.

During the decades following the Centennial celebration of 1876 through World War I, a series of laws were enacted designed to exclude undesirable immigrants regardless of country of origin. Other laws were enacted to exclude contract workers—a universal criterion which effectively excluded Orientals, for whom contract labor was common. At the same time there was a growing trend toward the explicit exclusion of certain national and racial groups.

At the same time, immigration continued to grow. In 1905 and 1910 there were record immigration flows of more than a million immigrants. The majority of these were from Southern and Eastern Europe, and most settled in the mining and manufacturing centers east of the Mississippi and north of the Ohio and Potomac rivers.

In 1904 the Congress appointed a distinguished commission to study U.S. immigration problems—the Dillingham Commission. In 1911 the Dillingham Commission issued a 42-volume report that reflected the restrictionist sentiments of the era and became the basis for immigration policy well into the middle of the century. "The Dillingham Commission Report" laid the foundation for the National Origins Act of 1924 which limited immigration to 150,000 annual visas to be allocated in proportion to the national origins of the White population of the United States in 1920. It laid the legislative base for a series of restrictive actions which reaffirmed the national origins quota. Immigration legislation was designed to preserve the White Northern European character of a mythological American nation.

The nationalism and isolationism that followed World War I gave new impetus to restrictionism. A series of actions by Congress reflected the national fear of the postwar influx of unassimilated aliens as well as a waning of the faith that the United States had a capacity to fuse all persons into a "nation of nations."

In 1917 (39 stat. 874) and 1918 (40 Stat. 1012) Congress passed legislation to further restrict immigration. The Asian immigration was stopped and a literacy requirement for all immigrants was established. By the 1920s the question was no longer whether to restrict immigration but how best to do it.

In 1924 Congress passed legislation establishing national origin quotas on immigration to be allocated to nations based on the distribution of national origins already present within the White population of the United States in 1920. Congress had finally acted to define the American nation and to make certain that its character would not change. While the 1924 law (ch. 190, 43 stat. 153) severely limited immigration from Europe and prevented it from Asia, the United States, mindful of the "good neighbor" policy, repeatedly articulated to the emerging Latin American nations that it did not limit immigration from any country in the Western Hemisphere. It did not take long for the small farmers in the American Southwest who were opposed to the importation of cheap Mexican labor to call for restrictions on immigration from Western Hemisphere countries, but it would take nearly half a century before such legislation would be enacted. In 1952 the controversial Walter-McCarren Act (66 stat. 163) revised and codified immigration and nationality laws, reflecting a new nationalism and fear of communism that had swept the nation following World War II. It essentially retained the national origins quota provisions and added an "inoperative" clause (66 stat. 182) which could restrict immigration from the Western Hemisphere.

The 1965 Amendments

Immigration from the Western Hemisphere did not reach significant numbers until the beginning of the twentieth century. When European immigration began to decline, immigration from Mexico grew—closely following the cycles of total immigration (Grebler et al., 1970).

Mexican workers were officially encouraged to come to the United States during World War II to fill the void left by American workers who had joined the war effort. From 1942 until 1964 the Bracero Program brought thousands of Mexicans as temporary farm workers into the United States as contract laborers. The program, which during peak years brought hundreds of thousands of Mexican laborers to work on U.S. farms, was always controversial. U.S. labor opposed it on the grounds that it depressed wages; humanitarians opposed it on the grounds that contract workers had little, if any, means of claiming the few rights they had. Restrictionists argued that Mexicans who came in as temporary workers stayed illegally to swell the growing U.S. population. From time to time, raids were carried out to find and deport the visa overstayers. During the infamous "Operation Wetback" raids, thousands of Mexican workers—including legal resident aliens—were sent back to Mexico with no concern for their legal or human rights.

Immigration continued to be a highly controversial issue. In 1964 President Lyndon Johnson called for immigration reform in his State of the Union address. The national-origins quotas of 1924, readjusted by Walter-McCarren in 1952, were consistent neither with the intense civil rights legislation nor with the growing U.S. commitment to the newly emerging nations in Asia and Africa. Since it was also a period of continuing economic growth, Americans could afford to believe the time had come for a new humanitarian immigration policy which would not discriminate on the basis of race and national origins and need not be concerned with economic implications of unrestricted immigration.

There was, however, growing concern with continuing immigration from Mexico. Between 1945 and 1965, over 1.3 million Mexicans became resident aliens. A continuing population growth and a slow economic growth in Mexico gave cause for concern. The "safety valve" implicit in the Bracero Program was closed when the program was ended in 1964.

The 1965 amendments to the Walter-McCarren Act were at the same time progressive and restrictive (PL 89-236, 79 stat. 911, 916). They abolished the national-origins quota applicable to the Eastern Hemisphere, ending the severe numerical limit on immigrants from Asian countries and the less severe limit on immigration from Eastern and Southern Europe. At the same time, they imposed numerical limits on the independent nations in the Western Hemisphere. They also dramatically changed the criteria for admission: kinship ties with a U.S. citizen or resident alien replaced the relatively greater emphasis on occupational skills in the 1952

Act. The 1965 amendments failed to address a number of problems and created others. They made no adequate provision for refugees. The act precluded adjustment of the status of Cuban refugees at a time when Cuban nationals were officially encouraged to flee Castro's revolution by the U.S. government. Subsequent legislation has failed to address the problems of refugees from Latin America. With the exception of those who have fled Cuba's communist government, most political refugees from Latin America come from countries which have friendly diplomatic ties with the United States.

Perhaps the most problematic results of the 1965 amendments are that for the first time restrictions were placed on residents from the Western Hemisphere. Mexican and other Latin American nationals continued to cross what had been for centuries a free and open border. A growing illegal immigration from Latin America became identified as the principle immigration problem—indeed, as a major national problem—in the following decade.

SCIRP and Simpson-Mazzoli

Additional legislation during the 1970s attempted to address the problems ignored—and a few created—by the 1965 amendments. Dissatisfaction with the confusing complexity of immigration legislation resulted in the creation of the Select Commission on Immigration Policy (SCIRP) in 1978. A panel of distinguished citizens, chaired by Rev. Theodore Hesburgh, president of Notre Dame University, was appointed by the president of the United States to study current immigration policies and recommend new ones. Its recommendations were embodied in the Simpson-Mazzoli bill, a controversial piece of legislation that called for employer sanctions against those hiring illegal aliens. In the spring of 1983 Simpson-Mazzoli, which had been hotly debated in the Congress and in the press, came to a vote in the Senate. The act passed in the Senate, but failed in the House. One year later in the summer of 1984, the House of Representatives passed its version by a narrow margin. The future of the Simpson and Mazzoli bill is uncertain because a compromise between the House and Senate versions has yet to be reached in committee. Hispanic civil rights groups and chambers of commerce were among the most vocal in opposing the legislation. Hispanics argued that the ease with which existing identification could be forced would lead the prospective employer to use the easiest and cheapest way of avoiding trouble: he would not hire anyone who looked Hispanic. Civil rights groups charged the provisions invited stereotyping.

The Simpson-Mazzoli legislation, designed to address the problems brought about by the 1965 amendments, was drafted at a time when Hispanic immigration was defined as a major social problem by the American people and the American press.

The New Immigration

Concern with the "new immigration" is based on one or more of three factors: the character of the immigration stream has changed; the nature of the American economy and institutions has changed radically; and the political climate and values of American society have changed (Tanton, 1979; Graham, 1980).

While immigrants come to America from all over the world, most Americans are especially aware of the continuing flow across the long border between the United States and Mexico and view with alarm demographers' predictions that Hispanics will be the largest minority group in the country by the end of the century.

Discussions of the Hispanic immigration center on the belief that Hispanic immigration is different from all previous ones. Hispanics are held to be radically different from all previous immigrants beause there are more of them, they are illegal entrants, unskilled and uneducated, poor, non-White, and they retain their language and culture, displaying a lack of commitment to American society and its values. Furthermore, Hispanics are coming into a labor market that cannot absorb them and settling into a nation divided by racial and civil rights issues.

Size of the Hispanic Immigration

Politicians, journalists, and scholars repeatedly argue that the United States is experiencing an unprecedented foreign flow (Teitelbaum, 1980). The fact is that the 808,000 people who were admitted legally in 1980 constituted a dramatic increase since this number had been radically augmented by refugees. These refugees, however, did not constitute a continuing immigration flow. By 1981 legal immigration had fallen to 697,000—close to the 600,000 legal entrants a year admitted during the 1970s when the average annual flow of legal immigrants made up only one-fifth of one percent of the American population. At the turn of the century, the annual flow often topped a million annually and made up over 1 percent of the U.S. population. In 1910 the foreign-born made up nearly 15 percent of the American population; in 1970, they constituted less than 5 percent. During the 1970s the American population grew by less than 1 percent a year. The roughly 4 million immigrants admitted during the 1970s accounted for 21 percent of that growth. From 1900-10 the population grew by more than 2 percent; immigrants accounted for 40 percent of that growth. Contemporary concern that the United States is experiencing a large and unprecedented immigration flow completely ignores the reality of the numbers.

Character of the Hispanic Immigrants

Illegal immigration is not solely Hispanic. It is believed that nearly half the illegal aliens in this country are from Mexico: the others came from other countries including Korea, Taiwan and the Philippines. Illegal immigration and Mexican immigration are two distinct issues. The reason immigration is perceived as Mexican immigration is the emphasis placed on apprehending Mexican aliens by the INS. Nevertheless the issue of Hispanic immigration cannot be addressed without addressing the issue of illegal immigration across the Mexican border. The border is largely unguarded and virtually unsealable.

It is obviously difficult to count the illegal immigrants residing at one time in this country. The Census Bureau estimated between 3 and 6 million illegal immigrants were in the United States in 1978. Some of these came long before 1968, many are persons who go back and forth and are not permanent residents (Cornelius, 1976). Estimates of the numbers of illegal immigrants in the United States range from 2 to 12 million, but some have estimated as high as 25 million (Siegal et al., 1980). As empirical evidence has become available the estimates have become more realistic and dramatically smaller. Recent analysis of Mexican Census data suggest the estimated number of Mexican illegal immigrants in the United States to be no more than 4 million, with the probable number being less (Bean et al., 1983).

The Hispanic immigrants are certainly no less educated or skilled than the many European immigrants who preceded them (Cafferty et al., 1983). The question is whether a mature American economy can assimilate people whose education and skills are less than those of the general U.S. population.

The most remarkable characteristic of immigrants in general is their economic success: the native-born sons of immigrants earn 5-10 percent more than equally educated native-born sons of native-born parents (Chiswick, 1977, 1979). Mexican immigrants are one exception: Mexican immigrants earn substantially less than other White immigrants; native-born men of Mexican origin earn less than other White men of the same immigrant generation (Chiswick, 1979).

Refugees, who have lower earnings than immigrants on arrival, approach but do not exceed the earnings of the native-born. Cuban refugees, since their skills were not readily transferable because of lack of knowledge of English, experienced dramatic downward occupational mobility, but their upward mobility was equally dramatic as they acquired linguistic and other skills (Chiswick, 1978; Portes et al., 1981).

Non-White immigrants were regarded as a special problem throughout the nineteenth century. Problems of race continue to be a great American dilemma. American society regards Hispanics as non-White regardless of skin color. Some Hispanics describe themselves as a racially distinctive "brown race." In fact, Hispanics do not constitute a single racial group; they include Whites, Blacks, American Indians, and Asians, as well as reflecting a high incidence of intermarriage among these groups.

It is interesting to consider the case of Puerto Ricans in this regard. Puerto Ricans are not immigrants; they are American citizens. They are part of the constant internal migration in America that is characteristic of an ambitious, restless people. They are citizens of the United States traveling within its national boundaries. Yet along with Mexicans and other Hispanics, they are seen as foreigners who take jobs and housing away from native-born Americans. The U.S. government has classified them as a minority, and both their detractors and their leaders describe them as members of a "brown" race.

The portion of the Puerto Rican population that classifies itself as non-White results from the mix of White Spanish conquistador and Black African slave. But this group does not, by any standard, constitute a separate race. Their lack of acceptance by majority society seems to indicate that it is easier for the White immigrant to be accepted by American society than the immigrant—or citizen—with a dark skin.

Some observers contend there is an especially tenacious loyalty to Hispanic culture that would slow down, if not entirely impede, "Americanization." It may well be that Hispanic immigrants have a special loyalty to their culture. However, the economic success of Cuban immigrants in Miami and of some Dominican immigrants in New York suggests that Hispanic culture, as such, is no obstacle to achievement. One may do quite well economically and preserve much of one's own culture. The durability of the ethnic cultures is amazing and subtle. To a greater extent than previously supposed, most Americans tenaciously cling to their ethnic culture. There is no evidence that Hispanics do so more than other immigrants.

One evidence of the retention of native culture is the retention of native language. Other groups, most notably the Germans, tried to maintain separate cultural enclaves complete with their own language schools, and fought the battle to retain their native culture with resourcefulness and vigor. Hispanics are currently doing so with much wider support in the elite nonimmigrant society because of the cultural values of the time. The civil rights militancy of the 1960s forcefully changed the passive acceptance of an inferior status by any group. Both a Supreme Court decision and Congressional initiatives made it politically possible to offer extensive bilingual training, although the views about what constitutes appropriate bilingual education programs are nearly as numerous as its advocates. Hostility toward bilingualism is powerful among many Americans, but there is little evidence that as Hispanics assimilate into majority society, Spanish language retention will persist.

There has always been a return migration flow from the United States. Indeed, in times of severe economic recession, emigration exceeded immigration. The circular migration that characterizes the travel between Mexico and the United States is seen as a major problem. Circular migration is characteristic among all nations which share common borders or even are close geographically. The circular migration flow among Latin American countries has existed for centuries. The illegal immigration to the United States from Mexico and Puerto Rico by nationals from the Caribbean and Central American countries may well be part of that flow. The sociological implications of circular migration are not clear, but while the flow may account for a large number of border crossings, census data and surveys of these Hispanic immigrants who have settled in the United States either legally or illegally show that the reality of the circular flow is much less than the mythology leads us to believe (Cornelius, 1976).

Character of the Receiving Country

Among those who advocate severely restricting immigration to the United States are those who do so arguing that changes in the economy and in American social policies and institutions make it difficult for this country to absorb continuing immigration. It is not that Hispanics are so very different from previous immigrant groups, but that they are coming to a very different country.

Mature Economy Cannot Absorb Them

There are those who argue that even if Hispanic immigrants exhibit the same willingness to work as previous immigrants, a mature economy cannot absorb them. A recent Urban Institute study challenges this argument. Southern California, the part of the country which received the greatest number of immigrants during the 1970s, also created jobs faster than any other and increased per capita income by 25 percent. On balance the economic benefits to the region outweighed the costs from the increased use of public services such as hospitals and schools (Fallows, 1983).

Between 1924 and 1965, when immigration from the Eastern Hemisphere was restricted, legal entitlements to income transfer benefits were extended in the United States. The current income transfer programs date from the 1930s, a time when more people were leaving than entering the United States and immigration was no longer regarded as a problem. The issue of legal entitlements for immigrants was designated as a major problem in the 1960s and has done much to fuel the restrictionists' debate. There is substantial evidence to show that immigrants make minimal use of these programs, but the argument is that immigrants contribute to the welfare burden whether they take jobs away from others or whether they go on welfare themselves.

Civil rights activities and a commitment to equal access for all Americans make it difficult to exclude immigrants from programs once they are here. It may be easier to keep them from coming altogether. There is also a problem of a changing concept of America and its promise: this is no longer viewed as a country of vast and inexhaustible resources but as one with severely limited opportunity for economic growth and natural bounty.

The "new" Hispanic immigration shares many characteristics with the "old" European immigration: immigrants are self-selected, hard-working entrepreneurial people who come to the United States to work. Many of the criticisms leveled at the Hispanic immigrants were made of the Southern and Eastern Europeans in the past. Some of today's arguments echo those of the Dillingham Commission, modified by a radically different political and social concept of human rights and equality. In spite of the similarities, however, today's migration stream is different: it is disproportionately Spanish-speaking; it is lower-skilled relative to the contemporary labor force; and it is relatively easier for today's Hispanic immigrants to cross the contiguous border than it has been and continues to be for other immigrants to travel to the United States.

Refugees

In the days of unrestricted immigration, many political refugees came to the United States without raising any questions of foreign or domestic policy. Restricted immigration policies raise the need to establish priorities for admission as political refugees. It was not until after the 1965 amendments, however, that these questions applied to refugees from Latin America.

The majority of refugees admitted to the United States since 1952 have been those fleeing communist governments. During the 1956 Hungarian uprising the federal government for the first time made special provisions for the settlement of refugees. It was not until 1959, when Cubans began to flee the Castro revolution, that the U.S. government made a major effort to aid the adjustment of refugees. The federal government coordinated efforts involving state and local government agencies, churches, private welfare agencies, and foundations. Refugees were provided with subsistence, English lessons, employment counseling, and education.

As Americans learned to coexist with communism, enthusiasm for admitting and aiding refugees waned. Under Walter-McCarren, they could be admitted only as regular immigrants; the 1965 amendments provided only a small quota for refugees. The Refugee Act of 1980 made it possible for refugees to be admitted on the basis of religion, ethnic, racial, and political persecution, increased the annual quota for refugees from 17,400 (6 percent of the worldwide ceiling of 290,000 visas) to 50,000, and also included a provision for the Attorney General to admit refugees as parolees.

A year later the "freedom flotilla," bringing thousands of Cubans who had been permitted by Castro to leave in anything that would carry them across the 90 miles to the Florida Straits, challenged the law. It was politically impossible to turn away the boats, and many of them were sailed by American citizens who had gone to Cuba to pick up Cuban relatives.

Cuban refugees were not as welcome in 1981 as they had been in the 1960s. Castro had allowed the politically undesirable as well as those who were creating social problems to leave the island. Some were social misfits and had criminal records. While there is some evidence that there were social misfits and criminals among the Cuban refugees in the 1960s, these were treated very differently. Those that were not claimed by families were sent to refugee camps. Governors of some Southern states who had welcomed Cubans to teach Spanish in their high schools in the early 1960s now feared for the safety of their women if Cuban refugee men were imprisoned at local military bases.

The "Marielitos," as those who sailed from the Cuban part of Mariel came to be called, were not welcome in any community—including the Cuban community in Miami. The reasons were complex but seemed to reflect the same restrictionist tendencies and fear of foreigners that continues to fuel the immigration debate.

Each successive wave of Cuban refugees has exhibited different characteristics. The first wave following the overthrow of Fulgencio Batista in 1959 included upper-class landowners, industrial entrepreneurs, and merchants. Following the Bay of Pigs there came larger numbers of middle-class professionals, technicians and white-collar workers (Fagen et al., 1968). Since 1972, middle-class exodus has given way to an increasing number of workers from a wide variety of educational, occupational, and socioeconomic backgrounds. It was the Marielitos in their dramatic exodus who made it clear that fleeing communism was no longer a good enough reason to be allowed to come to the United States. Since then, groups of refugees fleeing right-wing Central American governments have been consistently denied asylum.

Adoption of the UN Protocol resulted in a dramatic change in refugee policy. It makes the United States a country of first asylum and defines a refugee as anyone fleeing for fear of persecution from his country's government. This raises a number of highly problematic questions regarding Hispanic refugee populations. Refugees seeking entrance to the United States no longer need to be from Communist or Middle Eastern countries. The Central American refugee population raises a new difficult issue: if asylum is denied by the United States government, the refugee's fate becomes extremely precarious. The United States, however, will face diplomatic difficulties in granting asylum to refugees coming from a government which has American support.

Public Policy Issues

Regulation of the refugee flow poses very different problems than does that of general immigration. Refugees are admitted for humanitarian and political reasons; they are often admitted as a result of a cataclysmic—and often unexpected—event. The issue of Hispanics or refugees must be addressed in the context of creating a refugee policy responsive to the realities of the complex world of the late twentieth century. Two centuries of success by immigrants in America does not suggest the need for restrictive policies. However, the implications of this successful history of immigrants for the Hispanic immigrant is not clear to American policymakers.

There is evidence that there are differences in economic success by country of origin: Mexican immigrants earn less and achieve lower occupational levels than others. This does not necessarily doom them to a continuing lower economic status, but it does raise important questions which merit further study and discussion. Other related questions must also be asked:

Should the United States create a guest worker program to meet economic needs of both the sending and receiving country, since many who now immigrate here do so for economic reasons? Would it be more consistent with U.S. tradition to admit larger numbers of resident aliens and expect them to repatriate?

There is heated debate over how to stop illegal immigration, and this debate is fueled by the widly fluctuating estimates of the magnitude of this immigration, which range from 3 to 10 million. The size of illegal and legal immigration in any year in the United States is a poor guess at best. U.S. Census Bureau estimates fail to include any figure for emigrants or for illegal immigrants as does the INS. Demographers must be funded to work on informed projections. Demographers choose to ignore the subject because of the paucity of data available; funds must be made available for better data-keeping by INS.

All nations share a concern over limited global resources. The United States, which declared its frontier closed as recently as 1892 and added new territories well into the twentieth century, is understandably concerned about the limits of growth. Given this concern, we must ask: If immigrants bring new economic pressures, may they not also bring new ways of using and conserving resources? And if so, how is this best done?

Finally, there is a question that applies only to the Spanish-speaking: Will their assimilation into English-speaking culture be different from that of previous immigrants? And if so, what are the consequences for American society?

The work of Portes, McLead, and Parker (1978) shows that "the socioeconomic expectations of immigrants are neither flights of fancy nor purely subjective ambition . . . they appear governed by rational assessment of objective opportunities as determined by the individual's past experiences and his skills to cope with situations in the new country." After extensive interviews with Mexican immigrants and Cuban refugees, they concluded that while there were marked differences among the Spanish-speaking groups, the similarities were equally important. The qualities of belief in the work ethic, entrepreneurship, economic achievement, and political and social awareness shown by their respondents suggest that the Spanish-speaking may also share great similarities with other groups.

References

Bean, Frank D., Allan B. King, and Jeffrey Passel. 1983. "The Number of Illegal Migrants of Mexican Origin in the United States: Sex Ratio-Based Estimates for 1980." *Demography* 20 (February).

Bernard, W.S. 1977. *Immigrants and Ethnicity: Ten Years of Changing Thought.* New York: American Immigration and Citizenship Conference.

Cafferty, Pastora, Barry Chiswick, Andrew Greeley, and Teresa Sullivan. 1983. *The Dilemma of American Immigration: Beyond the Golden Door.* New Brunswick, N.J.: Transaction.

Chiswick, Barry. 1977. "Sons of Immigrants: Are They at an Earnings Disadvantage?" *American Economic Review* (February):376-80.

———. 1978. "A Longitudinal Analysis of the Occupational Marketability of Immigrants." In *Proceedings of the 30th Annual Winter Meeting, Industrial Relations Research Association*, ed. Barbara D. Denniss. Madison: IRRA.

———. 1979. "The Economic Progress of Immigrants: Some Apparently Universal Patterns. In *Contemporary Economic Problems*, ed. William Fellner. Washington: American Enterprise Institute.

_____. 1980. "An Analysis of the Economic Progress and Impact of Immigrants." Employment and Training Administration, U.S. Department of Labor. Mimeo.

Chiswick, Barry, ed. 1982. *The Gateway: U.S. Immigration Issues and Policies.* Washington: American Enterprise Institute.

Cornelius, Wayne A. 1976. "Mexican Migration to the United States: The View from Rural Sending Communities." Cambridge: Migration and Development Study Group of MIT. Mimeo.

Fagen, Richard R., Richard A. Brady, and Thomas J. O'Leary. 1968. *Cubans in Exile: Dissatisfaction and the Revolution.* Stanford: Stanford University Press.

Fallows, James. 1983. "Immigration: How It's Affecting Us." *Atlantic* 252 (November):45-106.

Glazer, Nathan, and Daniel Patrick Moynihan. 1970. *Beyond the Melting Pot.* Cambridge: MIT Press.

Gordon, Milton M. 1964. *Assimilation in American Life.* New York: Oxford University Press.

Graham, Otis. 1980. "Illegal Immigration and the New Reform Movement." *Immigration Papers II.* Federation for American Immigration Reform. February.

Grebler, Leo, Joan Moore, and Ralph Guzman. 1970. *The Mexican-American People.* New York: Free Press.

Greeley, Andrew M. 1974. *Ethnicity in the United States.* New York: Wiley.

Handlin, Oscar. 1951. *The Uprooted.* Boston: Little, Brown.

_____. 1957. *Race and Nationality in American Life.* Boston: Little, Brown.

Hansen, Marcus Lee. 1940. *The Atlantic Migration, 1607-1860: A Hisory of the Continuing Settlement of the United States.* Cambridge: Harvard University Press.

Higham, John. 1977. *Strangers in the Land: Patterns of American Nativism.* New York: Atheneum.

Immigration Act of 1917: Statutes at Large. 1917. Vol. 39.

Immigration Act of 1918: Statutes at Large. 1918. Vol. 40.

Immigration and Nationality Act of 1924: Statutes at Large. 1924. Vol. 43.

Immigration and Nationality Act of 1952: Statutes at Large. 1952. Vol. 66.

Immigration and Nationality Act of 1965: Statutes at Large. 1965. Vol. 79.

Julian, Samora. 1971. *Los Mojados: The Wetback Story.* South Bend, Ind.: University of Notre Dame Press.

Keely, Charles B. 1977. "Counting the Unaccountable: Estimates of Undocumented Aliens in the United States." *Population and Development Review* 3 (4):473-81.

Naturalization Act: Statutes at Large. 1970. Vol. 1.

Portes, Alejandro, Samuel A. McLead, Jr., and Robert N. Parker. 1978. "Immigrant Aspirations." *Sociology of Education* 51 (October):241-60.

Portes, Alejandro, Juan M. Clark, and Manuel M. López. 1981. "Six Years Later: The Process of Inoperation of Cuban Exiles in the United States, 1973-1979." *Cuban Studies/Estudios Cubanos* 11 (July).

SCRIP (Select Commission on Immigration and Refugee Policy). 1981. *U.S. Immigration Policy and the National Interest*. Final Report and Recommendations of the Commission on Immigration and Refugee Policy to the Congress and the President of the United States. March 1. Washington: U.S. Government Printing Office.

Siegel, Jacob S., Jeffrey Passel, and J. Gregory Robinson. 1981. "Preliminary Review of Existing Studies of the Number of Illegal Residents in the United States." Working document of the research staff. Washington: U.S. Select Commission on Immigration and Refugee Policy.

Tanton, John. 1979. "Rethinking Immigration Policy." In *Immigration Papers I*. Federation for American Immigration Reform. (January).

Teitelbaum, Michael. 1980. "Right versus Right: Immigration and Refugee Policy in the United States." *Foreign Affairs* 59 (Fall):40-41.

U.S. Commission on Civil Rights. 1980. *The Tarnished Golden Door: Civil Rights Issues in Immigration* (September).

3

Culture and Religion

William C. McCready

This chapter deals with the interaction between culture and religion in the lives of people from different Hispanic groups and suggests ways in which this may be important for understanding the contexts within which policy discussions take place. The unique immigration history of Hispanic groups is described and two special religious characteristics are analyzed: the lack of an immigrant clergy (at least as compared to earlier European immigrants) and the role of folk religion in people's lives. There is also material which clarifies the common assumption that "Hispanic equals Catholic" by showing that this too is a variable situation and has differing degrees of identification. Following this is a discussion of the role of intermarriage, cultural identity, and pluralism as they apply to various Hispanic groups and to the context for the formulation of social policies in the United States. The various conceptions and definitions of religious differences, group identities, and cultural differences form a base for the social policy context and influence the way policies are formulated and received. Religion and culture are cast as important elements in the mainstreaming process for Hispanics in this society. Finally, three policy issues are raised for consideration. The first is whether such services as health and education could not be better delivered to Hispanic communities if the policies which govern them took into account an understanding of religion and culture. The second is whether the cohesiveness of many Hispanic communities and neighborhoods can be considered a practical strength for many urban areas and be better used toward the common good. And the third is the extent to which the maintenance of a strong Hispanic identity brings increased richness and strength to the entire society. These are essential issues for a pluralistic society to consider and this chapter takes these matters a step forward.

It is important to provide a theoretical base for understanding the part that the interaction between culture and religion plays in the highly differentiated lives of various groups we call "Hispanic." Our definition of religion is linked with the work of anthropologist Clifford Geertz (1968:643) who has described religion as

> a system of symbols which acts to establish powerful, pervasive, and long-lasting moods and motivations in men by formulating conceptions of a general order of existence and clothing these conceptions with such an aura of factuality that the moods and motivations seem uniquely realistic.

In other writings Geertz discusses religion as both a model "of" reality and "for" reality. This represents the essential linkage between religion and culture. Culture is also both a model "of" and "for" reality. Simply put, a model "of" is something that relates the essential way things are—it is that conviction inside the self which knows, in a fundamental noetic manner, what is real. A model "for" is akin to a pattern or a blueprint. It is the map within the self which tells us which way to go and what to do. It is more connected with the propositional in life than with the definitional. The religious and cultural models are more closely intertwined in some cultures than in others, and it is the contention of this chapter that understanding this aspect of Hispanic life is important for several reasons.

First, because it is a defining characteristic of the various groups. The way life really is and the way it should be lived (the model "of" and "for") are clearly expressed in the religious perspectives which people espouse. Second, religion separated these groups from the host society. Third, religion can provide access to resources within the host society, if it is properly defined. Other groups who have come to this country have found this to be true, and we shall explore the differences between earlier migrations and contemporary ones in this regard. Finally, and perhaps most important, is the fact that religion and culture, interacting in lives and communities, often provide considerable motivation and inspiration for social change. It is within the interaction of religion and culture that people answer the important questions of their lives such as their purpose, worth, and identity. It is also within this context that the answers to such serious questions are passed along from one generation to the next. To attempt to understand a people and their social context without understanding something of these topics is to ignore an extremely important part of the whole. The motivating power of religion and culture stems largely from their ability to connect the individual both to a larger group or community and to a transcendent ideal reality. An example of this can be found in Robert Coles's description of his encounter with Ruby Bridges, a 6-year-old who was among the first Black children to integrate New Orleans's schools (Coles, 1964:356):

> Every day Ruby was picked up by Federal marshals and walked past crowds
> who shouted: "You don't deserve to live"; "You're worse than an animal."
> And yet each day she went to school. "Ruby, your teacher told me you were
> talking to the people in the mob. I wondered what you were saying to them."
> "I wasn't talking to them," she replied. "I was praying for them. They need
> praying for." "They do?" "Yes, that's what God would want me to do."

Coles tells this story as a response to the simple-minded notion that religion is "the opiate of the people." He describes Ruby's response to the hatred around her as accepting an offered moment of grace—a way of transcending the limits and boundaries which reason would say were placed around her immediate situation.

Historically, most groups of people who have immigrated to the United States have engaged in the development of a religious perspective, usually derived from that which they brought. One of the most important differences between Hispanics and the Europeans who preceded them had to do with the relative roles of the clergy. For the Europeans, their clergy provided "brokerage" services between the immigrants and the host society. Priests acted as political and economic community leaders as well as educators. They provided answers on how best to gain access to the larger society and how to reap the rewards of such access. The European immigrants built parallel institutions to the host society in terms of education and health care and supported them, generally without subsidy other than the tax exemptions granted to all such institutions. These efforts provided a separate institutional base for the immigrants which served them well during their period of transition. Strong-willed priest-leaders like Fr. Vincent Barzynski (Parot, 1981) contributed to historic changes in the ways in which specific immigrant communities related to the dominant host society. The fundamental role of the parish pastor has been described by several social scientists specializing in the early-twentieth-century immigrations (Wrobel, 1979; Tomasi, 1976).

In contrast, most Hispanic groups have few indigenous clergy and seldom do the clergy migrate with the people as was common in the European situation. As a result, although there are considerable resources in the "parallel institutions" of the Catholic Church, Hispanics are frequently unable to use them, know about them, or sometimes even to be welcomed by them (although this situation has improved dramatically in recent years). Instead, the Hispanic groups' relationship to organized Catholicism is somewhat at arm's length. As we shall see, folk religion abounds and the level of sophistication with regard to ways to manipulate and use the institutional church is quite low (Doyle, 1982).

Before detailing specifics in this regard, we shall first describe in more depth the interaction between religion and culture for the Hispanic populations and then discuss the contrasts between assimilation and pluralism with regard to cultural changes. Finally we shall draw some policy inferences from these observations in a concluding section.

Interaction between Religion and Culture

Although Hispanics are perceived as predominantly Catholic in terms of their religion, this perception needs to be examined as it applies to different groups in different locales. A study in Detroit in the late 1960s found that both Catholic and Protestant churches were perceived by immigrants to be the principal sources of support, both physically and emotionally (Choldin and Trout, 1969). Before exploring the denominational differences, the overall connection between religion and culture will be explored.

People from different cultures have devised many acceptable ways of communicating their religious feelings and sensibilities to each other and their children. Some people may feel that "high expression" signifies an intensity of belief and therefore they have raucous and noisy celebrations at their religious ceremonies. Others may feel that religion is so important that a more serious demeanor is required and they devise celebrations that are temperate and somber and more majestic than festive.

It is only when cultures are mixed within a society that these differences become relevant to the entire society. We can see the power of these kinds of differences when we realize that most conflicts in our modern world are essentially religious in nature. The Middle East, Southeast Asia, Ireland, many parts of the Indo-Soviet border—all attest to the intensity and power of cultural/religious differentiation in a multicultural setting. Religious identity, for some people, becomes a way of identifying with a culture or even with a nation. (The strong identity between being Catholic and being Polish is an extremely important part of contemporary Polish society.) However, it is not only those who display such a crystallization of identity who partake of the power contained in this interaction between religion and culture.

People who have been socialized into a specific cultural system which has a strong integration between religion and culture also derive considerable increments regarding their own personal sense of integration; a sense which can be most useful when confronting a new society and a different, unyielding culture. Many Hispanic groups socialize their members in such a way as to emphasize the primacy of familial relationships and obligations as well as the dignity of the individual and the necessity of engaging in personal contact when dealing with others (Doyle, 1982).

Like many immigrant groups before them, Hispanics stress the communal nature of life and the need to belong to a community in some way in order to be fully supported. Just as the individual needs to feel the strength of support that comes from belonging to a family, the family needs to experience the strength and support that comes from being accepted in a community. To the outsider the new immigrants appear to be clannish and secretive—from the inside, however, only membership in the group makes life bearable and worth living.

Various sociologists have devised models of the process of assimilation, and without going through all of them, we will draw upon the themes most common to all to provide the following description. The first generation was typically closest to the country of origin in terms of culture and life-style. Language was still that of the country of origin and communities were close-knit and bonded. The second generation was transitional and stood astride both cultures—the new and the old. Its members were frequently in conflict with both their parents and their children, and had little facility with their native tongue. The third and subsequent generations are very comfortable in the host society and move through it at their own determination. Some choose to become reacquainted with their cultural roots and heritage, but it is not seen as necessary. These have successfully made it into the mainstream.

Perhaps the most commonly used marker of this process is intermarriage (Alba, 1980). Endogamy is most prevalent in the early generations and steadily declines over time. After enough iterations, it is hypothesized that culture becomes so diluted that it can no longer be found within the society as a distinct entity. Some research has been done which indicates that cultural variations can be found which trace back to the culture of origin, even among the third generation (McCready, 1976). These studies indicate that college students could assess their family styles and after analysis could be segmented into discernible ethnic groups, each with their own particular characteristics. It appears that some things disappear with time and that others do not. This is the reason why the interaction of culture and religion is important.

One of the reasons that we conceive of culture as being diluted is that we think of it as it comes from the place of origin. Naturally, after some time the patterns, values, and memories which contain culture are going to change. However, it has yet to be determined just how this change takes place. Many analogies have been used to depict the experience of generations of immigrants in this society. We have studied assimilation, acculturation, melting pots, mosaics, multiculturality, pluralism, and many other variations on the same theme. While these may be valuable discussions, their relevance to policy has yet to be firmly demonstrated. However, a special case of the "dilution" question comes up when we begin examining the cultural persistence of characteristics within Hispanic groups.

The principal difference between Hispanics and others in this regard is the twin impact of their proximity to their homeland and considerable evidence already accumlated that their culture seems to endure longer than most. (Undoubtedly some of this is due to language, which is dealt with elsewhere in this book, but some of it is also due to the cultural "density" which is provided by the interlocking of culture and religion.) Because Hispanics may modify the host culture as much as they are modified by it, we need to consider the older models of how groups in our society relate to each other and to the common national "culture," if indeed there even is one.

Cultural pluralism is a model that has been successful at explaining the relationships between groups within our society in that it perserves the multicultural nature of reality while enabling groups to form coalitions rather than always competing with one another. While the assimilationist asks "how long until we are all alike," and the acculturationist asks "what is the underlying commonality which binds all these various groups together," the pluralist asks "how our multiculturality makes us a unique society." Differences are strengths rather than weaknesses in this context. Pluralists tend to look for what remains after the passage of time and several generations, while the others tend to look for what has disappeared. Both facts do happen and some things remain while others disappear, but the importance of these different perspectives is more than a matter of research emphasis or taste. Whether we concentrate on what has vanished or what is still here determines how we will frame our policies.

The need to focus on what has disappeared also has a converse side in that people feel a need to produce cultural conformity and evenness. The restrictions expressed in the Immigration Act of 1924 were a policy devised to produce an "American culture" rather quickly. The 1965 version of that law expressed an openness to cultural differences, made the act less restrictive, and opened the way for a great variety of immigrants from many different cultures. Instead of conformity, current policy seems destined to produce diversity. This challenges the assmilationist/pluralist dialogue anew and groups such as those of Hispanic origin are going to be greatly affected by the outcomes of the dialogue.

Religious Participation and Beliefs

Accurate data regarding the religious practices and beliefs of the Hispanic population are difficult to come by for two reasons. First, most of the data concerning Hispanics is derived from the Census, which cannot ask questions concerning religion; and second, too many researchers have felt that religion was a "given" for the Hispanic population—that it was not something that varied within the population. This stemmed from a bias that all Hispanics were Catholic and that all were relatively conservative in their attitudes and devout but noninstitutional in their religious practices. The available data, even though it is thin, does offer some insight and corrections regarding these impressions.

Even as far back as 1950 a significant proportion of Puerto Rican marriages in New York City were being performed in Protestant churches and by 1960, although there had been a decline due in part to efforts by the archdiocese to evangelize more effectively, the proportion was still high. (The figure for 1950 was 50 percent and by 1960 it had declined to 38 percent, according to data analyzed by Fitzpatrick in 1976.) By the 1980s most marriages involving Puerto Ricans in New York were civil marriages (Dohen, 1982) with approximately 40 percent being performed away from any church and the remaining 60 percent about evenly divided between Catholic and Protestant churches.

Less than 15 percent of the Hispanic respondents in the New York city study indicated that they felt marriage was a religious event. Only 14 percent said it was a "sacred thing," and less than 1 percent attached any real importance to being married by a priest (Doyle, 1982). Although a majority of respondents in this study identified themselves as Catholic (83 percent), it is not yet clear what these statistics may mean in terms of the religious identity of the next few generations of Hispanics. These figures concern Puerto Ricans and would be quite different for Mexicans, who are more closely connected to the Catholic Church. However, they are of value precisely because they differ from the existing model that contends that the linkage between Hispanics and the Catholic Church is virtually unbreakable.

There has been an underlying theme in much of the writing about Hispanic religion, for both Puerto Ricans and Mexicans, concerning the role of folk religion in their lives. The New York City study contains an interesting finding that while folk religion is important for most Puerto Ricans it is also strongly associated with institutional religion. Those who rank high on the folk scale also ranked high on the institutional scale and on both scales it was the Catholics who tended to be at the high end (Doyle, 1982).

As far as Mexican religious experiences and preferences are known, it appears that although there has been a good deal of proselytizing among Mexicans in specific geographic areas by Protestant sects, the impact of such activity has been minimal (Grebler et al., 1970). In one study in Toledo, Ohio, it was found that being affiliated with the Catholic Church ranked fourth among twenty attributes considered necessary to being a community leader (Soto, 1974). Previous studies have also indicated that Catholicism, rather than Protestantism, has been associated with upward mobility for Mexican-Americans (Peñalosa and McDonagh, 1966). Whether this is changing in the late 1970s and early 1980s is difficult to say and a good deal more research of this nature needs to be done. One indicator that affiliation with the Catholic Church may still be preferred and may express an association with upward mobility is the fact that during the early 1980s in Chicago, Hispanic candidates for the high-school and college-level seminary of the archdiocese presented themselves in increasing numbers almost every year (McCready, 1983). It remains to be seen whether this will result in more Hispanic ordinations, but it is certainly a trend worth watching.

Cultural Assimilation and Pluralism

A still apt description of pluralism can be found in the work of Horace Kallen (1949):

> The American way is the way of orchestration. As in an orchestra, the different instruments, each with its own characteristic timbre and theme, contribute distinct and recognizable parts of the composition, so in the life and culture of a nation, the different regional ethnic, occupational, religious and other communities compound their different activities to make up the national spirit. The national spirit is constituted by this union of the different. It is sustained not by mutual exclusions, nor by the rule of one over others, but by the free trade between these different equals in every good thing the community's life and culture produce. This is the relation that the Constitution establishes between the States of the Union; this is the relation that develops between the regions within the States and the communities within the regions. In all directions there obtain . . . a mutual give and take in equal liberty on equal terms. The result is a strength and a richness in the arts and sciences which nations of a more homogeneous strain and an imposed culture . . . do not attain.

The policy implications of the dialogue are quite clear. Assimilation can be seen as a weakening of our social fabric, a denial of a source of strength, while pluralism which reinforces our multicultural nature can be defined as increasing our social spirit and deepening our resources.

The increased ethnic consciousness and awareness that we have experienced in recent years attests to the resilience which these identities have in our society. It is not simply a matter of nostalgia, but rather of considerable importance as to how people identify themselves vis-à-vis other citizens and the host culture. The legitimation of different identities, initiated by Blacks during the 1960s, has been echoed by almost every other group in society. Just as Blacks have become a powerful cultural force in society, other groups have begun to assess their own positions. People of Hispanic origin are particularly prepared to engage in a pluralistic lifestyle because of the strength of their own cultural identity. This is due in part to the intertwining of culture and religion in Hispanic life.

A challenge to the pluralistic model has recently been initiated, not so much from an assimilationist perspective, although there is some of that in this approach, as from a neo-Marxian approach to the analysis of group behavior in society. Steinberg (1981) contends that ethnic identity which persists past the point of immigration for very long is the result of discrimination and social rejection rather than an effort to preserve something of value. This approach contends that if it were not for oppression and domination by the larger society, ethnic groups, particularly Blacks, would have long ago made it into the mainstream of American society.

This perspective concentrates on the economic and status differences between groups and clearly has utility when one is attempting to analyze the differential opportunities which groups may or may not experience. It is not useful, however, when assessing the importance or relevance of those characteristics which groups maintain over time as part of their valued heritage. It is difficult to weave culture, achievement, and religion into one comprehensive understanding of group life, but unless such an integration is attempted our policies and strategies will always be lacking one or more important and valuable characteristics. If we focus only on equalizing opportunity, as important as that is, we fail to encourage people to bring along with them, in their social and economic advance, that which ultimately makes their life valuable and worthwhile; we can commit true cultural deprivation. If on the other hand we support cultural maintenance to the detriment of economic advancement, we can commit discriminatory economic oppression.

The pluralistic perspective attempts to consider both types of opportunity as important and deserving of supportive policies. People should be able to advance socially and economically without having to give up their values and heritage if they do not wish to do so. For Hispanic groups in the United States these are critically important issues. For these groups the linkage between religion and culture is a potentially important one over which they ought to have the final say. A pluralistic perspective might well take the position that however people want to define themselves is none of the host society's affair. If they want to maintain cultural enclaves or build parallel structures, that is fine. If they want to combine their religion and culture into a unique lifestyle, that is also fine. The essential policy question is, how can the host society best provide that the cultural cost of achieving mainstream status be as low as possible.

The point that is slowly being made in contemporary society is that religion and culture and success are not necessarily incompatible. Hispanics have a considerably different tradition of religious practice than many within the American Catholic Church would endorse, and this is cause for deep concern on the part of many church officials (Doyle, 1982). However, it is also the case that the host culture has benefited from many Hispanic contributions. The American Catholic Church has learned a great deal about celebrating already from those of Hispanic origins. Many urban communities are learning about new styles of community organization from Hispanics who are most comfortable with the personal, the informal, and the motivational. Voter education and registration projects have benefited from uniquely Hispanic characteristics in the Southwest, West, and Midwest.

Much of what has been done is because of the cultural "density" in Hispanic life that is provided by the strong connection between religion and culture. To deny this density or to attempt to exclude it from our consideration of planning and agenda-setting would be to deny one aspect of Hispanic culture which is powerful, flexible, and adaptable, and socially useful in that it generates a great deal of motivation and inspiration for change and progress. In the final section of this chapter we will briefly discuss several policy-related issues of concern to the Hispanic population which are derived from the relationship between religion and culture. The issues that will be presented will be the role of the church, religion and community development, and the continuation of a specifically Hispanic identity within the U.S. population.

Public Policy Issues

The Catholic Church has attempted to relate to Hispanic immigrants and to those of Hispanic origin who have been in this country for many years in the absence of an indigenous clergy which was the model with which the church has been most familiar. Although many mistakes have been made and many opportunities lost, overall the record of attempting to work within the frame of resource reductions has been quite positive. There are three specific areas in which the role of the church might be beneficially expanded.

First, is the *delivery of services* especially tailored to the needs of Hispanics and which has the potential for being done better if it includes a religious perspective. The most likely candidates would be education and health care. Research has shown that Hispanic youngsters do very well in parochial schools even when they are from extremely disadvantaged homes (Greeley, 1981). It is also the case that health care is a great need among Hispanics, and the church already has considerable resources devoted to this area. One of the problems with the available services is that many

Hispanics do not know where they are or are uncomfortable in going to them. The church could be a leader in devising ways of presenting and delivering services that would reduce access problems. In the same vein, church schools have access to Hispanic homes that public schools do not. Therefore it behooves them to devise ways of using that access for the benefit of the Hispanic population. While it is true that in general Hispanics are not exceptionally devout in an institutional sense—they are not very likely to be frequent Mass attenders—they nonetheless value the church greatly and are comfortable in seeking it out for assistance. Because American Catholics have focused on Mass attendence as a primary criterion for devotion and because their officials, usually from a European tradition, have supported them in this, it is likely that many Hispanic Catholics will be considered "less than devout." This would be a great mistake and a waste of valuable resources for both the church and the Hispanic people. One of the benefits of closely examining the connections between culture and religion, for the members of the official church, would be that they could thereby avoid this potential pitfall.

Second, because of the cultural density mentioned, earlier Hispanics are more likely than many other groups to form *cohesive communities*, and this tendency could be of great value to many urban areas. One of the only resources which poor urban communities have is their population. When ways can be found to use the latent skills within the populations, many areas can be organized and can begin to develop economically. Sometimes the first resource that surfaces is anger or frustration, but even those can provide the fuel to generate effective organizations. Deep within many Hispanic communities is a strong commitment to each other produced partly by the blend of religion and culture. The commitment to the community can provide the initial spark for successfully developing and building self-sufficient and independently functioning neighborhoods. Part of the resistance to fully utilizing the religious dimension of community life comes from the way we educate our community organizers or from the way we select out those to whom the host society will listen. This is not a plea for listening to every Hispanic spokesperson cloaked in religion, but rather an exhortation to take account of religion in the "secular" business of community development. Properly done, this can be a powerful tool in helping to rebuild many of our older cities' neighborhoods.

Finally, there is the issue of the *persistence of Hispanic identity* which may not be as directly related to policy decisions as services or community development, but which ultimately may be much more important. Without a sensitivity on the part of educators, service providers, and policymakers to the desire on the part of many Hispanics to raise their children in a Hispanic context, we will run the risk of wasting our future cultural resources and richness and polarizing our already badly polarized society even further. Hispanics perhaps more than other groups are resisting the notion that to be an American means you have to be something other than what you are. This is something that most other immigrant groups dealt with and many paid what they now feel was too high a price for "becoming American." Our diversity is our strength and is as much a part of our society as is our commitment to freedom under law. Some groups have shown an extraordinary ability to preserve their heritage while entering the mainstream. Hispanics, partly because of the link between religion and culture, tend to be a group which passes along identity effectively. This is a rich cultural resource for our society and should not be abandoned or ignored. It is difficult to consider the design of a social policy which would produce or ensure this end, but it is equally difficult to consider the demise of an integrated identity.

Young people need to be able to develop their own identity, and if in the process they should also find themselves immersed in a rich cultural heritage, so much the better. Ultimately this strengthens our society by providing the diversity of experience that can allow us to empathize with, communicate with, and relate to people from very different cultural backgrounds. In the contemporary world this seems to be very much worth doing. The integration of religion and culture in the development of the social agenda would seem to be one of those aspects that may be easily overlooked, but which is fundamental to the creation of a solid foundation upon which to build.

References

Alba, Richard, and R. Kessler. 1980. "Patterns of Interethnic Marriage among American Catholics." *Social Forces* 57:1124-40.

Choldin, Harvey, and Grafton Trout. 1969. *Mexican Americans in Transition: Migration and Employment in Michigan Cities.* East Lansing: Michigan State University, Rural Manpower Center.

Coles, Robert. 1964. "Children and Racial Demonstrations." *American Scholar* 34 (Winter):349-92.

Dohen, Dorothy. 1982. "Marriage, Family, and Fertility Patterns among Puerto Ricans." In *Hispanics in New York: Religious, Cultural, and Social Experiences*, vol. 1. New York: The Office of Pastoral Research, Archdiocese of New York.

Doyle, Ruth. 1982. *Hispanics in New York: Religious, Cultural, and Social Experiences*, vol. 1. New York: The Office of Pastoral Research, Archidocese of New York.

Fitzpatrick, Joseph P. 1976. "The Puerto Rican Family." In *Ethnic Families in America*, ed. Charles H. Mindel and Robert W. Haberstein. New York: Elsevier.

Fitzpatrick, Joseph P., and Douglas T. Gurak. 1979. *Hispanic Intermarriage in New York City: 1975*. Hispanic Research Center. Monograph no. 2, New York: Fordham University.

Geertz, Clifford. 1968. "Religion as a Cultural System." In *The Religious Situation*, ed. Donald Cutler. Boston: Beacon.

Grebler, L., W. Moore, and R. Guzmán. 1970. *The Mexican American People*. New York: Free Press.

Greeley, Andrew. 1982. *Catholic High Schools and Minority Students*. New Brunswick, N.J.: Transaction.

Kallen, Horace M. 1944. *Americanism and Its Makers*. New York: Bureau of Jewish Education.

McCready, William C. 1983. "Analysis of Seminary Enrollment for the Archdiocese of Chicago." Unpublished paper.

———. 1976. "The Persistence of Ethnic Variation in American Families." In *Ethnicity in the United States: A Preliminary Reconnaissance*, ed. Andrew M. Greeley and William McCready. New York: Wiley-Interscience.

Parot, Joseph J. 1981. *Polish Catholics in Chicago, 1850-1920*. DeKalb, Ill.: Northern University Press.

Peñalosa, Fernando, and Edward C. McDonaugh. 1966. "Social Mobility in a Mexican-American Community." *Social Forces* 44:498-505.

Soto, John A. 1974. "Mexican American Community Leadership for Education." Ph.D. diss., University of Michigan, Ann Arbor.

Steinberg, Stephen. 1981. *The Ethnic Myth*. New York: Atheneum.

Tomasi, Silvano M. 1976. "The Ethnic Church and the Integration of Italian Immigrants in the United States." In *The Italian Experience in the United States*, ed. S. Tomasi and M. Engel. New York: Center for Migration Studies.

Wrobel, Paul. 1979. *Our Way: Family, Parish, and Neighborhood in a Polish American Community*. South Bend, Ind.: University of Notre Dame Press.

4

Toward a Model of Socialization for Hispanic Identity: The Case of Mexican-Americans

Marco A. Martínez

Socialization refers to the process by which individuals become members of multiple social systems. The study of socialization provides important information for understanding the position of groups in society. The failure of a group to perform well in American society is often attributed to the improper socialization of its members. This line of thought suggests that if members are socialized to the "American way," success will follow, but if socialization varies from this course, difficulties are sure to arise. Studies of socialization among Hispanics until recently have assumed that Hispanics are held back in American society because they are socialized into the Hispanic and not American culture. Marco Martínez presents a review of the literature of socialization as it relates to Hispanics, giving special attention to Mexican-Americans. Much of this literature lacks both an empirical base and a recognition of the heterogeneity of Hispanic groups. Perhaps most wanting is a comprehensive model of socialization for Hispanics. Many theoretical models used to study Hispanics are based on Western models of socialization which ignore important variables that influence the socialization process—ethnic history, cultural differences, socioeconomic status. Martínez offers a model of socialization which emphasizes the integration of development and systems theories. The model is rooted in the assumption that "human beings are pluralistic and multicultural by nature." This model is particularly cogent, since it recognizes that Hispanics are not socialized into a purely Hispanic or American culture but rather into a society where both cultures influence the development of the individual.

The study of socialization involves the understanding of how a child becomes a member of a community. The term socialization refers to the process by which individuals become members of multiple social systems, and is therefore a lifelong process. In this process of membership attainment, individuals develop the essential human skills of communication, language, self-awareness, and thought. These products and the process itself are fundamentally cultural in nature. The family, school, community, peers, occupation—all these social systems are interrelated and function in a context. Therefore, socialization into the family, for example, cannot be fully understood except as a joint process of the family and other systems and in the context of society. As the child and family are in constant interaction, so are the family and society. This means that the study of human growth is by its very nature multivariate and interdisciplinary.

The need for a comprehensive view of socialization is most urgent in the case of Hispanics. There are four major reasons: (1) information pertaining to socialization on Hispanics is limited; (2) the information available lacks integration; (3) there are no explicit theoretical formulations that can guide and integrate research on Hispanics; and (4) available information provides an inadequate and sometimes negative characterization of Hispanics. I provide evidence in support of these four assertions and for the need for a comprehensive model of socialization.

The search for information on socialization regarding Hispanics continues to be an excessively laborious task. In the recent "state-of-the-art" *Handbook of Child Psychology* (Hetherington, 1983) there is nothing on the subject. In a review of the pertinent literature on Mexican-Americans, Ramírez and Arce (1981:25) pointed out: "Current research on Chicano family life has originated primarily in response to the dearth of adequate empirical data. Prior to 1970, Chicano family literature was sparse and empirically deficient. It argued that the family was old-fashioned, structurally rigid, male-dominated, unresponsive to the demands of contemporary industrial society and detrimental to individual mobility and coping ability." There has been increasing empirical research during the last decade. These studies are being conducted mostly by Mexican-American (or Chicano) social scientists. However, as we will show, available information pertaining to socialization lacks integration.

Another salient feature of the negative characterization of Hispanic children and families is that they are treated as a homogeneous community. The term *Hispanics* is a generic form to refer to several groups (Puerto Ricans, Cubans, Mexicans, Hispanos, South Americans, and others) who share some characteristics in different degrees (culture, language, status in society) and are distinguished by significant inter- and intragroup diversity. Understood in this manner, research on socialization of Hispanics is at an embryonic stage.

We are confronted with the problem of how to capture the positive features and diversity in children's behavior in all their richness and how to give an accurate picture of Hispanics. This picture becomes possible if we change our idea of socialization and child development and if we take into consideration the fact that it represents a complex process characterized by the joint interaction of social and familial factors.

A crucial first task in this endeavor relates to the elaboration of a conceptual model that integrates and organizes existing information and provides a guide for future research. The central purpose of this paper is to introduce a conceptual model that integrates theoretical presuppositions and sets of variables to account for generalities and individual differences in human growth and behavior. The variables have been selected in part from theory and in part from research. The review of research studies serves the purpose of providing evidence of, and illustrating, the importance of the variables in the model, as well the model's comprehensiveness and usefulness. By necessity, thus, the literature to be reviewed is selective. The selection is further restricted to deal exclusively with literature pertaining to Mexican-Americans. This literature will function as a case study and to illustrate the heterogeneity within this group of Hispanics. We propose that the model to be presented can be applied to the understanding of all groups of Hispanics. This task, however, is a research program for the future. Implications for research and public policy will be discussed in the final sections of the chapter.

Model of Socialization

Theoretical Bases

It seems possible to outline a theory of socialization from ideas developed by Kaye (1982), Mead (1934), and Vygotsky (1962, 1978, 1981), among others. This theory can function as a foundation for the conceptual model to be proposed. In brief form, the three authors emphasize the sociocultural nature of socialization. Human growth can be characterized as a continuous process of socialization; it starts at birth and proceeds throughout life. The initial consideration is that the human organism is born with biological propensities and organization and becomes social through its encounters with human adults. The very nature of the human infant and of the adult evolved so as to facilitate socialization (Kaye, 1982).

Individuals develop their self and personhood by acquiring memberships in multiple social systems (Kaye, 1982); in social groups, communities, or 'the generalized others' (G.H. Mead, 1934); or in sociocultural collectives (Vygotsky, 1981). For G.H. Mead, "the organized community or social group which gives to the individual his unity of self may be called 'the generalized other'" (p. 154). In particular, Vygotsky emphasizes a historical perspective; everything that is human finds its origins in social relations. Even "in their own private sphere, human beings retain the functions of social interactions" (p. 164). Children begin to use the same forms of behavior in relation to themselves that others initially used in relation to them by a process of internalization. Mind is but the internalization of social dialogues. In G.H. Mead's (1934:155-56) words, "in abstract thought the individual takes the attitude of the generalized other toward himself."

Kaye (1982) argues that later instances of socialization might work because of the basic processes established in infancy. In the context of this broad theoretical construct, it is crucial to investigate the interrelations among the several social systems. Kaye (1982:219) suggests that an initial hypothesis "would be that processes of infant socialization are replicated by the human species at other ages and at other levels of social system."

We can visualize the process of socialization as a concentric arrangement of circles in which each circle is related to all others in the configuration. Each circle represents a social system depicting the multiple relationships of occupation, school, community, and peer group which ultimately define the human growth of the individual; the fundamental system is the family. That is, socialization does not proceed in an isolated sequential order: from family to peer, school, community, occupation, and so on. Family socialization is influenced by all other social systems to which the parents belong; and simultaneously, family socialization influences the initiation of the individual into all other social systems.

Pluralism and multiculturality are important aspects of the socialization process. Pluralism refers to the political divisions within which socialization occurs and multiculturalism refers to the sociological context for the same process. These divisions and contexts form a part of the foundation within which a person's identity develops, and they must be taken into account when we reflect upon the ways in which people learn their social roles and develop their psychological identities.

Human groups are pluralistic and multicultural by their very nature. Human beings are capable of learning the rules, languages, and other necessary skills to become members of diverse social systems and cultures simultaneously. By nature, human beings are flexible, opportunistic, and adaptable to different systems beginning in early childhood. The terms *pluralism* and *multiculturalism* describe basic characteristics of human nature and of the socialization process. Terms like *bilingual and bicognitive development, cultural diversity,* and similar others, are specifics of a more generic term, *socialization.*

This theoretical formulation of socialization forces one to assume a multivariate, interdisciplinary, and developmental perspective. This perspective leads to the proposition that multiple sociocultural, historical, political, and psychological factors need to be specified and interrelated in the unity of a framework. Furthermore, the framework should account for how change in one variable in the system will affect the other variables in the system.

Conceptual Analytic Framework

Human growth and behavior are explained as a function of the interaction of multiple variables. Each variable has multiple indicators and all variables are embedded in the matrix of variation ar͟ oss geographical space and extending over time. The model is fairly complex and comprehensive. It argues against the common research characterization of ethnic minority groups in terms of socioeconomic status, education, and ethnic membership variables (see Maccoby and Martin, 1983).

The argument underlying the model is that we need to specify the variables to be included on the bases of relevance to substantive theory, and ultimately of relevance to the phenomena one is attempting to explain. The primary aim of the model is to explain socialization among Hispanic groups, with initial consideration of Mexican-Americans as an illustrative case. One explains socialization by accounting for how children, for example, acquire the knowledge and behavior of their own families and communities. The explanation, furthermore, describes changes, universal and individual variations of the process accounted for by relationships among variables. An important consideration related to this aim is that following the proposed model we should understand Puerto Ricans, Cubans, and other Hispanic groups in their own terms. Once that was accomplished we could generalize and explore differences and similarities between and among groups and eventually build an empirical perspective about Hispanic socialization processes.

The model is developmental in perspective. A second hypothesis underlying the model is that the same framework, the variables and their interrelations, are necessary to explain the individual's progressive memberships in other social systems (school, occupation, etc.). In these instances of socialization, achieved development and behavior will be an important variable in understanding later processes of socialization. In other words, the child's membership in a particular family and community will influence his integration into a school system, for example, and will influence the school system itself. The reverse process will be also true. The child's membership in a particular school system will influence his membership in his family and community and will influence his family and community, and so on.

The proposed model has a transactional view. In the words of Sameroff et al. (1982:7), "the defining characteristic of the transactional model is that all elements in the system do in fact influence the development of all other elements. The elements do not merely sum or multiply to achieve a particular threshold level; rather, the social-psychological system undergoes fundamental change through the course of development."

This model provides the machinery to relate theory and hypotheses to observed data and to provide for the acceptance or rejection of theories based on empirical investigation. The model can also highlight not only what we know but what we do not know, and can provide guidance for future research.

Socialization Variables

The main purpose of this section is to show the usefulness of the proposed model of socialization by integrating pertinent research information into its framework. The review of the literature is selective and has several restrictions. Most importantly, it deals with family socialization; it considers variables to account for the child's integration into his family system. An attempt to contend with the multimembership process of socialization is far too complicated and beyond the space allotted to this paper, but ought to be pursued in a research agenda.

A second restriction is the exclusive focus on literature pertaining to Mexican-Americans. This literature has increased at a tremendous rate in the past decade. The rate of growth has created an urgent need for the integration of information. Additional elements characterize this section of the paper: (1) the literature was selected to illustrate critical issues and variables pertaining to the proposed model; (2) the literature's review was organized according to the variables of the model; (3) there is a great deal of overlap in discussing these variables, but it will be held to a minimum and used only to illustrate the need for a comprehensive and unitary framework.

Historical and Demographic Variables

Recent research has documented that Mexican-Americans are a highly heterogeneous population that varies along every classifying dimension (Estrada et al., 1981; Valdéz et al., 1983). An important factor accounting for such variability is history. Mexican groups in the United States have different histories of immigration and settlement. Some trace their roots to the Spanish and Mexican settlers who undertook the exploration and development of the Southwest long before the pilgrims arrived on the continent. American history in the Southwest began in 1848, when Mexicans were incorporated into the United States largely through military conquest (Camarillo, 1979). By the turn of the century, contrary to the arrangements established by Mexico and the United States in the treaty of Guadalupe Hidalgo, Mexicans had been dispossessed of their property and relegated to a lower-class status. Long-term residents of the region were reduced to being aliens in their native lands (Acuña, 1981; Sánchez, 1940).

Other groups of Mexicans are immigrants or children of immigrants who began to arrive in large numbers by the turn of the century. This immigration has had no interruption to the present (Burma, 1970; Bustamante, 1977; Taylor, 1934). Tyler (1975:4) has observed that "probably because Mexican-Americans are among the earliest settlers and also the latest immigrants, they are a paradox: native aliens. This apparent incongruity has made it difficult for most Americans to understand either the past or the present of Mexican-American life." The dearth of historical information has been a salient factor, beginning to be corrected, in accounting for the difficulty in understanding Mexican-Americans.

Substantial historical research on Mexican-Americans has been accumulated during the past decade. Neglected areas of historical inquiry have attracted increasing numbers of Mexican-American scholars (see Valdéz et al. [1983] for a review on historical research). Pertinent to our model are the works on the history of the Mexican-American family. In his review of this literature, Saragoza (1983) points out that the current historical evidence emphasizes the fundamental cultural variation and social differentiation among Mexican-American families. Crucial factors in the historical inquiry are variability across regions (including Mexico) and changes over time. Saragoza argues that the history of the Chicano family must be anchored in the context of the American economy. He claims that family socialization has been less in the hands of parents, barrios, or Mexican institutions, and more in the economic and political forces of society. Capitalism may have deeply affected the parent-child bond in the process of socialization. However, there are no data to indicate the nature of those changes and to explain how they have occurred. In future research we must ask "how Chicano families in different historical periods, in different socioeconomic contexts adapted differently to capitalism" (Baca Zinn, 1983:142), and how family socialization has responded differently to societal pressures.

General demographic characteristics of Mexican-Americans provide another dimension to their history. Much of this material is contained in a separate chapter in this book. It has been argued that demographic data and techniques are not yet adequate for studies of the Mexican-American population (Hernández et al., 1973; Sullivan, 1981). In brief, the quantitative data depict the Mexican group as a youthful population, rapidly growing, most likely living within extended families, bilingual at some level, and with its future well before it. Family formation, family socialization, schooling, and employment will continue to be crucial issues. Along with these generalities, we need to investigate the variability in the distribution of characteristics. A major empirical question in need of verification is how these historical and demographic factors are interrelated with others which we will now discuss, to account for differences in the process of multicultural membership of Mexican-Americans.

Socialization and Cultural Values

Cultural values are at the heart of understanding socialization and human growth. Socialization is very much a process of cultural development. Early studies of Mexican-American family socialization invariably focused on the analysis of cultural values; invariably also families were inaccurately and often negatively characterized. Although the information and perspective of the early investigators are beginning to be corrected (Andrade, 1983; Baca Zinn, 1979; Ramírez and Castañeda, 1974), the early studies continue to exert subtle influences on recent literature (Ybarra, 1983).

Kluckhohn and Strodbeck (1961) attempted to explain the condition of Spanish-Americans by means of "value orientations" or "cultural values." Numerous other authors followed the same formulation (Clark, 1959; M. Mead, 1953; Saunders, 1954; for a review of this literature see Vaca [1970] and Ybarra [1983]).

Several conclusions emerged from the early studies on Mexican-American families: (1) Mexican-American culture is rural and based on negative and detrimental values; (2) these cultural values are the main reason for the low socioeconomic and political situation of the group, and the strongest impediment to their acculturation and success; (3) Mexican-Americans have to renounce their culture in favor of the majority culture to be successful; and (4) the family continues to perpetuate the traditional culture through the socialization of its children.

The consideration of other factors could lead to dissimilar interpretations and conclusions and that is the central theme of this chapter. For example, in Knowlton's (1975:28) words, "this distress in northern New Mexico is not due to any genetic or cultural characteristic of the local Spanish-American inhabitants; it is due to the Spanish-Americans' loss of ownership or access to the natural resources of the region that have passed into Anglo-American or government hands."

Recent investigators (Murillo, 1976; Baca Zinn, 1979, 1983; Ybarra, 1983) have offered cogent critiques of the related literature, pointing out serious methodological flaws, specifically that of reducing family dynamics to crude accounts of cultural values alone. Baca Zinn (1979) suggested that cultural values become meaningful only when they are related to historical, economic, residential, and other structural factors. However, investigations following this suggestion with particular reference to family socialization are still to be developed.

Geographic Variables

There are two main aspects of these variables to consider. One relates to the immigration of Mexican families from different regions of Mexico to different regions of the United States. The second deals with the internal migration of Mexican-Americans from rural to urban areas, and from entirely different regions to others within the confines of the United States.

Recently, Camarillo (1979), García (1981), and Saragoza (1983), among others, have argued for the need to explain the family life of Mexican-Americans in the broad context of both Mexico and the United States. These authors suggested that we cannot claim that Mexican-American family socialization practices are an exclusive result of interaction with U.S. institutions and general lifestyle. Ramírez and Arce (1981) found that extended family and highly integrated extended kinship systems characterized the structure and function of Chicano families, even of families who were three or more generations removed from Mexico. Sena-Rivera (1979) contends that the extended family structure did not develop in the United States; it originated in Mexico and has persisted in the United States.

From a rural and regional minority population, Mexican-Americans have become a national minority and predominantly urban population, more geographically dispersed than at any other time (Tienda, 1983). There are variations among states. Most Mexican-Americans outside the Southwest reside in metropolitan areas; within the Southwest, Chicanos in New Mexico are the least urbanized, while the most urbanized live in California (Jaffe et al., 1970; for a review of research on Chicanos' internal migration, see Tienda [1983]).

Variations within small locations, like within cities, have been reported. Año Nuevo de Kerr (1975) analyzed the development of three Chicano neighborhoods that differed in their social composition and economic characteristics over time. She concluded that Chicano settlement experiences depended greatly on the sector of the city in which the community was established.

Most of the information available pertaining to Mexican-American family life comes from Mexican-Americans residing in the Southwest. It is frequently argued that regional differences are important (Saragoza, 1983).

With a few exceptions, little is being done to replicate Southwestern studies in the Midwest. An important factor in the Midwest communities, absent in the Southwest to the same degree, is the substantial contact of Mexican-Americans with other Hispanic groups. Marriages between people from different Hispanic groups are making it more possible for them to apply the term *Hispanic* or *Latino* to their children as a significant ethnic identification. These children are not only Mexican, Puerto Rican, or Cuban, they represent the new generation of Hispanics. We do not know how the family socialization practices for these children vary as compared to Mexican-American or Puerto Rican families. The situation of the Midwest promises to be an important area of research with respect in particular to socialization of Hispanics as a group.

Tienda (1983:176) concluded her review of the literature on internal migration of Mexican-Americans stating: "The most pressing research need in this area is to interpret their changing residential distribution by linking spatial with social dimensions in a coherent and systematic fashion. This requires information about the characteristics of places as well as the individuals who inhabit them."

Economic and Political Variables

A study by Grebler et al. (1970) represents the first major empirical work attempting to provide a comprehensive analysis of the social context of Mexican-Americans. They focused on family structure and examined a variety of socioeconomic and political variables. They found a basically egaliltarian division of household tasks between husbands and wives. Several other investigators have reported that an egalitarian power structure in decision-making and action-taking characterized most Mexican-American families (Hawkes and Taylor, 1975; Cromwell and Ruiz, 1979; Ybarra, 1983).

However, Grebler et al. (1970) argued that the socioeconomic inequality between Mexican-Americans and Whites and their limited assimilation to the larger society had its sources in the cultural values of the Mexican group. The last chapter of their book is dedicated to explaining how Mexican-Americans fall short of the majority White contemporary culture, and how this failure is due to remnants of traditional cultural values of Mexican-Americans. Others have followed Grebler et al.'s perspective (Anderson and Johnson, 1971; Carter, 1970; Moore, 1970).

These authors have failed to consider seriously the impact of other factors. For example, Frisbie and Neidert (1977) analyzed the structure of the relationship between minority group size and socioeconomic inequality. They found that neither Mexicans nor Blacks seemed to realize occupational benefits from increases in the proportionate size of their own group.

Their explanation was based on assumptions and indications of discrimination by the host culture. Frisbie and Neidert's findings are consonant with data from the U.S. Bureau of Census (1981), indicating that Mexican-Americans' average income is higher outside than inside the Southwest, where 86 percent of the total Mexican-American population resides. Galarza (1964) had similarly pointed out that the average income was higher for Mexican-Americans in California than in Texas, where the percentage of this group was higher and discrimination stronger.

Poston, Alvirez, and Tienda (1976) examined the earnings differences in groups of Anglo- and Mexican-American workers from 1960 to 1970. They found that an increase in the "cost" of being Mexican-American was apparent, since Mexican-Americans' economic position had not shown any significant increment. A similar trend has continued during the last decade (Massey, 1981).

Briggs, Fogel, and Schmidt (1977:55), among others, have argued that "much of the low income position of Chicanos is associated with their limited schooling" (see also National Commission for Employment Policy, 1982). Contrary to this claim, Poston et al. (1976:269) suggested that even though education is not the only determinant of earnings, they found it "difficult not to challenge the institutional mechanisms which may well be interfering with the ability of Mexican-Americans to improve their earnings potential with increased educational attainment" (see also U.S. Commission on Civil Rights, 1982).

The existence of structural and institutional discrimination has been documented with respect to education (Carter and Segura, 1979; Featherman and Houser, 1978; Vásquez, 1974) and labor market and unemployment rates (Barrera, 1979; Galarza, 1964; Graham, 1977; Burawoy, 1976; Piore, 1979).

The consideration of these socioeconomic and political factors, however, reveals only part of the picture. For example, the historical accounts of Mexican-Americans' struggle against oppression and their struggle to form labor (Acuña, 1981) and political organizations at the local and national levels (Pachon, 1983), are clear reminders of the interactional process among individuals, families, communities, and society. For future research, "we face the challenge of analyzing both those systems of social inequality within which family life takes place, and those adaptations Chicanos must make in order to survive" (Baca Zinn, 1983:144).

Linguistic and Educational Variables

The impact of family socialization on school socialization, or the analysis of school socialization per se, are beyond the scope of this paper. There exists a voluminous amount of literature on bilingual education, schooling, and child psychology bearing on these issues (Durán, 1983; Fishman and Keller, 1982; García, 1983).

Our purpose is to illustrate variables that relate to family socialization. One important variable is the type of schooling experiences that children receive and bring home with them. There is research evidence, for example, that negative attitudes from school personnel toward Mexican-American children's language (nonstandard or accented English or nonstandard Spanish) may impact negatively on the children's school experiences (Laosa, 1977; Ramírez, 1981), and may influence family life as well. The autobiography by Rodríguez (1981) illustrates the strong influence of school experiences and policies on family socialization. The literature on school-oriented family intervention programs relates to our concerns, and exemplifies the enduring negative characterization of ethnic minority families (Fantini and Cárdenas, 1980).

Another form of how schooling affects families is through the formal education that parents have received. Laosa (1982) concluded from a series of studies of Chicano mothers interacting with their children that mothers' educational attainment was the most critical factor in determining how they socialized their children for schooling. However, we argue that perhaps part of the family socialization is to prepare children for membership in other systems, yet family socialization is primarily the process of becoming a member of one's own family system. Following this reformulation, research programs will tend to focus on family life in its own terms, and to describe families and children in a positive fashion.

Communities and Families

The unit of analysis in studying family socialization could be a community, a region, or a large society; at a micro level, the unit could be a family, a mother-child dyad, or any other dyad. However, multiple factors should always be considered. The individual, thus, is not the proper unit of analysis.

An example of analysis conducted at the macro level is the series of studies by Ramírez and Castañeda (1974). They identified three distinct types of Mexican-American communities: traditional, dualistic, and atraditional. Each community was characterized by distinctive socioeconomic, cultural, and political factors, and also by specific family socialization practices. Seven variables were used in determining the variance between and within communities: (1) distance from the Mexican border; (2) length of residence in the United States; (3) identification with Mexican, Mexican-American, or Spanish-American history; (4) degree of American urbanization; (5) degree of economic and political strength of Mexican-Americans in the community; (6) degree of discrimination from the larger society; and (7) degree of contact with non-Mexican-Americans.

Ramírez and Castañeda noted that the seven variables contribute in varying degrees to changes and characteristics of Mexican-American communities in the Southwest. Following this framework, Ramírez, Castañeda, and Herold (1974) identified three Mexican-American communities in Southern California, and from these communities selected groups of schoolchildren and their mothers for an investigation. Mothers and children were administered tests to determine cognitive style, and the mothers also completed a socialization questionnaire and a Mexican-American family values questionnaire.

They found that in the traditional community most of its residents were Mexican-American; Spanish was the primary language; most of the residents were Catholic; there were close ties between most families; and there was strong identification with Mexican and Mexican-American heritage. In the dualistic community, Mexican-Americans were a minority with minimal economic or political influence; English was the primary language; and approximately 20 percent of the families were Protestant. The third community, atraditional, was located near downtown of one of the largest cities in the Southwest. All the residents were Mexican-Americans, but had more daily contact with the White majority community than residents of the other two communities. English was the primary language of most of the Mexican-Americans, and more than 30 percent were Protestant.

The investigators found that children reared in the traditional community were more field-dependent in cognitive style than children reared in the dualist and atraditional communities. In similar manner, the mothers in the traditional community were found to be more field-dependent and tended to agree with the field-dependent socialization and the traditional Mexican-American culture. Field-dependent individuals are described as being more influenced by the human element in the environment, less analytic in their thinking, and thus less adapted for schooling than field-independent individuals.

Ramírez and Castañeda's principal emphasis was to analyze cognitive styles among Mexican-American children; to explain differences in cognitive styles by means of social and family variables; and to explore the relationships between socialization practices of home and community and learning styles of children and the educational practices of schools. Their work generated a great deal of controversy, but also substantial interest in research mainly dealing with the development of educational programs for Mexican-American children (Carter and Segura, 1979).

From the point of view of our proposed model, some points are worthy of comment. The explanatory variables postulated by Ramírez and Castañeda are essentially identical to the variables in our model. We argue that critical differences separate the two models. In their framework, the variables are indices of competence, and describe outcomes rather than the processes underlying those indicators. Their variables describe situations, results: a particular learning style is the result of a given set of socialization practices. Identification and description of communities is made on the basis of current characteristics. Their measurement instruments also emphasize outcomes, not processes. These characteristics of the Ramírez and Castañeda framework are not necessarily incorrect, but they are incomplete.

A salient ingredient of our model is the variable "time," which emphasizes our theoretical interest in development, in processes, in asking how family socialization, for example, evolves over time. There is a difference between identifying and describing the patterns of family socialization and analyzing and describing how those patterns develop over time. If this is our interest, besides employing questionnaires and other self-report procedures, we will then resort to direct observation of interaction occurring and developing in time. As Vygotsky (1981) argued, behavior can be fully understood only as the history of behavior. Ramírez and Castañeda's framework, however, is valuable and should continue to be tested, particularly in other areas outside the Southwest. Kaye (1982) has pointed out that competency models, like the one by Ramírez and Castañeda, are important in specifying the variables to be incorporated into an accompanying process model. The two models, then, are complementary.

An important presupposition of our model is that understanding more about the processes of family socialization, rather than only its outcomes, will provide more valuable information for school socialization and for the transition and relationships between the two systems.

Family as a Unit of Analysis

In this section we will consider the family variables as related to the process of family socialization. Some basic research studies will be presented to illustrate our model.

Numerous studies have indicated that Mexican-American children are not as field-independent as White children (for a review of this research, see Kagan and Buriel [1977]). The concepts of field-dependent and field-independent refer to cognitive styles of individuals by which they relate to, classify, assimilate, and organize information from the environment. The thrust of the research evidence is that Mexican-Americans (tending to be more field-dependent) prefer social cooperation and nonanalytic or undifferentiated strategies of thinking and problem-solving in educational activities. In contrast, White children (who tend to be more field-independent) favor competition, independence, and analytic modes of thought in school interaction. The argument is made in the literature that variations in cognitive styles are closely related to patterns in socialization practices, and that for schooling purposes field-independence is more adaptive than field-dependence.

Another area of research has focused on achievement motivation. Madsen and Kagan (1973) investigated a group of twelve mother-child pairs from a small town of northern Mexico, and another group of twelve White mother-child pairs from Los Angeles. Both groups were observed in two experimental situations. The mothers either controlled the rewards given to the children for success or failure or selected achievement goals for the children. The authors concluded that the Los Angeles mothers behaved in ways that encouraged and modeled high achievement in their children, while the Mexican mothers reacted more to their children's feelings. In related studies comprising only U.S. samples, Steward and Steward (1973, 1974) found that White mothers facilitated assertive behavior in children more than Mexican-American mothers. Similar studies have described Mexican-American children as less competitive (Hoppe, Kagan, and Zahn, 1977; Kagan and Madsen, 1971), less rivalrous, less assertive, and more submissive (Kagan and Madsen, 1972). Kagan and Ender (1975) claimed that the differences found between the U.S. parents were not cultural but economic, and in the case of the Mexican mothers from northern Mexico, the differences were cultural. This group of mothers showed preference for boys and believed in fate and in external control, factors identified as central in Mexican culture, according to the authors.

Some difficulties with the foregoing programs of research were pointed out by Ramírez and Price-Williams (1976). These investigators examined White, Black, and Mexican-American fourth-grade children regarding achievement motivation and family identification. Their argument had three premises: (1) McClelland's (1961) definition of achievement motivation is rooted on a Western view of psychodynamics defining behavior as individually motivated; (2) contextual conditions are more important in the expression of achievement motivation; and (3) the particular form in which achievement is expressed is determined by the definition that culture assigns it. Ramírez and Price-Williams found Mexican-American and Black children expressed achievement motivation in the form of family achievement. The most important determinant, the authors suggested, may be the degree to which identification with the family is encouraged in socialization. Laosa (1978, 1980) has provided evidence suggesting that differences between White and Mexican-American maternal teaching strategies can be accounted for by differences in levels of formal schooling rather than by cultural differences or economic indices. In particular, Laosa (1981) found that White mothers employed inquiry and praise as teaching strategies more frequently than Chicano mothers. These mothers used modeling, visual cue, directive, and negative physical control more often than did White mothers. Laosa (1982:823) pointed out that "compared with the parent-child interactions in the average Chicano family, the parent-child interactions in the average non-Hispanic White family resemble much more closely the types of interactions one expects to find in a school classroom." Laosa (1981, 1982) speculated that the increased participation of Chicanos in formal education may have the effect of eliminating cultural and linguistic differences between the two groups to the point that differences in patterns of family interaction eventually disappear.

An alternative hypothesis is that these differences in family interaction patterns need not and will not disappear. For example, Martínez (1981) investigated how a group of mothers maintained conversations with their preschool children. The mothers were Mexican, Spanish-speaking, and on the average had only fifth-grade education. Martínez's study replicated Kaye and Charney's (1980, 1981) investigation conducted with White mothers who were much more educated, and their children. Both groups of mothers were equally successful in maintaining similar levels of conversations with their respective children. However, each group of mothers achieved sustained dialogues by different means. Mexican mothers utilized nonverbal and directive strategies, while White mothers stressed inquiry and expanding devices.

This is not to say that formal education is unimportant. Education is very important but is only one variable among others also of critical significance. As postulated by our model, changes in behavior and growth can only be explained by changes in all factors. Diversity and pluralism in society is as much the result of variation of multiple family and society factors as of the diversity and pluralism in the potential of human nature.

Some Implications for Research

We have proposed a conceptual model to assist in the analysis of the processes of socialization among Hispanics. An outline of theoretical presuppositions pertaining to socialization was elaborated. This theory functions as a foundation, and it integrates and organizes a viewpoint for the analytic framework. The characteristics, assumptions, and the multivariate elements of the analytic tool were discussed. Literature on Mexican-Americans related to family socialization was employed as a case study to demonstrate the explanatory and integrative usefulness of the conceptual model.

Recent reviewers of research on Mexican-Americans (Valdéz, Carmarillo, and Almaguer, 1983) have recurrently identified three urgent needs to be addressed by future investigations: (1) there is a rapidly growing amount of research information in need of integration; (2) research programs need to take a multivariate interdisciplinary perspective; and (3) there is a demanding need to develop explicit theoretical constructs relevant to Mexican-Americans. We have added an equally critical one: (4) the need to provide positive characterizations of Hispanic children, families, and communities. These needs embody a tremendous challenge to reformulate our thinking, to invigorate our commitment, and to establish interdisciplinary cooperation with the common aim of creating alternative models in dealing with those needs.

We postulate that our model represents an alternative perspective to address the problems of reductionism, disintegration, lack of theoretical and historical thrust, and negative portrayal that plague most of the literature pertinent to Mexican-Americans. The model can guide future research, particularly with respect to Hispanics. Much needs to be done within each variable of our framework, and much more in investigating how particular variables interrelate with each other, and ultimately with patterns and diversity in family socialization. A further step in the study of family socialization includes the analysis of the integration and relationships among the various social systems (family, school, peer, etc.). This investigation focuses on the phenomenon of multigroup membership by which individuals become pluralistic and multicultural and grow up as persons. This broadly stated research framework has numerous elements which can be examined independently or in the context of interdisciplinary cooperation. However, unless the research programs and their specific findings are embedded into a broad and comprehensive framework, the family socialization of Hispanics will never be understood well. The dearth of information regarding Hispanics looms considerably more than information on Mexican-Americans, not only in the area of family socialization but in many other discipline areas.

How much of the information accumulated on Mexican-Americans can be properly generalized to Puerto Ricans, Cubans, or other Hispanic groups? It is an empirical question which we urgently need to answer. Our framework can be applied to integrate and organize existing research data on each of the Hispanic groups. Once this step is accomplished, the formulation of hypotheses and the design and implementation of research programs can follow.

A critical objective of any investigation regarding family socialization among the various groups of Hispanics must include the analysis and description of generalities and variations that capture in a positive fashion the richness and diversity among Hispanic families.

Public Policy Issues

The most critical need to be addressed by policymakers involves the creation and development of mechanisms to improve our research data base on family socialization among Hispanics. Hispanics are a difficult challenge due to their tremendous diversity and our own limited knowledge of them. It is clear that policymakers cannot wait until our data increase in volume and relevance. However, some theoretical considerations can be of assistance immediately.

From the perspective of our model, public policy directed to family socialization among Hispanics must be responsible and must be innovative, if it wishes to be effective. To be truly responsible, policy must embody and address a multiplicity of factors, all critical in their internal relationship to family life. A policy is responsible when its formulation reflects the integrated and multifaceted reality of families growing within communities in the context of the larger society, and being mutually affected.

The structure of society cannot be taken as given. Public policies must address society factors and family variables in the same equation simultaneously. A policy geared to influence family attitudes toward schooling, for example, which neglects to consider school attitudes toward families, is not a responsible formulation. Current public policy is full of examples to illustrate the point. Significant changes in family socialization will arise only as a result of changes in all other society and family factors.

There is another way by which policy can be judged to be responsible. Public policy must clearly respond to the diversity between the various Hispanic populations. In a recent assessment of the national policy process, Pachon (1983:212) pointed out that policymakers continue to "have a startling lack of information on the Hispanic community." Historically, Pachon noted, they have failed to ask the question: How does policy X impact on the Hispanic community? Currently, they are still continuing to overlook the Hispanic community's characteristics of large extended families, bilingualism and biculturalism, and the implications of these factors for federal policies and programs. We argue that policy must still proceed one step further and ask: How does policy X impact on the various Hispanic communities? Obviously, there is a need to bring Hispanic families and their communities, with all their diversity, into the national policy forum.

Second, public policy must be innovative. To be innovative, policy must be oriented to emphasize strengths and develop positive characteristics, and not only to correct limitations or deficits of any kind. To be innovative, policy must have a longe-range focus and be based on coherent, comprehensive theories of human development. We argue that our conceptual model can assist policymakers to view their task in a more holistic, integrated, and developmental fashion. Policymakers should focus on helping families and communities to strengthen their forces and organization as means to attain self-control and positive and productive participation in society. In particular, we need a strong public policy framework that recognizes, encourages, and implements the development of the basic human predisposition for pluralism or multicultural membership of individuals. Taking this conceptual model into consideration can assist policymakers to be more effective in their formulations.

References

Acuña, R. 1981. *Occupied America: A History of Chicanos*, 2nd ed. New York: Harper & Row.

Anderson, J., and W. Johnson. 1971. "Stability and Change among Three Generations of Mexican Americans: Factors Affecting Achievement." *American Educational Research Journal* 8:285-307.

Andrade, S.J., ed. 1983. *Latino Families in the U.S.* New York: Planned Parenthood.

Angel, R., and M. Tienda. 1982. "Living Arrangements and Components of Household Income among Hispanics, Blacks and Non-Hispanic Whites in the U.S." *American Sociological Review.*

Año Nuevo de Kerr, L. 1975. "Chicano Settlements in Chicago: A Brief History." *Journal of Ethnic Studies* 2:22-31.

Baca Zinn, M. 1979. "Chicano Family Research: Conceptual Distortions and Alternative Directions." *Journal of Ethnic Studies* 7:59-71.

———. 1983. "Ongoing Questions in the Study of Chicano Families." In A. Valdez, A. Camarillo, and T. Almaguer, eds. *The State of Chicano Research on Family, Labor, and Migration.* Stanford: Stanford Center for Chicano Research.

Barrera, M. 1979. *Race and Class in the Southwest: A Theory of Racial Inequality.* Notre Dame: University of Notre Dame Press.

Briggs, V., W. Fogel, and F. Schmidt. 1977. *The Chicano Worker.* Austin: University of Texas Press.

Brown, G., M. Rosen, S. Hill, and M. Olivas. 1980. *The Condition of Education for Hispanic Americans.* Washington: National Center for Education Statistics.

Burawoy, M. 1976. "The Function and Reproduction of Migrant Labor: Comparative Material from Southern Africa and the United States." *American Journal of Sociology* 81:1050-87.

Burma, J. 1970. *Mexican Americans in the United States: A Reader.* Cambridge: Schenkman, Canfield.

Bustamante, J. 1977. "Undocumented Immigration from Mexico: Research Report." *International Migration Review* 11:149-77.

Camarillo, A. 1979. *Chicanos in a Changing Society.* Cambridge: Harvard University Press.

Carter, T. 1979. *Mexican Americans in School: A History of Educational Neglect.* New York: College Entrance Examination Board.

Carter, T., and R. Segura. 1979. *Mexican Americans in School: A Decade of Change.* New York: College Entrance Examination Board.

Clark, M. 1959. *Health in the Mexican American Culture.* Berkeley: University of California Press.

Cromwell, R., and R. Ruiz. 1979. "The Myth of Macho Dominance in Decision Making within Mexican and Chicano Families." *Hispanic Journal of Behavioral Sciences* 1:355-74.

Durán, R.P. 1983. *Hispanics' Education and Background.* New York: College Entrance Examination Board.

Estrada, L., F. García, R. Marcías, and R. Maldonado. 1981. "Chicanos in the United States: A History of Exploitation and Resistance." *Daedalus* 110:103-31.

Fantini, M.D., and R. Cárdenas, eds. 1980. *Parenting in a Multicultural Society.* New York: Longman.

Featherman, D., and R. Houser. 1978. *Opportunity and Change.* New York: Academic.

Fishman, J.A., and G.D. Keller. 1982. *Bilingual Education for Hispanic Students in the United States.* New York: Teacher College.

Frisbie, W., and L. Neidert. 1977. "Inequality and the Relative Size of Minority Population: A Comparitive Analysis." *American Journal of Sociology* 82:1007-30.

Galarza, E. 1964. *Merchants of Labor: The Mexican Bracero Story.* Santa Barbara: McNally & Loftin.

García, E. 1983. *The Mexican-American Child: Language and Social Development.* Tempe: Arizona State University Press.

García, M.T. 1981. *Desert Immigrants: The Mexicans of El Paso, 1880-1920.* New Haven: Yale University Press.

Graham, O. 1977. "Illegal Immigration." *Center Magazine*:56-66.

Grebler, L., J. Moore, and R. Guzmán. 1970. *The Mexican-American People: The Nation's Second Largest Minority.* New York: Free Press.

Hawkes, G., and M. Taylor. 1975. "Power Structure in Mexican and Mexican American Farm Labor Families." *Journal of Marriage and the Family*:807-11.

Hernández, J., L. Estrada, and D. Alvirez. 1973. "Census Data and the Problem of Conceptually Defining the Mexican American Population." *Social Science Quarterly* 53:671-87.

Hetherington, E.M., ed. 1983. *Socialization, Personality, and Social Development.* New York: Wiley.

Hoppe, C., S. Kagan, and G. Zahn. 1977. "Conflict Resolution among Field-Independent and Field-Dependent Anglo American and Mexican American Children and Their Mothers." *Developmental Psychology* 13:591-98.

Jaffe, A., R. Cullen, and T. Boswell. 1980. *The Changing Demography of Spanish Americans.* New York: Academic.

Kagan, S., and R. Buriel. 1975. "Field Dependence-Independence and Mexican American Culture and Education." In J.L. Martinez, ed., *Chicano Psychology*. New York: Academic.

Kagan, S., and P. Ender. 1975. "Maternal Response to Success and Failure of Anglo American, Mexican American and Mexican Children." *Child Development* 46:452-58.

Kagan, S., and M. Madsen. 1971. "Cooperation and Competition of Mexican, Mexican American, and Anglo American Children of Two Ages under Four Instructional Sets." *Developmental Psychology* 5:32-39.

_____. 1972. "Experimental Analysis of Cooperation and Competition of Anglo American and Mexican Children." *Developmental Psychology* 6:49-59.

Kaye, K. 1982. *The Mental and Social Life of Babies: How Parents Create Persons.* Chicago: University of Chicago Press.

Kaye, K., and R. Charney. 1980. "How Mothers Maintain 'Dialogue' with Two-Year-Olds." In D. Olson, ed., *The Social Foundations of Language and Thought: Essays in Honor of Jerome S. Bruner.* New York: Norton.

Kaye, K., and R. Charney. 1981. "Conversational Asymmetry between Mothers and Children." *Journal of Child Language* 8:35-49.

Kluckhohn, F., and F. Strodtbeck. 1961. *Variations in Value Orientations.* New York: Harper.

Knowlton, C. 1975. "The Neglected Chapters in Mexican American History." In G. Tyler, ed., *Mexican Americans Tomorrow: Educational and Economic Perspectives.* Albuquerque: University of New Mexico Press.

Laosa, L.M. 1977. "Inequality in the Classroom: Observation Research on Teacher-Student Interaction." *Aztlan* 8:51-67.

_____. 1978. "Maternal Teaching Strategies in Chicano Families of Varied Educational and Socioeconomic Levels." *Child Development* 49:1129-35.

_____. 1980. "Maternal Teaching Strategies in Chicano in Chicago and Anglo-American Families: The Influence of Culture and Education on Maternal Behavior." *Child Development* 51:759-65.

_____. 1981. "Maternal Behavior: Sociocultural Diversity in Modes of Family Interaction." In R.W. Henderson, ed., *Parent-Child Interaction: Theory, Research, and Prospects.* New York: Academic.

_____. 1982. "School, Occupation, Culture, and Family: The Impact of Parental Schooling on the Parent-Child Relationship." *Journal of Educational Psychology* 74:791-827.

Maccoby, E.E., and J.A. Martin. 1983. "Socialization in the Context of the Family: Parent-Child Interaction." In P.H. Mussen, ed., *Handbook of Child Psychology.* E.M. Hetherington, vol. ed., *Socialization Personality and Social Development.* New York: Wiley.

Madsen, M., and S. Kagan. 1973. "Mother Directed Achievement of Children in Two Cultures." *Journal of Cross-Cultural Psychology* 2:221-29.

Martínez, M.A. 1981. "Conversational Asymmetry between Mexican Mothers and Children." *Hispanic Journal of Behavioral Sciences* 3:329-46.

Massey, D. 1981. "Dimensions of the New Immigration to the United States and the Prospects for Assimilation." *Annual Review of Sociology* 7:57-85.

McClelland, D. 1961. *The Achieving Society*. New York: Free Press.

Mead, G.H. 1934. *Mind, Self, and Society*. Chicago: University of Chicago Press.

Mead, M. 1953. *Cultural Patterns and Technical Change*. Paris: UNESCO.

Mindel, C.H., and R.W. Habenstein, eds. 1976. *Ethnic Families in America: Patterns and Variations*. New York: Elsevier Scientific.

Moore, J. 1970. *Mexican-Americans*. Englewood Cliffs, N.J.: Prentice-Hall.

Murillo, N. 1976. "The Mexican-American Family." In N. Wagner and M. Haug, eds., *Chicanos: Social and Psychological Perspectives*. St. Louis: Mosby.

National Commission for Employment Policy, Report no. 14. 1982. *Hispanic and Jobs: Barriers to Progress*. Washington: NCEP (September).

Pachon, H.P. 1983. "Hispanic Underrepresentation in the Federal Bureaucracy: The Missing Link in the Policy Process." In A. Valdéz, A. Camarillo, and T. Almaguer, eds., *The State of Chicano Research on Family, Labor, and Migration*. Stanford: Stanford Center for Chicano Research.

Piore, M. 1979. *Birds of Passsage: Migrant Labor and Industrial Societies*. Cambridge: Cambridge University Press.

Poston, D., D. Alvirez, and M. Tienda. 1976. "Earnings Differences between Anglo and Mexican American Male Workers in 1960 and 1970: Change in the 'Cost' of Being Mexican American." *Social Sciences Quarterly* 57:618-31.

Ramírez, A. 1981. "Language Attitudes and the Speech of Spanish-English Bilingual Pupils." In R.P. Durán, ed., *Latino Language and Communicative Behavior*. Norwood: Ablex.

Ramírez, M., A. Castañeda, and P.L. Herold. 1974. "Acculturation and Cognitive Style in Three Mexican American Communities." Manuscript.

Ramírez, M., and A. Castañeda. 1974. *Cultural Democracy, Bicognitive Development and Education*. New York: Academic.

Ramírez, M., and D. Price-Williams. 1976. "Achievement Motivation in Children of Three Ethnic Groups in the United States." *Journal of Cross-Cultural Psychology* 7:49-60.

Ramírez, O., and C.H. Arce. 1981. "The Contemporary Chicano Family: An Empirically Based Review." In A. Baron, Jr., ed., *Exploration in Chicano Psychology*. New York: Praeger.

Rodríguez, R. 1981. *Hunger of Memory: An Autobiography*. Boston: Godine.

Sameroff, A.J., R. Seifer, and M. Zax. 1982. "Early Development of Children at Risk for Emotional Disorder." *Monographs of the Society for Research in Child Development* 47 (no. 7).

Sánchez, G. 1940. *Forgotten People*. Albuquerque: University of New Mexico Press.

Saragoza, A.M. 1983. "The Conceptualization of the History of the Chicano Family." In A. Valdéz, A. Camarillo, and T. Almaguer, eds., *The State of Chicano Research on Family, Labor, and Migration*. Stanford: Stanford Center for Chicano Research.

Saunders, L. 1954. *Cultural Differences and Medical Care: The Case of the Spanish-Speaking People of the Southwest*. New York: Russell Sage Foundation.

Sena-Rivera, J. 1979. "Extended Kinship in the United States: Competing Models and the Case of La Familia Chicana." *Journal of Marriage and the Family* 41:121-29.

Steward, M., and D. Steward. 1973. "The Observation of Anglo, Mexican, and Chinese American Mothers Teaching Their Young Sons." *Child Development* 44:329-37.

———. 1974. "Effect of Social Distance on Teaching Strategies of Anglo American and Mexican American Mothers." *Developmental Psychology* 10:797-807.

Sullivan, T. 1981. "The Democracy of Hispanic Populations in the United States: An Agenda for Research." Report prepared for the National Opinion Research Center, Chicago, Illinois.

Taylor, P. 1934. *Mexican Labor in the United States: Migrations Statistics IV.* Berkeley: University of California Press.

Tienda, M. 1983. "Residential Distribution and Internal Migration Patterns of Chicanos: A Critical Assessment." In A. Valdéz, A. Camarillo, and T. Almaguer, eds., *The State of Chicano Research on Family, Labor and Migration.* Stanford: Stanford Center for Chicano Research.

Tyler, G., ed. 1975. *Mexican Americans Tomorrow: Educational and Economic Perspectives.* Albuquerque: University of New Mexico Press.

U.S. Bureau of the Census. 1975. *Language Usage in the United States.* Advance report. Current Population Reports, series P.23, no. 60. Washington: U.S. Government Printing Office (July).

———. 1981. Current Population Reports, P-20, no. 361. *Persons of Spanish Origin in the United States, 1980.* Washington: U.S. Government Printing Office.

U.S. Bureau of Labor Statistics. 1981. *Employment and Earnings* 28: (January).

U.S. Commission on Civil Rights. 1982. *Unemployment and Underemployment Among Blacks, Hispanics, and Women.* Clearinghouse Publications 74. Alexandria: Publications Warehouse.

Vaca, M. 1970. "The Mexican American in the Social Sciences." *El Grito* 4:17-51.

Valdéz, A., A. Camarillo, and T. Almaguer, eds. 1983. *The State of Chicano Research on Family, Labor, and Migration.* Stanford: Stanford Center for Chicano Research.

Vásquez, J. 1974. Will Bilingual Curricula Solve the Problem of the Low Achieving Mexican American Student? *Bilingual Review* 1:236-42.

Vygotsky, L.S. 1962. *Thought and Language.* Cambridge: MIT Press.

———. 1978. *Mind in Society.* Cambridge: Harvard University Press.

———. 1981. "The Genesis of Higher Mental Functions." In J.V. Wertsch, trans. and ed., *The Concept of Activity in Soviet Psychology.* Armonk, N.Y.: Sharpe.

Ybarra, L. 1983. "Empirical and Theoretical Developments in the Study of Chicano Families." In A. Valdéz, A. Camarillo, and T. Almaguer, eds., *The State of Chicano Research on Family, Labor, and Migration.* Stanford: Stanford Center for Chicano Research.

5

Language and Social Assimilation

Pastora San Juan Cafferty

Language is a transmitter of culture; it is a mechanism by which individuals are socialized into society. The values, beliefs, and attitudes of society are communicated, and loyalty and allegiance to society are expressed. Language is inclusionary and exclusionary in its function: access to the benefits of society is limited for those who cannot speak or understand the language of society. Through much of the history of the United States the speaking of languages other than English has been seen as divisive and threatening to the common good. Non–English-speaking immigrants were encouraged to adopt English as their new tongue as a sign of their loyalty to the nation and as a method for their assimilation. Resistance to linguistic, and ultimately social, assimilation has characterized each immigrant group. Groups are distinguished by their degree of resistance, but all have wished to retain their native language and cultural identity in some form. The resultant diversity created conflict between immigrants and the native-born which manifested itself in the ebbing currents of reluctant tolerance and hostile intolerance. Hispanics are but the latest groups to enter into this process. In this chapter Pastora San Juan Cafferty discusses language and social assimilation issues that affect Hispanics in American society. She notes that Hispanics have a high rate of language retention. While the reasons for this are varied, a significant factor appears to be the cyclical migration patterns between country of origin and the United States which characterize much of the Hispanic population. Cafferty points out that although language retention is great among Hispanics, few are Spanish monolingual and those that are tend to be over forty. The debate over bilingualism is not whether the United States will become a bilingual society, but whether society should encourage the existence and maintenance of Spanish in the community, and if so, in what context it should do so. The debate is examined by breaking it down into three categories: political, social, and educational. Particular attention is given to the controversy over bilingual education since it is the focal point for much of the discussion.

The issue of Spanish-language retention among Hispanics is increasingly being framed solely in a sociopolitical context. One question that has defined the emotional debate in the Hispanic community and in the United States as a whole is not whether Hispanics should retain their native language, but what is society's responsibility to see that native language retention is facilitated for the Spanish-speaking. Another central question is to what extent is the Hispanic individual responsible for learning the language of majority society. As often happens with political debates the questions address the extreme: Should the United States become in law and in practice a country in which two or more languages have official status and are widely used in public life and equally maintained by educational and other institutions, or should the primacy of English be maintained to the extent that bilingual programs in schools and other public institutions should not be allowed?

The reality of Spanish retention and English acquisition lies in a less-well-defined area which changes dramatically from region to region and generation to generation. These questions must be asked in the context of contemporary American society, which is, essentially, English monolingual. There are historical as well as geographical, political, and economic reasons for this.

America recognized the importance of language in forging national identity early in its history. A nation founded in the late eighteenth century could well benefit from the linguistic experience of the various European nation-states which had painfully learned the relationship between linguistic and political and economic dominance.

In the nineteenth century, as successive waves of immigrants came to American shores, the importance of English in forging a national identity was affirmed. By the middle of the century, speaking English had become recognized as one of the important attributes of being an American. Since this was the most easily identified characteristic separating the native-born from the newly arrived foreigner, it became increasingly important.

America's geographic isolation in the nineteenth century—and its political and economic dominance in the twentieth—have reinforced English as the only national language. Americans are an English-speaking people who have little interest in and tolerance for other languages.

To understand the concern with the retention of Spanish language and culture among Hispanics in the United States, it is important to understand the historical concern of Americans to have all speak English as a common language; the history of native language retention among the European immigrants; and to discuss how Hispanics may or may not differ from other language communities in this country. Only then can one address the concerns expressed by society as a whole and by members of the Hispanic communities.

Role of the English Language

The young nation had briefly debated the wisdom of having English and French as its official languages. After considering the potential threat to the fledgling nation of the various ethnic groups, whose linguistic and cultural identity would prevent the formation of a single political entity, Congress declared English to be the official American language in 1786. Thus America chose to be a monolingual society as one of its first official acts as a new nation. It took this step deliberately to forge a single national identity from the many national groups that had come together to create a new nation-state. This policy of English monolingualism has been maintained for over 200 years through successive waves of European and Asian immigration. There has been little to challenge the dominance of English in America—and, indeed, in the world. There are no outside political or economic pressures to challenge English monolingualism. Waves of immigrants have initially posed a threat to English language dominance, but their successive linguistic assimilation has reinforced it.

English and European Immigrants

The flood of immigrants pouring into the new nation after 1776 led to the developing Anglo-Saxon race consciousness and to a distinction between those who had migrated before 1776 and the immigrants who came shortly thereafter. Those who migrated before 1776 were dubbed "colonists," and were praised as brave idealists who had migrated for religious and political freedom; the more recent "immigrants" were accused of coming to America only to benefit from the material prosperity the New World offered. Patriotic societies which excluded the new immigrants were founded at this time by the colonists.

Europeans had from earliest days migrated to America for a variety of reasons. A few had come seeking religious and political freedon, the majority had come seeking economic opportunity—particularly the privilege of owning land. Even those who sailed on the Mayflower numbered among them skilled laborers who were not of the Puritan faith. However, the mythology which idealizes the older immigrants at the expense of more recent arrivals has shaped attitudes toward immigration throughout American history. Early in the Colonial period, voices were raised in protest against some of the non-English elements that entered the Colonies. The

Scotch-Irish were viewed as a problem by the Quakers in Pennsylvania who found them to be aggressive and lawless. As early as 1729, a Pennsylvania statute sought to protect the colony against those likely to become public charges and to penalize those who brought in such elements.

Very early in American history, the English-speaking were identified as the most desirable settlers. The Colonies had been settled under the protection of the British Crown; the wealthy merchants who traded with the mother country, the holders of large tracts of land from the king, and the political rulers were all English-speaking. The powerful and wealthy spoke English. Nearly two centuries of British rule imprinted the British language and culture as that of the majority society.

The English-speaking assimilated easily into the society of the British colonies. Immigrants who did not speak English soon discovered the desirability of learning the new language. To speak English was proof of one's acceptance of American culture and values and of one's assimilation into American society. It was also desirable for economic and social mobility. The new immigrant had to learn English to communicate with his employer, to transact business, and to understand the laws. A common language was necessary for all settlers in the Colonies to communicate with each other. It was only logical that the language should be the English language of the mother country.

Linguistic and Cultural Assimilation

Strains of ethnocentrism and nativism at different periods in American history reflected derision and fear of foreign languages and foreign accents. Immigrants unable to speak and write English were classified as "illiterate" and often as "ignorant," and were subjected to social and economic sanctions. Employers often advertised for English-speaking workers in eighteenth-century broadsides. Papers and etiquette books published in the early nineteenth century stressed the importance of speaking English correctly to be accepted in polite society.

Societies view linguistic change as one of the prime targets for breaking down old loyalties and adapting to a new culture. The reverse is also true: retention of the native language provides an effective shield against assimilation. The right most often sought by groups struggling to maintain their ethnic identity in the face of assimilation into the dominant society is the provision of adequate education in the group's own tongue as well as recognition of the group's language as an official government language. It is not surprising, then, that a society which stressed the assimilation of immigrants would demand linguistic assimilation as well.

Native-Language Retention among Immigrants

The policy of English monolingualism in America has been justified for almost 200 years on the assumption that immigrants to America, who come to stay in a land promising political and religious freedom, will become citizens, and that their children will become a new generation of native Americans. While some immigrants did return, the majority came to stay. Early pamphlets and tracts extolling the virtues of migration to America were circulated throughout Europe. They all stressed the permanence of the migration. Indeed the journey was long and expensive. Most immigrants came with no notions of return.

While the majority of American immigrants have always come with the intention of settling permanently in America, there has always been a pattern of immigration and emigration, so that for every major stream, a counterstream developed (Ravenstein, 1885; Lee, 1966). The studies which exist regarding this pattern indicate that the decision to return or stay is directly related to the degree to which the immigrant adapted to American society. The relationship of native language retention as a factor in assimilation is little understood by linguists and anthropologists, while both acknowledge its reality and importance.

The Germans historically made the most successful efforts to retain their native language. This is the oldest and most persistent immigrant language community in the United States. It began in 1683 in Pennsylvania and still retains a vigorous dialect. Other immigrants organized their efforts at preserving language and culture around church and parochial schools. These included the French in New England and the Scandinavians and Dutch in the Midwest. While some of these were monolingual schools, the majority of them offered bilingual education. After 1800, the Germans, French, and Scandinavians continued to operate parochial schools, as did the new immigrants, particularly the Poles, Lithuanians, and Slovaks. That the effort to preserve language by immigrants in America is so closely aligned with efforts to preserve religious belief is evidence that language is seen as the catalyst in the preservation of cultural values. However, not all language preservation efforts were church-related.

Between 1840 and 1880, bilingual programs were offered in public schools. In addition to German bilingual education, there were French-English schools in Louisiana and Spanish-English schools in New Mexico. After 1880, only one group successfully maintained bilingual programs in the public schools—the Germans, who did so until 1917.

There is no evidence that bilingual programs were welcomed by the community at large. Rather, efforts at maintaining a bilingual community were always resisted in America. Bilingual programs existed in public schools due to political pressure exerted by ethnic communities; they were merely toleraated by the English-speaking. Bilingual programs were language programs offering little challenge to the melting pot theory of cultural assimilation.

The experience of the Germans in Ohio illustrates this. The Germans, who believed American public schools to be inferior to those they had left in Germany, founded their own German-language parochial schools in Ohio. In 1840, bilingual education was instituted in the public schools of Ohio not to encourage linguistic and cultural pluralism but to ensure that German children would also learn English. The Germans wanted their own schools to retain their ethnic identity; the state was willing to fund such schools to effect assimilation. Although German-language programs continued until World War I, not one single community maintained a language program adequately supported by the population it served that lasted over any extended period of time. The evidence suggests that bilingual public schools may have aided the process of assimilation.

Following World War I, all bilingual education efforts ceased in public schools, although bilingual programs continued in parochial schools. Having fought a war to save democracy and end all future wars, Americans asserted the uniqueness of their democratic experience and of all things American, including the American language. The political rhetoric, as well as the press and radio, denounced all things foreign and praised all things American. The European experience was described as decayed and corrupt, and those who had come to America were exhorted to cast off "the old man of Europe" and become "the new American man." There was little interest in foreign languages during the twenties, thirties, and forties. After 1945, foreign language efforts were focused on teaching English as a second language—to assimilate the immigrants who continued to cling stubbornly to their native tongues.

The Hispanic Migration Experience

Since language and cultural conflict may account for a good part of the Hispanic immigrant's problems, resolution of these problems is closely tied to mitigation of the conflict. Before addressing the conflict—and proposing policies and programs—one must determine how Hispanic immigrants differ from other American immigrants. Since the European migration was a major factor in the creation of the American nation, it has become the stuff of which myths are made. Most Europeans, like Hispanics, came seeking jobs and not all Europeans stayed. Migration from Europe has always been accompanied by a large-scale internal migration in which a majority of American citizens participate. But the cost and distance made the decision to return seem as irrevocable as the difficult decision to migrate.

Canadians, Mexicans, Central Americans, and Puerto Ricans

The poor and unskilled from all nations have made difficult journeys to America seeking jobs. However, in the case of Canadians, Mexicans, Central Americans, and Puerto Ricans the trip is relatively short. Like the majority of European immigrants, their desire to migrate was based on the economic advantages to be gained. Both Canadians and Mexicans can, and do, walk to their new home—come over by bus or truck—but proximity is a key factor in the decision to migrate, a factor which has not diminished in importance throughout the migration experience. Puerto Ricans began traveling by ship to New York in the nineteenth century. Following World War II, they could make the 6-hour trip for the price of a $35 plane ticket. Thousands saved and borrowed to come to work in the North; in other instances recruiters from farms in New Jersey and Connecticut gladly paid the airfare to guarantee cheap labor to harvest the crops.

The migration patterns for all four groups form a steady stream to the same communities throughout the nation. These patterns have varied little during the twentieth century, suggesting that both the promise of jobs and the comfort of joining relatives and friends in an unknown land is repeated from one generation to the next. In all groups, migration by whole families occurred; a family network was established so that family members were key sources of information. Family members who migrated first aided others in finding jobs and homes.

These groups have been largely rural as well as relatively homogeneous. Almost all have come as skilled or semiskilled labor. This suggests that the rural-urban migration is more than a simple process of leaving the farm in the homeland to travel to a city in the United States. Rather, the migrant first leaves his farm to find work in a city in his homeland and then travels on, seeking a better job with better pay in the United States.

While there is little national concern about the hundreds of thousands of Canadians who migrate to the United States, there is grave concern about a closely parallel Mexican migration. The two migration streams are similar: (1) both have resisted assimilation; (2) both have fled poor economic conditions and are drawn to economic opportunities here; and (3) both have returned to their homelands in large numbers, but those who have remained have retained their ties with their families and homelands. Given similar circumstances, the immigrant from Canada blends in to such a degree that his existence is largely ignored. However, the Mexican immigrant and Puerto Ricans with their darker skins and Spanish language are more visible.

Mexicans constitute the largest immigration stream among the Hispanics. While legal immigration from Mexico numbers in the thousands annually, illegal immigration is impossible to measure. Estimates of the number of illegal immigrants residing in America range from 2-10 million. A disproportionate number of these are Mexicans. Studies show that whatever the numbers, it is a circular migration. Circular migrants are those who travel between their homeland and a country where they seek work with regularity and often with little relationship to cycles in the economies of either nation. The illegal immigrant—like his legal counterpart—makes frequent extended visits to his homeland.

Puerto Ricans are American citizens traveling within national boundaries and form part of the same constant stream of internal migration in America. Yet along with the other Hispanics, they are seen as foreigners who take jobs and housing away from Americans on the mainland.

Other Hispanic Immigrants

Not enough is known about Hispanic immigrants. Cubans constituted a refugee migration which was initially welcomed. In the early 1960s when the American economy was strong and Americans accepted a commitment to receive people fleeing Communist rule, the federal government instituted a number of direct service programs to aid the Cubans. Many states and municipalities followed suit. Cubans clustered in southern Florida and northern New Jersey and were accepted by the majority society as a hard-working immigrant population which shared American middle-class values. In the 1980s, Cuban refugees, expelled by Castro, were not as readily welcomed either by majority society or by other Cubans who had preceded them.

Very little is known about the newest groups of Hispanic immigrants from Central and South America and the Caribbean. Some constitute part of the large illegal immigration stream. If they behave like the Mexicans and Canadians, they will also be circular migrants.

Spanish-Language Use among Hispanics

This constant Hispanic migration stream long in history and large in number results in the fact that Spanish is the most common language—other than English—spoken by persons in the United States. Among all non-English language users, Spanish is the language spoken in 35 percent of all households and by 44 percent of all persons (Estrada, 1980). Since 10 percent of all persons in the United States use a language other than English, this means that approximately 5 percent of all persons in the United States use Spanish as a primary language.

The small percentage of the population whose primary language is Spanish is surprising, since Hispanics have been forceful in demanding bilingual education programs, bilingual staff in agencies delivering emergency and social services, and bilingual official documents designed to ensure political participation. This advocacy of bilingual programs has resulted in the fear of those who oppose bilingual programs in schools and social service agencies that the United States—a nation which for over 200 years assimilated its immigrants into a common language and culture—will become linguistically (and thus politically) divided. The specter of a separated Quebec is conjured by those who fear there will be a Spanish-speaking nation in the Southwest separated by language and culture from the rest of the United States.

These fears have a complex basis. While there has always been language retention among immigrant groups in the United States, the Spanish-speaking have retained their native language more than has any other group (Fishman, 1966). There are a number of reasons which account for this phenomenon: the proximity of the Mexican border and the relative ease of travel of Mexican nationals and others from Spanish-speaking nations to the South, resulting in a continuing migration stream which constantly renews the linguistic tradition; the pervasiveness of the Hispanic heritage; the long and continuing isolation of the Spanish-speaking in the Southwest; and segregation patterns in American society which keep Hispanics isolated in a social and economic ghetto. Of these, only the renewal of the linguistic tradition by a constant migration stream has been successfully documented as being different from the experience of any other national group that came to America.

Spanish-Language Retention among Hispanics

The fact that only a small percentage of the general population speak Spanish and that among those Hispanics it is only the older members of a very young general Hispanic population who do so exclusively should answer the nation's concern with conserving the primacy of English. English is the language of the majority society and Hispanics—like other immigrants before them—speak English as they become part of that society. There is no evidence to the contrary. There is evidence, however, that Hispanics retain their native language more than did the European immigrants who came before.

Spanish is the most common non-English language spoken in the United States. However, only about 10 percent of the Hispanic population is Spanish monolingual. The large majority of these are persons over forty (Estrada, 1980). There is strong evidence that English-language usage increases as age decreases among the Hispanic population, even among bilinguals. Those who speak Spanish as their primary language tend to be older (Estrada, 1980). This is not suprising since English is the language of the market place and, as such, the language which Hispanics—like any other migrant group—speak when they enter the labor market. Spanish-language use has been shown, in contradictory evidence, to have both positive and negative effects on educational attainment and social mobility. There is also evidence that Spanish-language use is directly related to under-utilization of preschool programs, to higher attrition in both primary and secondary school, to overagedness, and to lower college attendance (U.S. Dept. of HEW, 1978). Other studies show that for those who manage to complete their studies, Spanish-English bilingualism is an asset which can result in greater income and job achievement (López, 1978).

Any discussion of bilingualism immediately becomes a discussion of bilingual education: mastering a language and understanding and appreciating a culture always involve a process of learning. The history of organized language consciousness, language loyalty, and language maintenance by different groups is a political history; it is the history of the formation of the large nation-states. The struggle for linguistic dominance is closely allied to the struggle for political and economic dominance among differing ethnic groups.

This may be why bilingualism—more specifically, bilingual education—is the issue most often discussed with respect to Hispanics in American society. The discussion is made more difficult for two reasons. One is defining the terms: the truly bilingual individual is able to read, speak, and understand two languages, but he may have either his native language—or the language he acquired—as the dominant language. At no time has there been a serious discussion that Hispanics in the United States should be monolingual in Spanish. The other is that the question of Hispanic's demand for bilingual programs and services is rightly seen as a political question.

The Question to Be Addressed

Before the complexity of bilingualism among Hispanics in America can be addressed, one must ask whether bilingualism should be encouraged in the United States as a matter of policy for any or all ethnic groups—whether institutions should exist which foster bilingualism and if so, whether these institutions should be supported not only by the ethnic group but by majority society.

If bilingualism is to be encouraged, one must ask whether the individual or the nation is to be bilingual. American society is strongly monolingual.

There are historical, economic, and political reasons for monolingualism, and there is no evidence that it is changing. There is some evidence that while there is strong native-language retention among a number of ethnic groups, there is no greater incidence of this retention now than there was at the beginning of the century.

There is evidence that native-language retention among Hispanics is decreasing (Estrada, 1980). This is often ignored for two reasons: there has always been greater native-language retention among Hispanics than among other immigrant groups, and the number of Hispanics in proportion to the rest of the U.S. population is continually increasing. Their number grew from between 9-12 million in 1970 to 14.6 million in 1980, according to census figures. This does not include the 3 million Hispanics in Puerto Rico. While many demographers predict that Hispanics will be the largest minority in American society by the end of the century, many sociologists and educators are concerned they will constitute a large linguistic minority.

In spite of this concern, there is little serious possibility that America will become a bilingual nation. English will continue to be the language of the marketplace except in the few places where large communities of Hispanics make it economically attractive and politically possible to foster a bilingual community. The American economy continues to demand English-language skills of those who wish to participate in it. The majority of immigrants came to America for economic reasons and will learn English to enjoy its economic benefits. The question is not whether America will become a bilingual society, but whether society should encourage the existence and maintenance of the Spanish language in the Hispanic community and if so, in what context. A related question is whether Spanish-language retention is detrimental to assimilation for the individual—and for the group—in an essentially English monolingual society.

In answering these questions it may be useful to discuss language in three different contexts: educational, political, and social. The educational is the most often addressed, for both majority society and members of the Hispanic communities recognize the importance of unusual education in the assimilation process. The political content of language refers to the individual's right to be informed about important activities in this society, such as the election of public officials, in order that he may fully exercise his rights. The use of language ranges from being able to access services and interact with peers in the workplace to complex social interactions.

The Educational Context

The difficulty in creating bilingual education policy is directly related to several issues. First is the decision, early in the history of the nation, that

America should have English as its single official language. Second, the public school system, for almost two centuries, did succeed in teaching English to successive waves of immigrants. While the public school never provided the ideal education which the mythology of history has credited it with, the ultimate proof of its relative success was the fact that the immigrant children did eventually learn English and adopted it as their only language.

In the United States no public institution has a greater impact on the individual's place in society than the school. This was the rationale for states and local communities to invest large sums to finance public school systems. Between the ages of six and eighteen most American children spend most of their time in schools. Their social contacts, their concepts of knowledge, and their social values are largely derived from the schools. Early educational success or failure will greatly determine the student's concept of self and of his position in society. The importance of assuring every American child an equal educational opportunity was the guiding principle in *Brown v. Board of Education.* Concluding that segregated schools were inherently unequal, the Supreme Court ruled state laws segregating Black and White students in the school system to be unconstitutional. The ruling was followed by a decade of civil rights activities that put an end to segregated schools. Leaders in the Black community repeatedly underscored the inequality of educational opportunity in segregated school systems and the importance of equal educational opportunity in achieving social and economic equality. In recent years, the Spanish-speaking community has also focused its civil rights efforts on the public schools. Its leaders have decried the lack of equal access to education for the Spanish-speaking in public schools.

Bilingual Education Efforts

In spite of the experience of bilingual programs in public and parochial schools for over a century, it was not until 1968 that public funds were again authorized for use in bilingual education programs. The Bilingual Education Act of 1968 established programs which teach the language and culture of minority students as well as the native language and culture (Title VII of PL90-247, 1968). Since then various states have taken actions which range from repealing laws which forbid the speaking of a language other than English on the school ground to enacting laws establishing programs in schools with substantial numbers of students with limited English-language skills. In 1974, the Supreme Court ruled that "students who do not understand English are effectively foreclosed from any meaningful education" and that steps must be taken to ensure equal educational opportunity (*Lau v. Nichols,* 1974).

Since the Bilingual Education Act passed in 1968, there have been fifteen years of controversy and political activism by proponents of bilingualism and bilingual education. The argument is easily made that Hispanics, like other immigrants, should learn the American language and thus assimilate into the mainstream of American society. But Hispanics argue their experience is different: they were in the Southwest as established Spanish-speaking communities long before those territories became part of the United States, and as circular migrants large numbers of Hispanics are traveling between two monolingual societies. English and Spanish become of equal value to the individual. In the case of Puerto Ricans, this migration is taking place within national boundaries. The first argument is highly political and addresses the question of English-language dominance and the imposition of the values of majority American society in opposition to the preservation of Spanish language and culture.

The political discussion is important but it is one of differing ideologies and can only be practically resolved in a democracy by the majority of society agreeing to foster the retention of native language and culture as a civil right. The question of the difference of the migration experience addresses issues of a pedagogical as well as sociological nature which can be examined from the viewpoint of what is best to help Hispanic individuals better interact with the various communities in which they live.

The concept of what constitutes sufficient education is not a pedagogical but a sociological concept which varies with time and place. Earlier immigrants to America needed to understand and speak English but often had little need for other educational skills to participate in the labor market. In today's highly technological service economy, a high-school diploma is often a minimum requisite for even entry-level jobs.

Hispanics lag well behind other groups in American society in educational achievement. Of the graduating age cohort in 1976, 87 percent of non-Hispanic Americans graduated from high school, while only 68 percent of all Mexican-Americans and 64 percent of all Puerto Ricans (on the mainland) did so. Concerning Hispanic achievement in postsecondary education, of the graduating age cohort in 1976, 34 percent of non-Hispanic Americans graduated from college with a bachelor's degree, while only 4 percent of Puerto Ricans (on the mainland) and 11 percent of Mexican-Americans did so (Cafferty and Rivera-Martinez 1981:23-26).

The importance of this lack of educational achievement is confirmed by the unemployment rates among Mexicans and Puerto Ricans on the mainland. While 8.2 percent of the majority population were unemployed in 1983, 13.5 percent of Puerto Ricans (on the mainland) and 12.6 percent of Mexicans were unemployed. The statistics are even more dramatic for teenagers: among youth, 20.4 percent of the majority population were unemployed, while 46 percent (base for this rate is 50,000 persons) of the Puerto Ricans (on the mainland) and 24 percent of Mexicans were unemployed (Greene and Epstein, 1984).

Bilingual Education Legislation

The Bilingual Education Act of 1974, which superseded the 1968 act, was more explicit in intent and design. Children no longer needed to be from low-income families, a criterion that had previously prevented the law from meeting the needs of large numbers of children. The 1974 act also provided a definition of a bilingual education program:

> instruction given in, and study of, English and to the extent necessary to allow a child to progress effectively through the educational system, the native language of the children of limited English-speaking ability, and such instruction is given with appreciation for the cultural heritage of such children, and, with respect to elementary school instruction, such instruction shall, to the extent necessary, be in all courses or subjects of study which will allow a child to progress effectively through the educational system.

In yet another legislative action related to bilingual education, the Equal Education Opportunity Act of 1974 listed six actions that the Congress defines as denials of equal educational opportunity. Among them is the failure of an educational agency to take appropriate action to overcome language barriers that impede equal participation by its students in its instructional program.

This act provided for the initiation of civil action by individuals who have been denied equal educational opportunity. Thus it provided for the first time a direct statutory right of action to non-English-speaking persons seeking equal educational opportunity through the institution of effective bilingual programs in public schools.

While efforts at the federal level have been limited, the implementation of bilingual education programs at the state level has been even more limited. Most state statutes define bilingual education as a transitional process to make the student a fluent speaker of English. Only two states, New Mexico and Texas, define bilingual education as the preservation of the native language and culture as well as the acquisition of English-language skills.

In 1974 the Supreme Court ruled that Chinese students who did not know English well enough to be instructed in the language were excluded from receiving an education by a school system which did not provide instruction in their native language. Justice Douglas delivered the opinion of the court:

Under these state-imposed standards there is no equality of treatment merely by providing students with the same facilities, text books, teachers, and curriculum; for students who do not understand English are effectively foreclosed from any meaningful education.

Basic English skills are at the very core of what these public schools teach. Imposition of a requirement that, before a child can effectively participate in the educational program, he must already have acquired those basic skills is to make a mockery of public education. We know that those who do not understand English are certain to find their classroom experiences wholly incomprehensible and in no way meaningful.

The Civil Rights Act of 1974 and the *Lau v. Nichols* case have been used by proponents of bilingual education as an argument for mandated bilingual education programs. In fact, they offer no pedagogical guidelines. All they do is mandate compensatory education for non-English speakers.

Also in 1974, Aspira of New York, Inc. obtained a court decree making selection of Spanish-surnamed and Spanish-speaking children for Language Assessment Battery (LAB) Test mandatory. Before the consent decree, bilingual programs were not being given to all the children, only to those identified by the office of the superintendent. The court made it mandatory to give bilingual programs and education to all students who need it by giving all Spanish-surnamed and Spanish-speaking children the LAB test to determine which children need bilingual programs. It is too early to judge the effect of mandatory bilingual education on the Puerto Rican schoolchildren of New York, but the Aspira decree has set a precedent which could be significant for other cities.

The Department of Health, Education, and Welfare memorandum of May 25, 1970, stipulated that school districts with more than 5 percent national origin minority group children have a legal obligation to provide equal educational opportunity for language minority students (U.S. Commission on Civil Rights, 1975). Although the memorandum requires school districts to provide some form of language program to meet the needs of language minority children, it does not specify what type of program this should be. When a district has not provided an educational program for language minority students, the department has strongly suggested that a curriculum be developed which does not penalize language minority students for their language and culture.

Educational Approaches

Presently there are several types of educational approaches which attempt to deal with the difficulties of language minority students. The first, English as a Second Language (ESL), attempts to make non-English-speaking children proficient in English by providing supplementary instructional sessions in English for a specified time. Instruction in all other classes is in English. ESL differs from foreign language instruction in that it is designed to meet the immediate communication needs of the students by providing them with skills needed to communicate with teachers and peers in the classroom. The ESL approach seems to work best in communities where children receive enough exposure outside of school to function as native speakers of English in a relatively short time.

Another strategy is that of bilingual education, which offers instruction in both languages in varying degrees: (1) transitional bilingualism, in which the child is placed out of the program after gaining basic mastery of the English language; (2) monoliterate bilingualism, in which aural-oral skills in both languages are taught, but reading and writing is taught in English only, as in the case with some American Indian languages; (3) partial bilingualism, in which fluency and literacy are offered in both languages, but the native language is restricted to certain subject areas, such as music and gym; (4) a full bilingual program, in which both languages are used as media of instruction for all subjects. An important characteristic of the full bilingual program is that these programs utilize both languages and teach about both cultures on an equal basis.

The premises behind ESL and bilingual education programs are drastically different. Bilingual programs are designed to build on a child's existing native-language skills to develop English-language skills while maintaining and enhancing native-language skills. Generally, classes requiring cognitive development are taught in the native language until the child has mastered the English-language. Afterwards both languages are used as the media of instruction. ESL programs are designed solely to teach English-language skills so that the student can function in an English monolingual school system. There is no effort to maintain native language and culture.

Opponents of special treatment of language minority students argue that bilingual programs will not provide enough incentives for the student involved to learn English quickly. They also cite a lack of evidence that these programs will be successful. This is difficult to address because most attempts to evaluate bilingual education have been very poor.

Most evaluations of bilingual programs fall into two categories: those which attempt to prove that bilingual programs accomplish their objectives and those which attempt to evaluate the effect of the program on acquisition of the second language. The bilingual programs which have been evaluated appear to be meeting many of their objectives without hindering the development of English-speaking skills.

Evaluation of Bilingual Programs

Early research in bilingualism in the United States found that bilingual students were handicapped in terms of intellectual functioning. These early findings have been consistently used as an argument against bilingual education. However, reviewing the research on Spanish-speaking bilinguals in the Southwest, Natalie Darcy (1963) found that bilingual subjects who had received lower scores on verbal and nonverbal group tests did not differ significantly from English monolinguals on a nonverbal intelligence test when socioeconomic status was controlled.

Several programs have shown that Hispanic students in a bilingual curriculum can progress at a faster rate than Hispanic students in an English-only curiculum. In a Texas project, this was the result obtained. The San Antonio Independent School District, between 1965 and 1966, concluded that the children receiving instruction in both English and Spanish made gains in English vocabulary and grammar superior to those made by children in the special English-only program. Yet here too, the thrust of the curriculum was the student's eventual transference to English as a primary language rather than the maintenance of his first tongue (Cafferty and Rivera-Martínez, 1981).

A similar result was obtained in a program operating in the El Paso public school system between 1966 and 1967. In this project, children receiving instruction in Spanish showed that they could achieve skills in English at a level equal to that of children receiving instruction in English (Saavedra, 1969).

In an Illinois experiment, children enrolled in a bilingual education program were compared to students in an ESL program. The results disproved the theory that children learned more English in a monolingual program (Seelye et al., 1973).

In 1970, the Edgewood Independent School District of San Antonio demonstrated the effectiveness of bilingual education with preschoolers. To determine effectiveness, the intelligence quotient (IQ) of children aged three to five was measured at various stages of the bilingual program and compared to that of children in two other preschool programs similar in all aspects except being monolingual. Again, the findings supported the use of a bilingual curriculum. Significant gains in IQ were achieved by children in the bilingual program, as opposed to the children in the regular nursery school program. By the time they entered first grade, children in the bilingual program could communicate equally well in English and Spanish.

In their evaluation report on bilingual centers founded in 1972, the Chicago Board of Education found that students taught in Spanish performed just as well as students taught in English. At the end of the program, results derived from test data and various evaluation instruments indicated that Spanish-speaking students in a program with a bilingual instruction component did much better than their counterparts in programs with no bilingual education component. The students in bilingual programs exhibited more positive concepts of their own worth and a higher level of aspiration.

In spite of the positive results of bilingual education programs provided by these few studies, it is impossible to draw conclusive proof of the success of bilingual education at present. However, recent analysis of the research literature on second-language acquisition and second-language learning seems to indicate that bilingualism has a positive effect on cognitive functioning.

While it can be argued that an individual benefits psychologically from knowing and appreciating his native language and culture, it may be just as strongly argued that society should not fund programs of cultural enrichment for linguistic minorities at the expense of the majority population.

The issue of creating and implementing bilingual educational policy for Hispanics is complicated by the fact that in a society committed to equality for all, it is difficult to distinguish among different types of immigrants who may have different needs. The permanent immigrant may need bilingual education only as a transition to English-language skills, while the circular migrant may need maintenance programs.

For the past two centuries, educational policy and the public school system have been seen as key components in bringing about social assimilation in successive generations of immigrants. Public school education distinguished the American native from immigrant parents and provided him with the opportunity for economic and social advancement. Equality of education was seen as a prerequisite to equality of opportunity. It is in this context that one must address the issue of bilingual institutions and Hispanics in contemporary American society.

Political Context

The issue of how to provide equity for those who do speak English in American society is perhaps more difficult than that of how best to teach English to those who do not. If American society is English-dominant, should it create bilingual programs to serve the needs of those who do not speak English? If so, should these institutions be for everyone? Should they be everywhere? If not, for whom and where should they exist? These questions are not unrelated to the issue of bilingual education: if individuals are truly bilingual, they will need a minimum of bilingual institutions. However, there is at minimum a period of transition when the individual functions best—if not exclusively—using his native language.

The question of provision of bilingual services ranges from providing signs in English and Spanish in public transit to funding bilingual programs in social service agencies and printing bilingual ballots. Churches and social service agencies have traditionally offered services in the native language to immigrant communities. Society has always recognized that individuals are best served in the language they know best. The question is whether American society should, as a matter of public policy, foster bilingual institutions.

While there have been a number of successful efforts by Hispanic as well as by other language communities (notably Asian) to review potential participation by having bilingual (and in some cases multilingual) ballots and election literature required by law, these are transitional efforts in that they are designed to bring immigrants into the mainstream by encouraging potential participation. Although much is made of the "new linguistic militancy," these efforts are not new. English literacy was not universally required for either voting or citizenship until the twentieth century. It was not until 1926 that the last state barred the franchise to lawful residents, and not until 1950 that Congress required English literacy as a condition for citizenship.

The Mixta consent decree in California (Asociación Mixta, 1975) established the right to accessibility to social services for those who do not understand English by mandating that provisions be made for bilingual staff and literature in federally funded programs. While there has been social opposition demanding that those in America speak English, it is difficult to argue that legal residents should have to speak English to avail themselves of fire, police, health care, and other emergency and social services.

In 1976, after a Christmas Eve fire which killed a number of children in the predominantly Mexican community of Pilsen in Chicago, Mayor Richard J. Daley announced that all emergency personnel employed by the City of Chicago would have to learn basic Spanish. Those investigating the tragic deaths had determined that some children would have been saved if they had understood the fire fighters. The fire fighters' union promptly threatened to go on strike. There were many irate letters to the editor of the daily papers supporting the fire fighters' position that Hispanics should have to learn English to avail themselves of any services offered by American society.

Hispanic civil rights organizations both at the grass roots and at the national level emphasize the importance of Spanish language to facilitate access to programs and ensure equity of participation. MALDEF, the Mexican American Legal Defense and Education Fund, founded in 1968 in Denver, sponsors a community education program to let grass roots groups know how they can use the nation's institutions to obtain services. PRLDEF, the Puerto Rican Legal Defense and Education Fund, founded in New York in 1972, has frequently joined MALDEF demanding publicly funded bilingual services at their intersessions. The courts have mandated bilingual election materials in New York City, Philadelphia, and Chicago, as well as in parts of New Jersey and in a number of localities in the Southwest. Connecticut welfare offices provide bilingual written matter and bilingual social workers as a result of a PRLDEF suit.

The private sector has traditionally been more responsive to the needs of the non-English-speaking in American society. The history of bilingual education for countless generations of immigrants was a parochial school history. Churches have traditionally provided native language services and recognized the importance of language in fostering the preservation of cultural and religious values. Settlement houses—founded to assist immigrants newly arrived to America—provided services in their native language. The private social sector continues to be more responsive to the needs of Hispanics who do not speak English. This may be appropriate. However, the large Hispanic immigration has taken place at a time when important changes in the role of the public and private sectors were taking place. As public funding increases for services, individual dependence on public agencies increases as well. Today the question is no longer what is the best language in which to address the needs of a non-English-speaking individual and community, but is it appropriate for an English-monolingual society to create and fund bilingual institutions.

Language usage in public institutions has become a volatile political issue as Hispanic communities demand a range of actions which would recognize Spanish as a semiofficial language and include federally funded language training programs provided for federal, state, and local civil servants; translations into Spanish of all governmental forms, brochures, manuals intended for the general public; simultaneous translation provided for Hispanic clients by the criminal justice system; translation of all legislation, significant public speeches, and other government documents.

As Hispanic community leaders make demands for an increasing recognition of Spanish in a number of institutions, American society reacts with varying degrees of concern. While the school is not the only institution which Hispanic community leaders have demanded be bilingual, it is the only one which poses a threat to a society that fears the spread of bilingualism and biculturalism, for it is the only institution which may perpetuate the foreign language and its foreign culture.

Social Context

The most important—and most often spoken—question is whether American society should encourage bilingualism in the sense of two monolingual cultures. This could occur where there is a high enough density of Hispanics—in certain areas of the Southwest, of the Northeast, or in South Florida. Such monolingual communities already exist. They are often socioeconomic as well as linguistic ghettos abandoned by successive generations of the young who seek economic advancement and achieve social and linguistic assimilation in the greater society.

There are three possibilities for the speakers of a minority language in any society: give up the native language and thus reduce, if not eliminate, the ethnic identity it articulates; reduce the handicap to the speakers of the minority language by instituting changes in the educational system and by adopting the minority language for certain public processes; or abandon the society by emigration or revolution. Thus bilingualism can be a permanent characteristic of a society resulting from sustained multilingual contact or an intermediate stage for members of minority language communities in transition from linguistic pluralism to monolingualism.

Historically in the United States, bilingualism has been an intermediate step for the immigrant. First- and second-generation immigrants may continue to speak the native language among themselves but English is the only means of communication with majority society. Eisenstadt (1955) defines two stages of assimilation: *cultural assimilation,* which is the adaptation to values, norms, patterns of behavior, and expectations without which the individual is unable to function in society; and *social assimilation,* which is the absorption of the newcomers into the host society as accepted members of social groups ranging from club memberships to marriage. The research of Gordon (1964), Greeley (1974), Glazer and Moynihan (1970), indicates that assimilation takes place in incremental stages. The ethnic culture may subsist for several generations even though social assimilation is well underway.

The question of linguistic assimilation becomes central to that of cultural assimilation since a common language can support both by maintaining relationships within the ethnic group and maintaining a group identity separate from majority society. Lieberson (1970) contends that in the United States, maintaining a distinct native language is probably more closely linked to ethnic differences than is religion. Murguia (1975) argues that in the assimilation model the immigrant faces class and cultural—but not racial—prejudice. As he rises in economic status the immigrant assimilates by adopting the norms and mores of the host society. Intermarriage often takes place.

Murguia argues, however, that the Mexican-American experience cannot be analyzed using this model. He argues that a colonizer model similar to that used by Fannon (1968) and Memmi (1965) in analyzing the French colony of Algeria is more appropriate in studying the Mexican-American experience. Similar arguments have been suggested regarding the Puerto Rican experience.

It is valuable to distinguish between linguistic retention—which depends on literary, cultural, and emotional values—and linguistic assimilation— which depends on political and economic values (Haugen, 1956). Richard Rodríguez (1982), in his moving autobiography, makes the distinction between private language—used with one's family—and public language— used in social activities. He argues that while Spanish may remain the private language of Hispanics, it is only when English—the public language—becomes dominant that a Hispanic individual can achieve social assimilation and economic success. His book was lauded by opponents of bilingual education and condemned by its advocates. In fact, it is not a pedagogical work evaluating bilingual education programs but a poignant autobiography of the immigrant experience.

The reality is that the United States is not a bilingual society; the majority of Americans have no need to be bilingual. While one can argue the cultural and educational advantages of learning a second language, for the majority of Americans such knowledge is not an absolute need.

For native speakers of a language other than English, learning English is necessary to function fully in American society. For most immigrants to America, this requires a transitional bilingual program. These individuals will learn English through their native language. They may or may not choose to preserve their native language, but it can be argued that society should not bear the cost of such cultural and linguistic maintenance. It is not essential to the individual for participation in society. Given the limited resources available for education, it is difficult to make the case for maintenance of bilingual programs at public expense.

It could be argued that the best way to assimilate an individual into American society is bilingual education. Even those who are not advocates of bilingual education agree with Joshua Fishman (1966) that the schools seldom succeed in language maintenance; education in both the native and majority language results in the dominance of the majority language. The bilingual individual would choose the language of the majority society. There is little danger of bilingual education resulting in a monolingual Hispanic community alienated from majority society. The chief Americanizing force in the past has been access to opportunity.

Summary and Conclusions

The issue of English monolingualism and native-language retention in America has always been problematic. Since language and culture are intertwined, one would assume that a society which speaks of itself as "a nation of immigrants" and extols the contributions of various ethnic groups to its culture would encourage linguistic diversity as an expression of cultural pluralism. Yet the opposite is true: native language retention is regarded as dysfunctional. The speaking of English—to the exclusion of the native tongue—has long been associated with the opportunity for social and political advancement.

Successive groups of immigrants, however, have preserved their linguistic and cultural identity with various degrees of success. Their success, despite efforts to eradicate the native language and culture by majority society, is dramatic evidence of the immigrant's need to preserve his native language and culture while becoming an American.

It can be argued that while ethnic differences are sometimes not accompanied by linguistic differences, it is rare to find two different language groups in society where speakers are not in two different ethnic groups: the ethnic group's greatest identification becomes its language. Linguistic assimilation is evidence of—as well as motivation to—cultural assimilation.

Public Policy Issues

The issue of native language retention among the Spanish-speaking and its implications for their successful cultural, social, and economic assimilation into mainstream American society must be addressed in the context of 200 years of the American experience, but with a clear understanding of the characteristics Hispanics have and do not have in common with other important groups.

Before questions of the relative value of language and cultural retention to successful social and economic assimilation can be answered, other questions must be addressed:

- What does American history tell us about the relative values of assimilation, acculturation, bilingualism, and biculturalism?
- What is the social responsibility and benefit in maintaining native language and culture?
- What is the role of educational institutions in fostering bilingualism and biculturalism? Or alternatively, assimilation and acculturation?
- What are the benefits of present bilingual institutions (schools, social science agencies, churches) to the Hispanic community? To society as a whole?
- To what degree is native language retention beneficial or detrimental to the Hispanic individual? To the Hispanic community? To American society?

To address these issues, empirical research must be done. Equally important, the thinking of philosophers, historians, linguists, and educators must be brought to bear on the questions.

References

Asociación Mixta v. Hew. 1975. Civil No. C-72-382-Saw nD. Cal. July 15.

Bruckner, D.J.R., ed. 1980. *Politics and Language: Spanish and English in the United States.* Chicago: University of Chicago, Center for Policy Study.

Cafferty, Pastora San Juan, and Carmen Rivera-Martínez. 1981. *The Politics of Language: The Dilemma of Bilingual Education for Puerto Ricans.* Boulder, Colo: Westview.

Coleman, James S. 1977. *Parents, Teachers, and Children: Prospects for Choice in American Education.* San Francisco: University of California Press.

Cornelius, Wayne A. 1979. "Mexican Migration to the United States: The View from Rural Sending Communities." Cambridge: Migration and Development Study of MIT.

Darcy, Natalie. T. 1963. "Bilingualism and the Measurement of Intelligence: Review of a Decade's Research." *Journal of Genetic Psychology* 103 (December):259-82.

Eisenstadt, S.N. 1955. *The Absorption of Immigrants.* Glencoe: Free Press.

Epstein, Envin, 1970. *Politics and Education in Puerto Rico: A Documentary Survey of the Language Issue.* Metuchen, N.J.: Scarecrow.

Epstein, Noel. 1977. *Language, Ethnicity, and the Schools: Policy Alternatives for Bilingual, Bicultural Education.* Washington: Institute for Educational Leadership, George Washington University.

Estrada, Leabordo F. 1980. "Language and Political Consciousness among the Spanish-Speaking in the United States: A Demographic Study." *Politics and Language: Spanish and English in the U.S.* Chicago: University of Chicago Press.

Fannon, Franz. 1968. *The Wretched of the Earth.* New York: Grove.

Fishman, Joshua. 1966. *Language Loyalty in the United States.* The Hague: Winston.

Fishman, Joshua et al. 1971. *Bilingualism in the Barrio.* Bloomington: Indiana University.

García, R. 1976. *Learning in Two Languages.* Bloomington: Phi Delta Kappa Educational Foundation.

Glazer, Nathan, and Daniel Patrick Moynihan. 1970. *Beyond the Melting Pot.* Cambridge: MIT Press.

Gordon, Milton M. 1964. *Assimilation in American Life.* New York: Oxford University Press.

Greeley, Andrew M. 1974. *Ethnicity in the United States.* New York: Wiley.

Green, Gloria P., and Epstein, R.K., eds. 1984. *Employment and Earnings.* vol. 31 no. 1 (January). U.S. Department of Labor. Washington: U.S. Government Printing Office.

Haugen, Einer. 1956. *Bilingualism in the Americas: A Bibliography and Research Guide, No. 26.* American Dialect Society.

Kloss, Heinz. 1977. *American Bilingual Tradition.* Rowley, Mass.: Newberry.

Lambert, Wallace F., and G. Richard Tucker. 1972. *Bilingual Education of Children.* Rowley, Mass.: Newberry.

Lau v. Nichols. 1974. 414 U.S. 563, 566.

Lee, Everett S. 1966. "A Theory of Migration." *Demography III* 3 (no. 1):55.

Lieberson, Stanley. 1970. *Language and Ethnic Relations in Canada.* Toronto: Wiley.

López, David. 1978. "Rates of Language and Maintenance Shift." *Sociology and Social Research* 62 (no. 2).

McLaughlin, Barry. 1978. *Second-Language Acquisition in Childhood.* Hillsdale, N.J.: Lawrence Earlbaum.

Memmi, Albert. 1965. *The Colonizer and the Colonized.* Boston: Beacon.

Murguia, Edward. 1975. *Assimilation, Colonialism, and the American People.* Austin: University of Texas Press.

Petersen, William. 1958. "A General Typology of Migration." *American Sociological Review* 13 (June):256-66.

Public Law 90-247. 1968. Title VII.

Ravenstein, Ernest G. 1885. "The Laws of Migration." *Journal of the Royal Statistical Society* 48 (June): 167-235.

Ridge, Martin, ed. 1981. *The New Bilingualism: An American Dilemma.* Los Angeles: University of California Press.

Rodríguez, Richard. 1982. *Hunger of Memory.* Boston: David R. Godine.

Saavedra, Barbara Heiler. 1969. "Applied Language Research Center, El Paso Public School." *Modern Language Journal* 53 (February):97.

Seelye, H. Ned, Rafaela Elizondo de Weffer, and K. Balasubramonian. 1973. "Do Bilingual Education Programs Inhibit English Language Achievement? A Report on the Illinois Experiment." Paper presented at the 7th Annual Convening Teachers of English to Speakers of other Languages, San Juan, Puerto Rico, May 9-13.

Senior, Clarence. 1961. *The Puerto Ricans: Strangers, Then Neighbors.* Chicago: Quadrangle.

U.S. Commission on Civil Rights. 1975. *A Better Chance to Learn: Bilingual and Bicultural Education.* Washington: Clearinghouse Publication no. 51 (May).

U.S. Department of HEW. National Center for Statistics. 1978. *The Condition of Education.* Washington: Government Printing Office.

Veltman, Calvin. 1979. *The Assimilation of American Language Minorities: Structures, Pace, and Extent.* Report to the National Center for Education Statistics.

von Maltitz, Frances. 1975. *Living and Learning in Two Languages.* New York: McGraw-Hill.

Weinberg, Meyer. 1977. *A Chance to Learn.* Cambridge (England): Cambridge University Press.

Wilson, Kenneth. 1979. "The Effects of Integration and Class on Black Education Attainment." *Sociology of Education* 52 (April):84-98.

Wilson, Kenneth, and Alejandro Portes. 1980. "Immigrant Enclaves: Labor Experiences of Cubans in Miami." *American Journal of Sociology* 86:295-319.

6

Hispanics And Education

Neil Fligstein and *Roberto M. Fernández*

In this chapter the authors discuss the relevant literature concerning research on the educational achievement of persons from various Hispanic backgrounds and suggest a model for examining the differences. Education is posited as an intervening variable between social and familial background and the persons' current social status. One of the points which is stressed is the general lack of sufficient data with which to address this question. After summarizing the available research concerning the educational achievement of Mexican, Puerto Rican, Cuban and other-Hispanic persons, the authors use data from the Department of Labor's National Longitudinal Survey (NLS) to propose and test their model of the way in which the variables of background and education are related. The NLS is by no means defined as a perfect data set, but is does have a large number of Hispanic respondents and enough variables of the type required to begin this analysis. After presenting and discussing the model the authors focus on the impact of two factors which appear to have special significance for the educational achievement of Hispanic persons: their place of birth and their ability to speak English. In a final section of policy recommendations the authors focus attention on the need to develop policies which address the problem of school completion, which continues to be an obstacle for many Hispanic youth. The problem is further targetted as the completion of high school since these data indicate that once a person completes high school, Hispanic youth are more likely than non-Hispanic White youth to go on to college. The authors suggest that it is this sort of focusing the question that must be done in order to sufficiently understand the educational achievement patterns of Hispanics.

The reasons for low educational achievement by Hispanics in the United States are the subject of much speculation and surprisingly little research. To understand how and why Hispanics achieve less education than non-Hispanics, it is necessary to consider a variety of elements, some of which are unique to the situation of Hispanics, while others reflect the general process of educational attainment in the United States. To arrive at a theoretical model of this process, one must examine (1) the general model of educational attainment, (2) the unique situation of Hispanics, and (3) the special role that language may play in the low educational achievement of Hispanics and the possible ameliorating consequences of bilingual education or "English as a second language" programs. Once this model is specified, an attempt is made here to evaluate its efficacy utilizing data from the 1979 National Longitudinal Study. This chapter concludes with recommendations for social policy and further research.

General Model of Educational Attainment

Formal education is often seen as a process intervening between an individual's family of origin and later occupational and economic attainments (Jencks et al., 1972; Featherman and Hauser, 1978). The amount of education an individual receives is a product of a complex process which involves a number of factors. These include one's background, intelligence, academic performance, school setting, parental and teacher encouragement, and occupational and educational goals.

The most important set of factors thought to affect an individual's educational attainment is the individual's background (Jencks et al., 1972; Mare, 1980). Higher-income families in which parents have more education and high occupational status tend to support children in educational endeavors, because the parents realize that for their children to have a similar lifestyle they must obtain an education that prepares them for some career. Parents of less affluent families may emphasize education less, because the cost of college and higher education relative to the prospective returns on this investment does not justify the expenditure. The four variables usually used to index these background factors are father's education, mother's education, father's occupational status, and parental income. It has been found that all these variables equally affect the child's educational attainment (Sewell and Hauser, 1975; Shea, 1976). This suggests that a variety of mechanisms are operating to convert socioeconomic background into educational attainments. Parental income would seem primarily to most affect their ability to pay for their offsprings' education and related expenses. The parents' educational attainment appears to tap the value parents place on education for their children. Father's occupational status is also a rough indication of the value placed on education. In professional occupations education is seen as the means necessary to achieve the end, i.e., entrance into a profession. However, education is not as important for employment opportunities in blue collar occupations.

Sewell and Hauser (1975) have tried to clarify more precisely how various social-psychological processes intervene between background and educational attainment. Their work has tried to assess how the advantages of background are channeled through social-psychological mechanisms to affect eventual educational attainment. The basic theoretical notion is that an individual's educational attainment will be influenced by relations to other people. Certain of these people will assume differential significance in children's lives and help shape their educational goals. Three groups are seen as relevant to this process: parents, peers, and teachers. It has been found that parents and peers are the most important significant others. Hauser (1971) and Otto and Haller (1979) conclude that the major mechanism by which background is translated into educational achievement is parental attitude about what the child's educational goals should be.

Two other variables that help explain educational achievement are intelligence (or scholastic ability) and academic performance (Sewell and Hauser, 1975; Jencks et al., 1972). Intelligence measurement, however, is related in a problematic fashion to background ethnicity and language. High intelligence is more likely to be measured in students who share middle-class backgrounds and values than in those from different ethnic groups that hold nonstandard values, speak other languages, and have different cultural experiences (Aguirre, 1979; Cordasco, 1978).

The school itself is thought to aid educational attainment in a number of ways. For instance, class size, facilities, and teacher motivation are factors that could affect educational attainment. Most students of the subject conclude that there is very little independent impact of schools after holding constant student background and neighborhood factors (Jencks and Brown, 1975; Hauser et al., 1976). In looking at Blacks, research on high school contextual effects and school desegregation has been more successful (Thornton and Eckland, 1980; Patchen et al., 1980; Wilson, 1979). For Hispanics, there is also evidence that suggests that school-level variables have an independent effect on scholastic achievement. Carter and Segura (1979) stress that since teachers assume Hispanics are poor students, they behave in a manner that hinders the student's ability to achieve.

The last important factor in the educational attainment process is an individual's educational and occupational aspirations. There is evidence that the best predictor of completed schooling is educational aspirations (Sewell, Haller, and Portes, 1969; see Alexander and Cook, 1979, for a different view). Occupational aspirations also determine education, as career plans may require a degree. Both educational and occupational aspirations are determined to a large extent by background, significant others' expectations, intelligence, academic performance, and the school environment.

In sum, research on educational attainment in sociology has clearly demonstrated that social background affects educational outcomes primarily through the transmission of values and attitudes toward education. Parents provide economic, psychic, and emotional support for their children that translates into educational achievement. Schools appear to selectively reinforce those students who have this kind of motivation and give them encouragement to succeed. Through this kind of complex social-psychological process, student aspirations for education and occupations are shaped and their behavior follows. The other key pattern to note is that students with higher measured intelligence tend to have higher educational attainment, as do those with higher grades. Academic performance itself is a function of background and values as well as intelligence. Both intelligence and grades are also related to background in that some components of these factors originate in the advantages of growing up in a middle-class environment (Sewell and Hauser, 1975).

In addressing issues that affect Hispanics in the United States, the complexities of these factors are increased by the diversity of the Hispanic population. The various Hispanic groups have arrived in America at different times under varying conditions, and their educational attainments have been shaped by these differences and by the culture of each group. Past research has shown that Hispanic subgroups differ in their educational achievement (Nielsen and Fernández, 1981; Jaffe et al., 1980; Levitan et al., 1975; National Center for Education Statistics, 1980).

Mexican-Americans

Most scholars have argued that Mexican-American students have been systematically discriminated against in school. Legally, Mexican-Americans were not subject to discriminatory racial laws. In practice, however, Mexican-American students have attended segregated schools and often their educational facilities are understaffed and lack basic resources (Weinberg, 1977a; Carter and Segura, 1979). Most studies (Carter, 1979; Carter and Segura, 1979; Vásquez, 1974) see student underachievement and alienation as a direct consequence of the inferiority of the school setting for Mexicans.

School delay has been the basic mechanism by which schools have intentionally or unintentionally lowered Mexican-American students' probability of high-school completion. By having students repeat grades, schools have made alternatives to schooling more attractive to Hispanic students (Carter and Segura, 1979). Carter and Segura see this process as one in which the Mexican students are pushed out of school because they encounter a difficult school situation where they are expected to fail. The other part of this process is that as school becomes less attractive, job opportunities become more so.

An issue that remains to be explored is the effect of cultural differences on educational attainment of Mexican-Americans. The central argument usually put forward is that Mexican-American culture contains values that are not conducive to educational attainment. This point of view has both a positive and negative connotation. Some have argued that the Mexican-American child is culturally deprived since he experiences little intellectual stimulation, has a negative self-image, and the value of education is not stressed by his parents (Bloom, Davis, and Hess, 1965; Gordon and Wilkerson, 1966; Heller, 1966). Mexican-American culture has been characterized as family-centered, patriarchal, and oriented toward the extended family. The primary cultural values are thought to be machismo, fatalism, and orientation toward the present. Educators have tended to view Mexican-American students as victims of their culture, and their low educational achievement is thought to reflect these values and orientations. However, most empirical evidence does not support this view of the Mexican family (see for example Coleman et al., 1966). Further, there is no evidence that Mexican students have a lower self-image than White students (DeBlassie and Healey, 1970).

Ramírez and Castañeda (1974) argue that each culture possesses distinct cognitive styles by which it relates to and organizes the world. Mexican-Americans are what they call "bicultural," and have a cognitive style that they refer to as "field-dependent." By "bicultural," they mean that Mexican-Americans have had to adjust to two cultures and therefore have the capacity to express themselves in the cognitive styles of both their own culture and the dominant White culture. "Cognitive style" refers to learning styles, incentive-motivation schemes, and human relational and communication styles. The dominant values of Mexican-American culture are thought to be identification with family, community, and ethnic group, personalization of interpersonal relations, status and role definition in family and community, and Mexican-Catholic ideology. According to Ramírez and Castañeda, these differing cognitive styles result in different learning styles. For instance, Mexican-American children learn better in cooperative rather than competitive settings. They are also more other-oriented and rely more heavily on family, community, and friends for self-perception. Field dependence implies that Mexican-American children do better on verbal tasks and tasks that relate to other people, while White children do better on analytic tasks.

Ramírez and Castañeda's argument suggests that the cultural differences between Mexican-Americans and majority American society reflect different values as to what is important in relating to other people. They do not see Mexican-American children as culturally deprived; rather, they exist in a different culture that has its own set of rules and justifications and whose practices are antithetical to dominant White middle-class culture.

These cultural differences, combined with the negative perception and treatment of Mexican-American students by schools, go a long way toward explaining why Mexican-Americans experience low educational attainment. Given a hostile school environment and the pressures of needing to work to help support a household, it is not surprising that Mexican-Americans leave school at an early age (Haro, 1977; Laosa, 1977).

Puerto Ricans

Puerto Ricans are American citizens by virtue of the commonwealth status of Puerto Rico. Thus Puerto Rican migration to the United States is really a form of internal migration. The 1910 Census reported that only 1,513 persons born in Puerto Rico were living on the mainland. There have been a series of waves of Puerto Rican migration since then, which have tended to correspond to the ups and downs of the U.S. and Puerto Rican economies. Between 1940 and 1950 the number of Puerto Ricans living on the mainland tripled. It then doubled during the decade of the 1950s. Presently there are 2,013,945 persons of Puerto Rican birth living on the mainland. The major cause of the migration to the mainland appears to be the continuing poverty on the island and perceived opportunities for employment in the United States.

While schools in Puerto Rico presented difficulties for children because of their lack of resources as well as the issue of instruction in English or Spanish, schools in the mainland have presented even more problems. The issue of language is probably the key problem for Puerto Rican children, and is complicated further by the fact that there is circular migration between the island and mainland. The question of bilingual education may be the major education issue for Puerto Ricans. It has been argued that Puerto Rican children must have a basic knowledge of both English and Spanish because they are part of a circular migration stream between the island and mainland. (Cafferty and Rivera-Martínez, 1981). Within the Puerto Rican community there are differences of opinion as to what constitutes appropriate education and in which language instruction should take place. Many who plan to stay on the mainland agree with the schools' attempt to teach the children in English. Others argue that bilingual-bicultural education is not only a necessity, but a nonnegotiable demand.

Most observers agree that the two basic explanations of the Puerto Rican dropout rate are language and the fact that students are forced to repeat grades (Cafferty and Rivera-Martínez, 1981). Students who do not speak

English have difficulties learning and are more likely to fail a grade and be held back. Thus they fall behind their peers and become increasingly alienated from school.

Cubans

The flow of immigrant Cubans to the United States has political rather than economic origins (Wilson and Portes, 1980; Pedraza-Bailey, 1980). While Puerto Ricans came to the mainland for economic reasons and Mexican-Americans have either lived for many generations in the United States or else have recently immigrated for economic reasons, Cubans came to the United States mainly to escape the Castro regime. About 37,000 people arrived in the United States between 1959 and 1961. After the Bay of Pigs incident, immigration increased rapidly. By the end of 1962 there were about a quarter of a million persons admitted from Cuba. In 1965, President Johnson announced an "open door" policy that allowed Cubans who wanted to emigrate to do so, bringing about a second wave of immigration with the result that in 1976 the U.S. Immigration and Naturalization Service (1977) reported that 661,934 Cubans had arrived in America. There have been continued migrations, so that the total Cuban population is 803,226 according to the 1980 Census.

Unlike Mexican-Americans or Puerto Ricans, Cubans have received federal aid to help them adjust to the American environment since their arrival. President Eisenhower initially allocated $1 million for programs to aid the resettlement process. President Kennedy extended these programs to include aid for (1) transportation costs from Cuba, (2) financial assistance to needy refugees, (3) financial assistance to states and local governments for public services such as education, (4) costs of resettlement outside Miami, and (5) employment and training costs for refugees.

Pedraza-Bailey and Sullivan (1979) document how the federal government aided in retraining Cubans and teaching them English, as well as setting up bilingual programs in public schools in Miami. In the 1960s, this plan appeared to be working. There are now significant numbers of Cubans in New York, New Jersey, and California. However, as early as 1973 there was evidence that Cubans were returning to Miami (Clark, 1977; Wilson and Portes, 1980). Wilson and Portes (1980) argue that the major reason for this was the attraction of the Cuban community to other Cubans. They suggest that Miami forms an ethnic enclave where Cubans dominate economically and politically. Spanish is the dominant language and Cuban culture is preserved. This enclave contains great economic wealth, as many Cubans who arrived in America brought substantial financial assets with them. This enclave also forms a natural location for new immigrants who are looking for employment and security in a new land.

Cubans have had historically higher educational attainment than Puerto Ricans and Mexican-Americans (Jaffe et al., 1980). As recent immigrants, Cubans have the highest language retention among these groups. While in terms of achievement Cubans appear to be the most successful of any Hispanic group, they are the least linguistically assimilated of any Hispanic group. The most straightforward explanation of this phenomenon is that Cubans have formed an ethnic enclave in Miami (Wilson and Portes, 1980). The issue of language is also very important to Cubans. They have been able to exert control over their local schools with the aid of the federal government in order to preserve their linguistic and cultural heritage (Pedraza-Bailey and Sullivan, 1979).

Other Hispanics

There are numerous other groups in the United States that have Hispanic origins. These groups come from various countries in Central and South America as well as the Caribbean. Their class origins tend to be heterogeneous. Those who are professionals and managers tend to have few problems assimilating and they easily experience upward mobility (Stevens, Goodman, and Mick, 1978; Chiswick, 1978). Others leave for political reasons and many of these have a relatively easy time of adjusting to the new environment of the United States. Those who have few skills and are often undocumented (e.g. Dominicans and Salvadoreans) fare much worse. These groups have high educational attainment which reflects their social origins (Jaffe et al., 1981).

The Issue of Language and Bilingual Education

For all the Hispanic groups and indeed for all immigrant groups, the preservation of language and culture upon finding oneself in a new culture is of paramount importance. Recently, in the sociological literature, there has been an enormous resurgence of interest in the question of second language usage and preservation of various ethnic heritages (Greeley, 1974; Lieberson, 1981; Estrada, 1980; Glazer and Moynihan, 1975). The basic conclusion of the new ethnicity literature is that ethnic identity is important to many Americans, and the preservation of language, culture, and ethnic ties has not diminished in importance as the earlier melting pot theorists had predicted. For Hispanic groups, the key focus has been on bilingual education. This refers to all programs that potentially affect the language use or ability of non-English speakers. Unfortunately, much of the discussion of bilingual education has tended to take place at a rhetorical level that often reflects the value choices of various interest groups. The goals of any program oriented toward non-English speakers are themselves value choices which reflect official policy framed by the ability of various organized subpopulations to obtain programs that meet their defined needs. In the following sections, we (1) briefly review various bilingual education programs, (2) suggest the goals of such programs and the political and cultural implications those goals reflect, (3) discuss the history of bilingual education in recent years in the United States, and (4) consider the effectiveness of various types of bilingual education programs in achieving their goals.

Types of Bilingual Education Programs

Most bilingual education programs in the United States have as their goal the teaching of English to non-English speakers (Llanes, 1981; Gaarder, 1977; Epstein, 1977; Paulston, 1978). This goal has followed from the major federal legislation that has brought bilingual education into existence. Most bilingual education programs are transitional. The major issue is how best to transform the non-English speaker into an English speaker without having the person fall behind in school, get frustrated in school, and/or drop out of school. The debate on bilingual education has had two components: first, whether the goal of transitional bilingual education is valid; and second, how best to achieve the transition to English with the least harm to the child in terms of impairing his chance to learn and achieve. The various bilingual programs that have been suggested and used in practice usually reflect one side or another of this debate. When no program exists the term *submersion* is used. Submersion is the process whereby non-English-speaking children are placed in classrooms where English is spoken. This means that the child is given no language help and he must either learn English or fail. There are four models of bilingual education programs: structured immersion, English as a second language, transitional bilingual education, and bilingual-bicultural education. The first three clearly focus on providing transitional language capabilities, while the last has as its goal the maintenance of the mother tongue and culture while learning English.

Structured immersion is the method whereby the teacher instructs the class in English but students are free to ask questions in either English or their mother tongue. The teacher usually answers questions in English. The curriculum is structured such that no prior knowledge of English is assumed when new material is introduced. This means that the student is simultaneously learning English and the new content material.

English as a second language (ESL) is the method whereby students are placed in classes taught in English for most of the school day. During part of the school day, students are given English instruction designed to help them understand English. For this ESL instruction, the mother tongue may or may not be used.

Transitional bilingual education is the method whereby students are initially taught in their mother tongue and gradually brought into English instruction. Usually the ESL component is attached to the bilingual program to facilitate a more rapid movement into English instruction. The goal of this kind of education is to ensure that students do not fall behind in class while they are learning English. After a time, students have the instruction in the mother tongue phased out and all instruction is done in English. The principal difference between transitional bilingual education and the other methods of instruction is that students begin learning in their mother tongue.

Bilingual-bicultural education refers to an educational program whose goal is not just rapid movement into English as an instructional medium, but also to maintain and enhance speaking and writing ability in the mother tongue, thereby maintaining the mother culture. All the programs assume that without command of English children will be unable to complete schooling and/or succeed in American society.

Under the mandates of the Civil Rights Act and Supreme Court decisions, the federal government is responsible for providing students with an environment where they can learn English. Educational policies directed toward language reflect a broad spectrum of opinion from viewing submersion as the best approach to seeing bilingual-bicultural programs as the only solution. Endorsement of any approach depends on what one defines as the goal of the educational process and an appropriate way of achieving that goal. The fact that much confusion exists about what constitutes the best way to achieve English proficiency reflects as much the cross-cutting purposes of local communities, their leaders, and their constituencies as it does this society's lack of knowledge and information about what an effective program is.

Social and Legal History of Bilingual Education

Bilingual education has a long history in America. The nineteenth century was a period of language tolerance. However, when the massive migrations of Eastern and Southern Europeans began in the 1880s, language issues and problems came to the fore. By 1923, English was mandated by thirty-two states as the sole language of instruction in schools (Brisk, 1981; Cordasco, 1976). Some schools tried to prevent the teaching of any language other than English. This policy of English as the sole language of instruction in public schools regardless of schoolchildren's linguistic background persisted until the 1960s.

The major force underlying recognition of the rights and needs of speakers whose mother tongue was other than English were the linguistic minorities themselves (Anderson and Boyer, 1970; Fishman and Lovas, 1970). Various groups have demanded their right to learn and maintain their own language and culture. It is these demands that are at the bottom of the whole bilingual education issue.

Political pressures, particularly by Mexican-Americans, brought about legislation which became Title VII of the Elementary and Secondary Education Act (Bilingual Education Act) of 1968. Seventy-two programs were started in 1969 to aid the education of children of limited English-speaking ability who came from low-income families. Funding for these programs has grown from $7 million in 1969 to $150 million in 1980 (bilingual programs in 1981 received $157 million, while under the current administration budget estimates for such programs were $134 million in 1982 and $95 million in 1983). In 1974, Title VII was amended to eliminate the income requirements and also allocated funds for bilingual teacher training, for the preparation and dissemination of materials. This led to the formation of the Office of Bilingual Education. The goals of the act remained compensatory, in the sense that the purpose of the legislation was to provide for the transition from a language other than English to English. This has been the major thrust of federal aid to bilingual education from its inception. In 1978, amendments were added that gave additional funds to aid speaking as well as writing proficiency, provided funds for research purposes, and began Spanish language programs to aid Puerto Rican children returning to Puerto Rico.

The most important legal case in the bilingual education controversy was the 1974 Supreme Court decision in *Lau v. Nichols*. The basic issue in the case involved Chinese parents in San Francisco who sued the school board on grounds that their children, who spoke Chinese, were unable to take advantage of the educational system. The Supreme Court ruled that the Civil Rights Act of 1964 guaranteed persons the right to equal benefit from any education program aided by the federal government. The court agreed that schools must provide some compensatory education for students who were not native speakers of English to be in compliance with the Civil Rights Act. While the Supreme Court did not specify what kind of remedy they would accept, the Office of Civil Rights came up with a set of guidelines now known as the "Lau Remedies" which recommend transitional bilingual education. School districts and critics have argued that they are too restrictive, and that schools should pursue programs that are both cost-effective and relevant to their population (Epstein, 1977). Transitional bilingual education where multiple languages are present or where very few students need language training is argued to be too costly.

Effectiveness of Bilingual Education

There is great difficulty in evaluating the various programs, as they have different goals and different outcomes; they vary as to quality of instruction and amount of money spent on a per capita basis, and students are involved for differing amounts of time. Further, the target populations differ in that some programs are oriented toward different Hispanic groups while others are targeted at various other ethnic minorities. Finally, evaluation is made all the more difficult by lack of standardization of testing and of appropriate experimental controls so that background and desire to be in the bilingual education program are controlled appropriately. Also, there is often little baseline evidence of performance, so that testing the effectiveness of various programs is difficult.

In spite of these shortcomings, it is possible to make some generalizations about the effectiveness of various bilingual programs. Most of the studies done evaluate the scores on English or math proficiency tests of students who are nonnative English speakers enrolled in different kinds of bilingual education programs. The assumption is that test scores measure academic success and that such success will directly translate into additional years of schooling. In a thorough review of the literature, Baker and de Kantor (1981) conclude that there have been few if any studies that attempt to evaluate whether various bilingual education programs aid in keeping students in school and thereby increase Hispanic educational attainment.

The general conclusion is that some form of program, whether it be transitional bilingual education, structured immersion, or English as a second language, seems to aid the English and math scores of nonnative speakers of English (Baker and de Kantor, 1981). The evidence concerning which strategy of teaching the majority language works best is a bit more confused, but the bulk of the evidence suggests that it depends on the program and the situation of the minority language (e.g. Spanish speakers in the United States). The weight of the evidence suggests students do better when they are introduced to schooling in their native tongue first and then eased into English instruction (Carsud and Curtis, 1980; McConnell, 1980; Golub, 1981). In the situation where students know the dominant language and are taught the minority language, structured immersion appears to operate as the best strategy (Barik, Swain, and McTavish, 1974; Lambert and Tucker, 1972; Cohen, 1974). The reason structured immersion seems to work has to do with the position of the language minority in society as well as the goal of instruction.

In the situation where minority language groups are taught through structured immersion rather than in transitional bilingual education, it has been found that they do better in the latter (Skutnabb–Kangas, 1979; Ramírez and Politzer, 1975). The apparent explanation is that students from the minority language are placed in an alien cultural setting and this works to reinforce their feelings of insecurity and inadequacy in that setting (Ramírez and Castañeda, 1974; Carter and Segura, 1979). To make the transition to bilingualism more effective, it is often the case that it is necessary to reassure students and make them gradually move toward speaking and instruction in the dominant language. In the case of dominant-language students learning a second language, there are obvious motivational factors at work (see Lambert and Tucker, 1972). Students probably want to learn the second language and their parents value that skill. In that situation, structured immersion or submersion serves a positive function.

A number of studies show that transitional bilingual education programs have little or no effect on English or other proficiency skills (Ramos et al., 1969; Ames and Bick, 1978; Baker and de Kantor, 1981). These results might initially seem to contradict our original conclusions, but there is one plausible explanation. Bilingual education programs and their evaluation techniques differ radically from situation to situation. That they are effective in some situations and not in others says more about the specific program than about the general idea of providing aid to students who are making a transition from one language to another. The important point is that effective bilingual programs do make a difference in the English and math proficiency of students, while poorly conceived and executed programs do not. The quality of the teaching and the amount of support, both from parents and administrators, are important components for the effectiveness of any program. That students who go through some kind of program do better than those who go through none is enough justification for different kinds of programs. The choice of program is more problematic, although transitional bilingual education seems to make sense because it attempts to make the transition to English as easy as possible for the child. Structured immersion programs have been shown to be ineffective in those situations where the language minority group is taught in the dominant language. Transitional bilingual education appears to be more effective in this case for reasons already mentioned. While there appears to be evidence that bilingual education programs aid in making the transition to the dominant language, there is little or no evidence as to their effect on completed schooling.

Model of Educational Attainment

We shall now propose a model of educational attainment and how such a model would be modified to take into account the special situation of the various Hispanic groups. There are two parts to this model: variables that have been found to pertain to all subpopulations and variables that can be expected to disproportionately affect Hispanics. The background characteristics common to all groups include number of siblings, father's education, mother's education, father's occupation, and family income. The parental education measures and father's occupation index both the socioeconomic status of the family and parents' attitudes about the desirability of education. The family income measures the ability of the family to pay for education. Number of siblings indicates how many children the family income has to be spread over. Controlling other factors, the larger the family, the more likely that the respondent will be drawn out of school and into the labor force to help support the family (see Rumberger, 1981 for a similar argument). We also include a measure for gender since past research has shown males and females vary in their educational attainment (Alexander and Eckland, 1974). The social-psychological measures of parental, peer, teacher, and respondent's educational aspirations and expectations would also be expected to affect educational outcomes. However, in the data set utilized here, these measures were unavailable.

From the review of the experiences of various Hispanic groups, two additional types of background variables need to be included: migration history and linguistic practices. In both cases, past research has shown mixed results concerning educational attainment.

Some studies found that immigrants tend to be a highly motivated, self-selected group, and hence show higher achievement, perhaps after an initial disadvantage due to language and customs (Chiswick, 1978). This high level of motivation may be passed on to the immigrants' children, thus explaining why progeny of more recent migrants achieve higher educational attainment (Fernández, 1982; Nielsen and Fernández, 1981). Kimball (1968) and Baral (1979) suggest that long-time residents may become "ghettoized" and therefore achieve poorly compared to more recent migrants. Others (e.g. Featherman and Hauser, 1978) find that immigrants are at a socioeconomic disadvantage and attribute this to difficulties of language and culture. In addition, the 1970 Census data indicate that immigrants have lower levels of education (Jaffe et al., 1980) prior to immigration, which can translate into lower educational achievement for the child.

Past research has established that Spanish speakers in a predominantly English-speaking society experience difficulties in school and work due to language (García, 1980; Tienda, 1981). However, other studies have found that bilingualism is an asset, both in school (Peal and Lambert, 1962; Fernández, 1982) and in certain job markets (López, 1976).

Much of the discrepancy in these findings may be due to the varying conceptions and measures of linguistic practices employed by the different studies. Although not enough data exists on the issue, it seems reasonable to incorporate language measures into models of educational attainment for Hispanics.

A set of school-level variables are important predictors of educational transitions. These include whether the school is public or private, its racial and ethnic composition, and the measures of school quality such as drop-out rate and teacher/student ratio. Recently, Coleman (1981) has shown that minorities in private schools tend to do better than those in public schools (but see Lewis and Wanner [1979] for contrary evidence). Measures of school racial composition (percent Black and Hispanic) are included because past research on school integration has shown small but positive effects on scholastic achievement for Blacks (Wilson, 1979; Lewis and St. John, 1974). No similar research exists concerning Hispanics. However, the importance of segregation issues for Hispanics (see Noboa 1980) requires testing whether similar effects can be discerned with available data by including percent Hispanics in our model. As a general measure of the holding power of the respondents' high school, the percent who drop out are used as a predictor of these educational transitions. Lastly, in accord with the extensive literature on school effects (e.g. Coleman et al., 1966; Bidwell and Kasarda, 1975; see Spady [1976] for a review), the number of teachers per student in the respondents' high schools are used as a school resource measure.

In addition to these general school-level variables which should affect both Whites and Hispanics, the model incorporates curriculum measures that should be important for Hispanics, i.e., whether the student was enrolled in an "English as a second language" program or some form of transitional bilingual education program. It is essential to assess whether these programs aid in increasing educational attainment.

Finally, community level variables are considered. The local unemployment rate of the respondent's area of residence can be considered a measure of the pull factors in the local labor market that might draw youth out of school (see Duncan, 1965; Edwards, 1976). Another community-level variable, urban residence, is significant because of the greater number of nonschool options available in cities.

Our goal is to examine models that include variables relevant to the general model of attainment as well as variables specific to the Hispanic experience. Because of data limitations, the model estimated must exclude certain variables. Thus all results presented here are tentative, due to specification error. The National Longitudinal Survey (hereafter NLS) is the most useful data set for our purposes, since it contains family background information, school information, and some information on local areas. The NLS is limited as it suffers from serious missing data problems on many variables and lacks measures on a number of other key variables. Further, the data set is restricted to those aged 14-22 in 1979. However, given these limitations, the NLS appears to be the only data set with a large enough number of Hispanics and sufficiently wide array of measures to allow an examination of the reasons for Hispanic educational attainment.

The analytic strategy is to examine the causes of schooling outcomes for relevant age cohorts for Whites, Mexicans, and all other Hispanics. The dependent variables include school delay, dropping out or staying in high school, and entering college. The analysis is restricted to only two Hispanic groups as there were too few cases to allow for a more detailed examination of Cubans, Puerto Ricans, and other Hispanics. A more extended discussion of these results and others can be found in Fligstein and Fernández (1982, 1984). The following summary is based on tables appearing in the appendix to this chapter.

Table A.1 presents means and standard deviations for the three subpopulations by ethnic group. We have broken down ethnicity into all groups previously discussed even though the actual analysis places Cubans, Puerto Ricans, and other Hispanics in the same group. This is done to see how different the various groups are on the different variables.

In terms of school completion rates, Whites, Cubans, and other Hispanics (here defined as Central, Caribbean, and South American) have higher rates of school attendance and high-school completion than Mexican-Americans and Puerto Ricans. Puerto Ricans have the lowest rates. These differences are quite striking.

When we consider rates of college attendance, we find that Hispanics are more likely than Whites to attend college once they have a high-school diploma (Puerto Ricans are an exception). This suggests that the primary barriers to Hispanic educational attainment are encountered early in the education life course—high school and prior—and that those Hispanics who survive to finish high school are a highly select, motivated group.

Comparing the mean values on parental education, Cuban parents have educational levels nearly equal to those of White parents while other Hispanics, Puerto Ricans, and Mexican-Americans trail behind. Other interesting comparisons concern siblings' language, SMSA location, school characteristics, and the distribution of bilingual education and ESL courses. Mexican-American and Puerto Rican respondents tend to come from large families while other Hispanics and Whites come from smaller families. Cuban respondents have the fewest siblings. Puerto Ricans, Cubans, other Hispanics, and Mexican-Americans all tend to be concentrated in SMSAs, while Whites are much less likely to be located in SMSAs. About 7 percent of all Hispanics were Spanish-monolingual (as indexed by the Spanish interview variable). This means that most Hispanic youth have learned some English. Hispanic youth are concentrated in high schools, and except for Cubans, tend to be in schools with higher dropout rates than Whites'. Finally, none of the Cubans sampled had been enrolled in ESL or bilingual education courses in high school, while 2-16 percent of the other Hispanic groups reported such enrollment. One can conclude that these programs have touched only a small fraction of Spanish-speaking Hispanics. In sum, Cubans and other Hispanics appear demographically most similar to Whites, while Mexican-Americans and Puerto Ricans seem least similar.

The differential causes of school delay appear in Table A.2. For Whites, both parents' education significantly affects school delay and the more education the parents have, the less delay the student experiences. Male respondents have more school delay, and respondents from large families also experience more delay. For Whites, being born in a foreign country increases the probability of school delay. There is also a statistically significant effect of the teacher/student ratio: students who attended schools with more teachers per student tend to be less grade-delayed. Presumably teachers are able to spend more time with students individually, so that students are less likely to fail.

The school delay regression for Mexican-Americans shows that those in large families and those of foreign birth experience delay. Also, if one has an immigrant mother one experiences less grade retention. The effect of mothers is seen throughout the Mexican-American equations, as mother's education and mother's nativity are strong causes of educational attainment. Among the school and social environment variables, three effects are statistically significant. Respondents who live in an SMSA are less likely to experience school delay. A high unemployment rate causes less school delay, implying that Mexican-American students may be trading off schooling for work and leaving school when work is available. Finally, Mexican-Americans in private schools are less delayed than those in public schools. There were no statistically significant effects for enrollment in bilingual education or ESL courses.

In the model for school delay for all other Hispanic groups, two significant effects appear: mother's education and number of siblings. Mother's education appears to lessen school delay while number of siblings increases it. When the school and social environment variables are added, one additional effect appears. Respondents who attended an ESL course were more likely to be in school. This is the only curriculum effect in all the models presented here and it suggests that, at least for this group, ESL programs lessen school delay.

In comparing Mexican-Americans and Whites on the causes of school delay, three major conclusions are evident. First, parental education operates to lower school delay for Whites, but has little effect for Mexican-Americans. This suggests that school delay for Mexican-Americans is not directly related to socioeconomic background and may reflect other conditions. Second, being nonnative increases school delay for Mexican-Americans almost half a year more than for Whites. Nonnative origins is a serious cause of delay for Mexican-Americans. Finally, immigrant mothers have children with less school delay for Mexican-Americans, lending credence to the importance of mothers in the educational process for Mexican-Americans.

Table A.3 contains results on whether a respondent completed high school or dropped out. For Whites, the largest effects appear to be those of parental education. This strongly confirms that parental education is a key determinant of children's finishing high school. Young men are less likely to complete high school than young women, and this could reflect their greater opportunities in the labor market. Respondents from larger families (as measured by number of siblings) were also less likely to finish high school, suggesting the importance of family obligations on school continuation decisions. Four of the school effect variables bear a statistically significant relation to finishing high school. Respondents in schools with Hispanics or with high dropout rates tended to finish high school less frequently. Again, this could reflect school quality, social environment, or a number of other factors. The teacher/student ratio also positively affected the probability of high-school completion. More teachers means more attention per student and greater likelihood of high school completion. Finally, controlling other factors, attending a private school also significantly increases chances of high school completion. Whether this is due to private schools' selecting better students who are less likely to drop out or to aspects of the school environment that encourage high achievement cannot be discerned.

Turning to the results for Mexican-Americans, we see that mother's education significantly increases the likelihood of high school completion, while father's education does not. This suggests, again, that Mexican-American mothers play a key role in their children's educational outcomes. The more siblings a respondent has the less likely he or she is to complete school. Finally, persons of foreign birth finish high school less frequently. Neither of the language measures affect high school completion. When the school and social environment variables are added, only the percent of Hispanics in the school significantly affects high school completion. Mexican-Americans in Hispanic schools tend to complete high school more frequently, and this could imply that a Mexican-American student culture aids high school completion. Again, there are no statistically significant effects of bilingual education or ESL courses.

We next consider causes of high school completion for those other Hispanics over eighteen. There are two statistically significant effects: father's
education and Spanish interview. The higher the father's education, the
more likely the respondent is to finish high school. Being interviewed in
Spanish implies that a respondent will be less likely to finish high school.
The school and social environment variables have statistically significant
effects.

The major comparison to consider is between Whites and Mexican-
Americans. In general, the background variables are more powerful predictors of high school completion for Whites. Both parents' education
strongly affects high school completion for Whites, while only mother's
education does so for Mexican-Americans. White males are much less
likely to complete high school than White females, while Mexican-American females and males are equally likely to do so. Being in a Hispanic high
school aids school completion for Mexican-Americans and deters it for
Whites. Foreign-born Mexican-Americans are also more likely to finish
high school than foreign-born Whites. Taken together, these results imply
that Whites' high school completion is highly related to their family of
origin and sex, while Mexican-Americans' completion is determined
mostly by their mother's education and their nativity.

The final set of equations to consider concerns the determinants of
college attendance, given that the respondent finished high school. These
models are certainly misspecified, since parental income is left out of the
equation. Since college costs money, this serious omission is problematic.
The results appear in Table A.4.

The equation for Whites shows both measures of parental education
positively affect the likelihood of college attendance. Respondents from
larger families are less likely to attend college. Note that this variable could
proxy for the family's ability to pay for college. Two interesting effects
emerge concerning nativity. If either of one's parents was born in a foreign
country, one is more likely to attend college. This may be due to immigrants' high levels of motivation (Nielsen and Fernández, 1981; Fernández,
1982; Chiswick, 1978). These effects are quite provocative. Only one of the
variables concerning school and social environment significantly affects
college attendance. If one attends a private school, one is more likely to go
to college.

We now turn to the determinants of Mexican-American college attendance, given that respondents completed high school. Only two family
background variables affect college attendance: mother's education and
mother's nativity. Mexican-Americans with immigrant mothers are more
likely to go to college, while the higher the mother's educational attainment
the more likely the respondent is to attend college. When the measures of

school and social environment are added, there are no interesting substantive effects.

Lastly, we consider the causes of college entrance for those other Hispanics who finish high school. The model has no statistically significant effects. The major differences across groups center on two factors: the lack of effects of various variables for Hispanics and the importance of those variables for Whites, and the fact that mothers appear more important to Mexican-American college attendance while both parents are important to Whites. Hispanics who go to college are survivors of an educational system that tends to work against them.

Discussion of the Results

The differences across groups, particularly between Mexican-Americans and Whites, are striking. The major differences in social background center on place of birth and native language. Mexicans who are foreign-born and speak Spanish are less likely to achieve high educational levels. Since their parents have low educational attainment, Mexican-Americans also face these additional disadvantages. The other Hispanic analyses reveal similar patterns, although to a much lesser extent. Further, there is very little evidence for the effects of bilingual education or ESL on schooling outcomes. This could reflect the heterogeneity of those programs.

These results are exploratory. The sample sizes were small and many measures were problematic. In particular, the language measures were poor and the amount of missing data on the transcript and school data was substantial. Measures of ESL and bilingual programs, where they did exist, were also crude. Therefore all conclusions are tentative. More data needs to be collected to examine group differences. It is clear from the descriptive statistics that Puerto Ricans and Mexicans are in a much worse situation regarding education than Cubans and other Hispanics.

Family background appears to be the major explanation of White educational attainment. Parental education and number of siblings significantly affect staying in school, graduating from high school, and attending college. Other interesting effects concern parental nativity. Teacher/student ratios affect school delay and high school completion. Respondents in private schools tend to complete school more frequently and attend college more often than those in public schools.

Statistical analysis of aggregate groupings of Cubans, Puerto Ricans, and other Hispanics can produce little useful information. The groups are too diverse and hence the data too heterogeneous. It is important to run these models by ethnic subpopulation to see if the results hold. Unfortunately, this data set cannot allow this detailed analysis.

Public Policy Issues

The various Hispanic groups have fared differently in the U.S. educational system. The differences appear to be related to three factors: (1) each group's socioeconomic position; (2) lack of exposure to English; and (3) foreign nativity, which reflects unfamiliarity with American culture. In addition, school delay is a major cause for Hispanics failing to graduate from high school. Those Hispanics who finish high school are more likely than Whites to attend college. The real educational barrier for Hispanics appears to be high school completion.

Most data on language usage is problematic, and even less is known about the quality and quantity of programs aimed at teaching English to Spanish speakers. Further, no data set currently exists that allows for detailed analysis of Cubans, Puerto Ricans, and other Hispanics in terms of their educational attainment. The lack of adequate data hampers any judgments on causal analysis of relevant factors for all groups. Nonetheless, a number of policy recommendations are tentatively possible.

- It is necessary to study the effects of language and language programs and what makes programs work.
- Measures to increase educational attainment for Hispanics should focus on high school. The high rate of high school noncompletion for Hispanics is most problematic. In particular, programs oriented toward lessening school delay, increasing the number of teachers, and generally making it easier for non-English speakers and recent immigrants to adjust seem most promising.
- Aid should be particularly directed toward Puerto Rican and Mexican-American students. These groups have extremely low rates of high school completion.
- Programs should be set up to teach English to recent immigrants.

Appendix

The data is the 1979 National Longitudinal Survey. Results were produced using ordinary least squares regression for school delay and logistic regression for high-school completion and college attendance. Variables were coded as follows: School delay is defined as the median age in the population in the highest grade the respondent completed; the age of the respondent at the highest grade completed. High-school completion is coded 0 if the respondent did not finish high school and 1 if he did. College attendance is coded 0 if the respondent did not attend college and 1 if he did.

The independent variables are entered into the analyses in two sets: family background and school and social environment. In our theoretical discussion, we suggested variables relevant to the general population and variables relevant to Hispanics. Here, we incorporate both types of measures into family background and school and social environment variables.

There are nine measures of family background included in the model. They are: father's and mother's education and years of schooling; a dummy variable coded *0* if the respondent was female and *1* if the respondent was male; three dummy variables coded *0* if the respondent, his/her mother, and his/her father were born in the United States, and coded *1* if they were born elsewhere; a dummy variable coded *0* if the interview was conducted in English and *1* if it was conducted in Spanish, and the number of siblings in the respondent's family. No measures of family income and father's occupation were included because of high levels of missing data (over 40 percent).

The school and social environment measures reflect the social ecology of the surrounding area. The local community is indexed by two measures: the local unemployment rate in 1979 and a dummy variable coded *1* if the respondent was living in an SMSA and *0* if not.

The school variables are of two types: school environment and curriculum. School environment measures the quality of education and the racial/ethnic composition of the school. Only one of the school variables has relatively high nonmissing data. This is a dummy variable coded *0* if the respondent attended a public school and *1* for a private school. The other school variables were not assessed for about half of the sample. In order to use the data available, it was necessary to construct a dummy variable called "nonresponse school items" that is coded *0* if the respondent has no school data and *1* if data exists. All variables utilizing the school data are coded *0* if the data was missing. If those who responded were not systematically more likely to have stayed in school, completed school, or entered college, then this dummy variable should not statistically significantly affect the outcome. From our discussions with the people who collected the data, there is no reason to believe that such bias exists. The four measures of school environment are the percent in high school who were Hispanic, the percent in high school who were Black, the percent of students who dropped out of high school, and the students/teacher ratio.

The curriculum data for individuals was collected independently of the rest of the NLS data. Only about 40 percent of the respondents have this data, which are taken from high school transcripts. A dummy variable called "nonresponse transcript" was created and it was coded *0* if the respondent did not have transcript data and *1* if he did. Here too, *0* was assigned to the missing transcript data. We should thus be able to assess if the presence of transcript data is systematically related to the outcomes. The two curriculum variables are coded at the individual level and they are dummy variables coded *0* if the respondent did not take a course entitled "English as a Second Language" or "Bilingual Education" and coded *1* if he did.

More information on the sample data and analytic strategy is available in Fligstein and Fernández (1982, 1984).

TABLE A.1

Means and Standard Deviations of Various Variables for Whites, Mexican-Americans, and All Other Hispanics, and for Puerto Ricans, Cuban-Americans, and Other Hispanics, for Three Subpopulations (those aged less than 18, those older than 18, and those who have completed high school)

Variable	White						Mexican-American						All Other Hispanics[a]					
	A[b]		B		C		A		B		C		A		B		C	
	x̄	S.D.	x̄	S.D.	x̄	S.D.	x̄	S.D.	x̄	S.D.	x̄	S.D.	x̄	S.D.	x̄	S.D.	x̄	S.D.
Percent in high school	.90	.30					.83	.38					.87	.34				
Percent high school graduate			.83	.37					.57	.49					.66	.48		
Percent enter college					.58	.49					.66	.48					.63	.48
Father's education	11.73	3.95	12.03	3.60	12.55	3.43	7.29	4.60	6.90	4.67	8.02	4.56	9.47	4.57	9.22	5.03	10.50	4.93
Mother's education	11.58	2.56	11.89	2.62	12.28	2.45	7.07	3.99	6.96	4.31	8.17	4.21	8.89	3.85	8.98	4.17	9.89	4.38
Sex of respondent	.50	.50	.46	.50	.46	.50	.47	.50	.48	.50	.47	.50	.53	.50	.46	.50	.45	.50
Number of siblings	3.20	2.17	3.22	2.08	3.04	1.92	4.96	2.76	5.16	2.92	4.36	2.37	3.63	2.79	4.02	3.18	3.31	2.70
Nativity	.04	.19	.03	.17	.03	.17	.25	.43	.28	.45	.13	.34	.25	.43	.39	.49	.44	.50
Father's nativity	.05	.22	.05	.22	.05	.22	.41	.49	.45	.50	.36	.48	.35	.49	.43	.50	.50	.50
Mother's nativity	.06	.24	.05	.22	.05	.22	.45	.50	.47	.50	.39	.49	.36	.48	.44	.50	.51	.50
Language as child	.11	.31	.13	.34	.13	.34	.93	.26	.94	.23	.93	.25	.93	.25	.95	.22	.95	.22
Spanish interview	.02	.14	.02	.13	.02	.13	.05	.21	.07	.25	.03	.18	.04	.19	.06	.23	.01	.09
SMSA location	.64	.48	.68	.47	.69	.46	.71	.46	.80	.40	.80	.40	.94	.22	.97	.18	.96	.20
Local unemployment rate	6.34	2.16	6.14	2.18	6.12	2.20	6.64	3.20	5.97	2.71	6.07	2.53	6.21	1.99	6.19	2.00	6.03	1.95
Nonresponse school items	.54	.50	.51	.50	.53	.50	.47	.50	.40	.48	.49	.50	.36	.48	.34	.48	.40	.49
Percent Hispanic in school	3.18	8.86	2.89	8.53	2.77	7.88	31.82	32.60	28.13	33.87	35.13	35.39	18.65	26.01	13.62	21.42	14.20	21.68
Percent Black in school	6.31	12.77	5.63	11.75	5.68	11.45	4.11	9.71	3.23	9.17	2.84	6.76	12.06	17.43	9.88	17.67	9.20	15.75
Percent dropout in school	11.04	21.13	8.28	14.72	7.90	13.72	13.16	19.70	9.98	15.33	11.69	15.65	13.07	21.87	9.72	14.80	9.97	13.99
Teacher/student ratio	.04	.02	.04	.03	.03	.03	.03	.03	.03	.03	.04	.03	.03	.03	.03	.03	.03	.03
Public/private	.06	.24	.08	.27	.09	.29	.04	.19	.03	.18	.04	.19	.09	.29	.13	.33	.16	.37
Nonresponse transcript	.70	.46	.66	.47	.69	.46	.58	.49	.44	.50	.53	.50	.52	.50	.42	.49	.47	.50
ESL course	.00	.05	.00	.05	.00	.04	.04	.19	.03	.16	.02	.15	.07	.26	.03	.16	.02	.13
Bilingual education	.02	.13	.02	.05	.02	.15	.07	.26	.05	.22	.06	.24	.06	.24	.01	.10	.01	.09
Percent Cuban													.19	.39	.21	.41	.29	.46
Percent Puerto Rican													.51	.46	.39	.49	.30	.46
Percent Other Hispanic													.30	.46	.39	.49	.41	.49
N	3,465		2,280		1,871		587		296		173		306		180		117	

TABLE A.1 (Continued)

Variable	Cuban-American						Puerto Rican						Other Hispanic					
	A[b]		B		C		A		B		C		A		B		C	
	x̄	S.D.	x̄	S.D.	x̄	S.D.	x̄	S.D.	x̄	S.D.	x̄	S.D.	x̄	S.D.	x̄	S.D.	x̄	S.D.
Percent in high school	.91	.28					.81	.40					.92	.27				
Percent high school graduate			.89	.31					.49	.50					.69	.47		
Percent enter college					.65	.49					.57	.50					.67	.48
Father's education	11.47	4.27	11.89	5.13	12.12	5.34	8.08	4.42	7.22	5.13	8.89	5.39	10.52	4.29	9.79	4.02	10.54	3.89
Mother's education	10.81	3.52	11.61	3.57	11.85	3.65	7.94	3.84	7.11	3.90	7.71	4.49	9.26	3.56	9.45	3.90	10.08	4.13
Sex of respondent	.54	.50	.53	.51	.47	.51	.52	.50	.46	.50	.49	.51	.53	.50	.41	.50	.42	.50
Number of siblings	1.69	.93	1.84	1.24	1.88	1.25	4.45	3.09	5.21	3.46	4.17	2.79	3.48	2.41	4.00	3.00	3.69	3.01
Nativity	.53	.50	.79	.41	.79	.41	.00	.00	.03	.17	.06	.24	.50	.50	.54	.50	.90	.31
Father's nativity	.92	.28	.95	.23	.97	.17	.02	.14	.03	.17	.06	.24	.55	.50	.56	.50	.46	.50
Mother's nativity	.89	.30	.87	.34	.88	.33	.03	.16	.01	.12	.03	.17	.59	.48	.65	.48	.50	.51
Language as child	.93	.25	.97	.16	1.00	.00	.97	.18	.99	.12	.97	.17	.88	.33	.90	.30	.90	.31
Spanish interview	.00	.00	.00	.00	.00	.00	.03	.18	.08	.28	.00	.00	.08	.27	.06	.23	.02	.14
SMSA location	.98	.13	1.00	.00	1.00	.00	.95	.21	.96	.20	.94	.24	.90	.30	.96	.20	.94	.24
Local unemployment rate	5.25	1.56	4.99	1.37	5.06	1.44	6.49	2.04	6.93	1.83	6.67	1.68	6.36	1.97	6.09	2.14	6.25	2.21
Nonresponse school items	.29	.47	.29	.46	.29	.46	.35	.48	.37	.49	.43	.50	.41	.50	.35	.48	.46	.50
Percent Hispanic in school	23.47	32.37	9.95	21.52	9.03	20.31	15.66	22.80	14.73	21.92	17.11	24.26	14.46	26.17	20.60	20.95	15.69	20.41
Percent Black in school	5.42	7.92	5.82	10.72	5.76	10.71	13.61	19.65	12.76	20.64	11.06	16.81	13.72	17.01	9.17	17.13	10.27	17.74
Percent dropout in school	8.47	12.20	9.92	12.53	10.26	12.71	11.15	19.85	9.99	16.24	9.43	14.76	19.25	27.97	9.38	14.58	10.17	14.56
Teacher/student ratio	.03	.02	.03	.03	.03	.02	.03	.03	.02	.03	.03	.03	.04	.03	.03	.03	.03	.03
Nonresponse transcript	.56	.50	.45	.50	.44	.50	.44	.50	.38	.49	.37	.49	.64	.48	.44	.50	.56	.50
ESL course	.00	.00	.00	.00	.00	.00	.05	.21	.03	.17	.00	.00	.16	.37	.04	.20	.04	.20
Bilingual education	.00	.00	.00	.00	.00	.00	.06	.23	.00	.00	.00	.00	.10	.30	.03	.17	.02	.14
Public/private	.19	.39	.18	.39	.21	.41	.08	.27	.03	.17	.06	.24	.07	.25	.20	.40	.21	.41
N	59		38		34		155		71		35		92		71		48	

a. Includes Puerto Ricans, Cuban-Americans, and other Hispanics.

b. A = Less than or equal to 18 years old, B = Greater than 18 years old, C = High school graduates.

Source: 1979 NLS.

TABLE A.2
Results of a Set of LOGIT and OLS Regressions for Whites, Mexican-Americans, and Other Hispanics, for Those 18 Years of Age and Younger

Dependent Variable: School Delay[b]

Variable	Whites b	Whites SE(b)	Whites b	Whites SE(b)	Mexican b	Mexican SE(b)	Mexican b	Mexican SE(b)	Other Hispanics b	Other Hispanics SE(b)	Other Hispanics b	Other Hispanics SE(b)
Father's education	-.02†	.004	-.01†	.004	-.02	.01	-.02	.01	-.01	.01	-.01	.01
Mother's education	-.03†	.005	-.033†	.006	-.02	.01	-.01	.01	-.05†	.016	-.05†	.02
Sex of respondent	.19†	.02	.18†	.02	.17*	.08	.16*	.07	.02	.10	.02	.09
Number of siblings	.03†	.02	.03†	.006	.06†	.015	.06†	.02	.03	.02	.03	.02
Nativity	.18*	.08	.17*	.08	.66†	.11	.69†	.11	.23	.19	.23	.19
Father's nativity	-.06	.07	-.05	.07	.04	.11	.04	.11	-.21	.22	-.21	.22
Mother's nativity	.02	.07	.02	.07	-.23*	.11	-.19	.11	-.10	.22	-.10	.22
Language as child	.04	.05	.04	.05	.13	.15	.13	.15	.10	.20	.10	.21
Spanish interview	.15	.08	.13	.08	.23	.19	.23	.19	-.28	.26	-.28	.16
SMSA location			-.06*	.03			-.26†	.09			-.18	.24
Local unemployment rate			-.006	.006			-.06†	.01			.05	.03
Nonresponse school items			.009	.03			.03	.10			.10	.14
Percent Hispanic in school			-.001	.001			.000	.001			.002	.002
Percent Black in school			.000	.001			.002	.004			.001	.003
Percent dropout in school			.002†	.001			-.002	.002			.003	.003
Teacher/student ratio												
Public/private			-1.31*	.54			-.15	2.20			-4.05	2.79
Nonresponse transcript			-.02	.05			-.42†	.19			-.07	.17
ESL course			-.05	.03			.20	.11			-.31	.13
Bilingual education			-.14	.10			.21	.17			-.43	.27
Cuban ethnicity									-.07	.16	.13	.17
Puerto Rican ethnicity									-.08	.16	-.14	.16
Constant	.89		.98		.62		1.25				1.07	
R²	.07		.08		.20		.25				.21	
D												
N	3,465				587				311			

NOTE: * = p < .05; † = p < .01.
a. Results from logistic regression.
b. Results from OLS regression.
Source: 1979 NLS.

TABLE A.3
Results of a Set of LOGIT and OLS Regressions for Whites, Mexican-Americans, and Other Hispanics, for Those 19-22 Years of Age

Dependent Variable: High School Completion[a]

Variable	Whites				Mexican-Americans				Other Hispanics			
	b	SE(b)	b	SE(b)	b	SE(b)	b	SE(b)	b	SE(b)	b	SE(b)
Father's education	.15†	.02	.141	.02	.03	.04	.02	.04	.10*	.05	.14*	.06
Mother's education	.24†	.03	.23†	.03	.10*	.04	.12*	.46	.03	.05	.02	.07
Sex of respondent	-.34†	.12	-.37†	.13	-.02	.27	-.05	.29	-.34	.36	-.33	.43
Number of siblings	-.14†	.03	-.13†	.03	-.13†	.05	-.15†	.06	-.11	.06	-.09	.07
Nativity	.38	.48	.47	.51	-1.75	.42	-1.51†	.47	-.58	.79	-1.42	1.06
Father's nativity	1.54†	.47	1.54†	.49	.16	.40	.41	.43	.01	.89	.50	1.04
Mother's nativity	-.33	.39	-.16	.41	.57	.40	.41	.43	.01	.89	.50	1.04
Language as child	.13	.22	.11	.22	.42	.60	.40	.63	.81	.75	.89	.95
Spanish interview	-.63	.39	-.67	.40	-.23	.57	.36	.68	-2.59*	1.14	-2.14	1.18
SMSA location			.07	.14			.48	.39			-2.23	1.38
Local unemployment rate			.02	.03			.04	.06			-.03	.11
Nonresponse school items			.21	.16			.34	.41			.95	.61
Percent Hispanic in school			-.02*	.006			.014*	.006			.00	.01
Percent Black in school			-.001	.005			-.02	.02			-.025	.014
Percent dropout in school			.01†	.004			.002	.01			-.001	.016
Teacher/student ratio			9.67†	2.91			-7.17	9.21			16.60	12.12
Public/private			1.94†	.53			.16	.88			.08	.75
Nonresponse transcript			.30	.16			.69	.39			.20	.54
ESL course			-1.37	1.27			.06	.93			1.71	1.28
Bilingual education			.75	.74			1.28	.84			-.15	3.06
Cuban ethnicity									.70	.67	.33	.73
Puerto Rican ethnicity									-.62	.54	-.05	.64
Constant	-2.17		-2.69		-.06		-1.25		-.31		.71	
R²			.15				.26				.29	
D	.13				.20				.21			
N	2,280				296				204			

NOTE: * = p < .05; † = p < .01.
a. Results from logistic regression.
b. Results from OLS regression.
Source: 1979 NLS.

TABLE A.4

Results of a Set of LOGIT Regressions for Whites, Mexican-Americans, and Other Hispanics, for Those Who Graduated from High School

Variable	Whites		Dependent Variable: Mexican-Americans				College Attendance Other Hispanics	
	b	SE(b)	b	SE(b)	b	SE(b)	b	SE(b)
Father's education	.19†	.02	-.05	.05	-.06	.06	.07	.05
Mother's education	.18†	.03	.16†	.06	.17†	.06	-.03	.06
Sex of respondent	-.02	.10	-.32	.36	-.49	.38	-.22	.39
Number of siblings	-.12†	.03	-.06	.08	-.04	.09	-.02	.08
Nativity	.23	.40	-.96	.62	-.62	.73	-.02	.08
Father's nativity	1.08†	.35	.53	.54	.45	.58	-.54	.66
Mother's nativity	.78†	.36	1.39†	.53	1.26*	.59	1.43	.82
Language as child	.16	.18	-.48	.75	-.58	.79	.04	.78
Spanish interview	.23	.41	-.96	.62	-.62	.73	-1.82	1.15
SMSA location	.18	.12			.78	.49	-.10	.48
Local unemployment rate	-.04	.03			.12	.08		
Nonresponse items	.09	.13			-1.24*	.55		
Percent Hispanic in school	.014	.007			-.00	.007		
Percent Black in school	.002	.004			-.06	.03		
Percent dropout in school	.00	.004			.03	.02		
Teacher/student ratio	.53	2.12			12.65	12.64		
Public/private	.97†	.21			.28	1.23		
Nonresponse transcript	.11	.13			.13	.46		
ESL course	-.32	1.47			-2.66	1.45		
Bilingual education	.13	.34			.45	.97		
Cuban Ethnicity							-.56	.60
Puerto Rican Ethnicity							-.01	.55
Constant	-3.96		.21		-1.06		1.60	
D	.16		.12		.19		.10	
N	1,871		173				133	

NOTE: * = p < .05; † = p < .01.

Source: 1979 NLS.

References

Aquirre, Adalberto. 1979. "Intelligence Testing and Chicanos: A Quality of Life Issue." *Social Problems* 27 (December):186-95.

Alexander, Karl, and Martha Cook. 1979. "The Motivational Relevance of Education Plans: Questioning the Conventional Wisdom." *Social Psychology Quarterly* 42 (no.3):202-13.

Alexander, Karl, and B.K. Eckland. 1974. "Sex Differences in the Educational Attainment Process." *American Sociological Review* 39:668-82.

Ames, J.S., and Pat Bick. 1978. "An Evaluation of Title VII Bilingual/Bicultural Program, 1977-78." Brooklyn School District of New York.

Anderson, Theodore, and Mildred Boyer. 1970. *Bilingual Schooling in the U.S.* Washington: U.S. Government Printing Office.

Armor, David. 1972. "School and Family Effects and Black and White Achievement: A Reexamination of the USOE Data." In F. Mosteller and D.P. Moynihan, eds., *On Equality of Educational Opportunity*. New York: Vintage.

Baker, Keith, and Adriana de Kantor. 1981. *"Effectiveness of Bilingual Education: A Review of the Literature."* Report to the U.S. Department of Education, Washington.

Baral, David. 1979. "Academic Achievement of Recent Immigrants from Mexico." *NABE Journal* 3:1-13.

Barik, H.C., M. Swain, and K. McTavish. 1974. "Immersion Classes in an English Setting." *Working Papers on Bilingualism*: 38-56.

Bidwell, Charles, and J. Kasarda. 1975. "School District Organization and Student Achievement." *American Sociological Review* 40 (February):55-70.

Blau, Peter, and O.D. Duncan. 1967. *The American Occupational Structure*. New York: Wiley.

Bloom, Benjamin, Allison Davis, and Robert Hess. 1965. *Compensatory Education for Cultural Deprivation*. New York: Holt, Rinehart & Winston.

Brisk, Maria. 1981. "Language Policies in American Education." *Journal of Education* 163:3-15.

Cafferty, Pastora San Juan, and Carmen Rivera-Martínez. 1981. *The Politics of Language*. Boulder, Colo.: Westview.

Carliner, Geoffery. 1976. "Return to Education for Blacks, Anglos, and Five Spanish Groups." *Journal of Human Resources* 11:172-84.

Carter, Thomas. 1970. *Mexican Americans in School: A History of Educational Neglect*. New York: College Entrance Examination Board.

Carter, Thomas, and Robert Segura. 1979. *Mexican Americans in School: A Decade of Change*. New York: College Entrance Examination Board.

Carsdud, Karen, and John Curtis. 1980. "Evaluation of Achievement Outcomes: Austin's Experience." Paper presented at the National Conference on Longitudinal Evaluation of Bilingual Programs, Austin, Texas.

Chiswick, Barry. 1978. "The Effect of Americanization on the Earnings of Foreign-born Men." *Journal of Political Economy* 86:897-921.

Clark, Juan. 1977. "The Cuban Exodus: Why?" Miami: Cuban Exile Union. (mimeo).

Cohen, A. 1974. "The Culver City Immersion Program: The First Two Years." *Modern Language Journal* 3:95-101.

Coleman, James S., et al. 1966. *Equality of Educational Opportunity*. Washington: U.S. Department of Health, Education, and Welfare.

————. 1981. *Public and Private Schools*. Report to the National Center for Education Statistics.

Cordasco, Francesco, ed. 1976. *Bilingual Schooling in the U.S.* New York: McGraw-Hill.

Cordasco, Francesco, 1978. *The Bilingual-Bicultural Child and the Question of Intelligence*. New York: Arno.

DeBlassie, Richard, and Gary Healey. 1970. *Self-Concept: A Comparison of Spanish-American, Negro, and Anglo Adolescents Across Ethnic, Sex, and Socioeconomic Variables*. Las Cruces: New Mexico State University.

Duncan, Beverly. 1965. "Dropouts and the Unemployed." *Journal of Political Economy*. 73:121-34.

Duncan, O.D., D.L. Featherman, and B. Duncan. 1972. *Socioeconomic Background and Achievement*. New York: Seminar Press.

Edwards, Linda. 1976. "School Retention of Teenagers over the Business Cycle." *Journal of Human Resources* 11 (Spring):1-13.

Epstein, Noel. 1977. *Language, Ethnicity, and the Schools*. Washington: George Washington University.

Estrada, Leobardo. 1980. "Language and Political Consciousness among the Spanish-Speaking in the U.S." In D.J.R. Bruckner, ed., *Politics and Language: Spanish and English in the U.S.* Chicago: Center for Policy Studies, University of Chicago.

Featherman, David, and R.M. Hauser. 1978. *Opportunity and Change*. New York: Academic.

Fernández, Roberto M. 1982. "Bilinguals and Scholastic Achievement: Some Baseline Results." Paper presented at the American Sociological Association meetings in San Francisco.

Fishman, Joshua. 1976. "Language Maintenance in a Supra-Ethnic Age: Summary and Conclusions." In F. Cordasco, ed., *Bilingual Schooling in the U.S.* New York: McGraw-Hill.

Fishman, Joshua, et al. 1971. *Bilingualism in the Barrio*. Bloomington: University of Indiana Press.

Fishman, Joshua, and John Lovas. 1970. "Bilingual Education in a Sociolinguistic Perspective." *TESOL Quarterly* 4:215-22.

Fishman, Joshua, V. Nahirny, J. Hofman, and R. Hayden. 1966. *Language Loyalty in the U.S.* The Hague: Mounton.

Fligstein, Neil, and Roberto Fernández. 1982. "The Causes of Hispanic Educational Attainment: History, Patterns, and Analyses." A report to the National Commission on Employment Policy.

_____. 1984. "Educational Transitions of Whites and Mexican-Americans." In M. Tienda and G. Borjas, eds., *Hispanics in the Labor Market*. New York: Academic.

Fogel, Walter. 1966. "The Effect of Low Educational Attainment on Incomes: A Comparative Study of Selected Ethnic Groups." *Journal of Human Resources* 1 (Fall):22-40.

Gaarder, A. Bruce. 1977. *Bilingual Schooling and the Survival of Spanish in the U.S.* Rowley: Newbury House.

García, Steve. 1980. "Language Usage and the Status Attainment of Chicano Males." Center for Demography and Ecology Working Paper no. 80-2. Madison: University of Wisconsin.

Glazer, N., and D. Moynihan, eds. 1975. *Ethnicity: Theory and Experience*. Cambridge, Mass.: Harvard University Press.

Gordon, Edmund, and Doxey A. Wilderson. 1966. *Compensatory Education for the Disadvantaged*. New York: College Entrance Examination Board.

Greeley, Andrew. 1974. *Ethnicity in the United States*. New York: Wiley.

Haro, Carlos. 1977. "Introduction." *Aztlan* 8:1-10.

Hauser, R.M. 1971. *Socioeconomic Background and Educational Performance*. Washington: American Sociological Association.

Hauser, R.M., W.H. Sewell, and D.F. Alwin. 1976. "High School Effects on Achievements." In W.H. Sewell, R.M. Hauser, and D.L. Featherman, eds., *Schooling and Achievement in American Society*. New York: Academic.

Heller, Celia. 1966. *Mexican-American Youth: Forgotten Youth at the Crossroads*. New York: Random House.

Jaffe, A.J., Ruth Cullen, and Thomas Boswell. 1980. *The Changing Demography of Spanish Americans*. New York: Academic.

Jencks, Christopher, et al. 1972. *Inequality*. New York: Basic Books.

Jencks, Christopher, and Marsha Brown. 1975. "Effects of High Schools on Their Students." *Harvard Educational Review* 45:273-324.

Jensen, Arthur. 1980. *Bias in Mental Testing*. New York: Free Press.

Kimball, W.L. 1968. "Parent and Family Influences on Academic Achievement among Mexican-American Students." Ph.D. diss., Department of Education, UCLA.

Kjolseth, Rolf. 1972. "Bilingual Education Programs in the U.S.: For Assimilation or Pluralism?" In B. Splosky, ed., *The Language Education of Minority Children*. Rowley, Mass.: Newbury House.

Lambert, W.E., and G.R. Tucker. 1972. *Bilingual Education of Children*. Rowley, Mass.: Newbury House.

Laosa, Luis. 1977. "Inequality in the Classroom: Observational Research on Teacher-Student Interactions." *Aztlan* 8:51-68.

Liebowitz, A.H. 1980. *The Bilingual Education Act: A Legislative Analysis*. Rosslyn, Va.: National Clearinghouse for Bilingual Education.

Lieberson, Stanley. 1981. *Language Diversity and Language Contact*. Palo Alto: Stanford University Press.

Levitan, Sar; W.B. Johnston, and R. Taggart. 1975. *Minorities in the United States.* Washington: Public Affairs.

Lewis, L.S., and R. Wanner. 1979. "Private Schooling and the Status Attainment Process." *Sociology of Education* 52 (April):99-112.

Lewis, R., and N. St. John. 1974. "Contributions of Cross-Racial Friendship to Minority Group Achievement in Segregated Classrooms." *Sociometry* 37:79-91.

Llanes, José. 1981. "The Sociology of Bilingual Education in the U.S." *Journal of Education* 163:72-84.

López, David. 1976. "The Social Consequences of Chicano Home/School Bilingualism." *Social Problems* 24:234-46.

Mare, Robert. 1980. "Social Background and School Continuation Decisions." *Journal of the American Statistical Association* 75:295-305.

McConnell, Beverly. 1980. "Effectiveness of Individualized Bilingual Instruction for Migrant Students." Ph.D. diss., Washington State University.

National Center for Education Statistics. 1980. *The Condition of Education for Hispanic Americans.* Washington: U.S. Government Printing Office.

Nielsen, François, and Roberto M. Fernández. 1981. "Achievement of Hispanic Students in American High Schools: Background Characteristics and Achievement." Report to the National Center for Education Statistics.

Noboa, Abdin. 1980. "Hispanics and Desegregation: A Summary of ASPIRA's Study of Hispanic Segregation Trends in U.S. School Districts." *Metas* 1 (Fall):1-24.

North, David. 1978. "Seven Years Later: The Experience of the 1970 Cohort of Immigrants in the U.S. Labor Markets." Report to the Employment and Training Administration. Washington: U.S. Department of Labor.

Otto, Luther, and Archibald Haller. 1979. "Evidence for a Social-Psychological View of the Status Attainment Process." *Social Forces* 57:887-914.

Patchen, Martin, G. Hoffman, and W. Brown. 1980. "Academic Performance of Black High School Students under Different Conditions of Contact with White Peers." *Sociology of Education* 53 (January):33-51.

Paulston, Christina. 1978. "Theoretical Perspectives on Bilingual Education Programs." In James Alatis, ed., *International Dimensions of Bilingual Education.* Washington: Georgetown University Press.

Peal, E., and W. Lambert. 1962. "Relationship of Bilingualism to Intellectual and Applied Psychology." Monograph, *Archives of General Psychiatry* 27 (no. 546):1-23.

Pedraza-Bailey, Sylvia. 1980. "Political and Economic Migrants in America: Cubans and Mexicans." Ph.D. diss., Department of Sociology, University of Chicago.

Pedraza-Bailey, Sylvia, and Teresa Sullivan. 1979. "Bilingual Education in the Reception of Political Immigrants: The Case of Cubans in Miami." In R. Padilla, ed., *Ethnoperspectives in Bilingual Education Research: Bilingual Education and Public Policy in the United States.* Ypsilanti: Department of Foreign Languages and Bilingual Studies, Eastern Michigan University.

Ramírez, A.B., and R.L. Politzer. 1975. "The Acquisition of English and the Maintenance of Spanish in a Bilingual Education Program." *TESOL Quarterly* 9:113-24.

Ramírez, Manuel, and Alfredo Castañeda. 1974. *Cultural Democracy, Bicognitive Development, and Education*. New York: Academic.

Ramos, M., J.V. Aguilar, and B.F. Sibayan. 1969. *The Determination of Language Policy*. Quezon City (The Philippines): Alemor/Phoenix.

Rogg, Eleanor. 1974. *The Assimilation of Cuban Exiles*. New York: Aberdeen.

Rumberger, R. 1981. "Why Kids Drop Out of High School." Paper presented at the meetings of the American Educational Research Association in Los Angeles.

Sewell, W.H., A. Haller, and A. Portes. 1969. "The Educational and Early Occupational Attainment Process." *American Sociological Review* 22:67-73.

Sewell, W.H., and R.M. Hauser. 1975. *Education, Occupation, and Earnings: Achievement in the Early Career*. New York: Academic.

Shea, Brent. 1976. "Schooling and Its Antecedents: Substantive and Methodological Issues in the Status Attainment Process." *Review of Educational Research* 46:463-526.

Skutnabb-Kangas, T. 1979. *Language in the Process of Cultural Assimilation and Structural Incorporation of Linguistic Minorities*. Arlington, Va.: National Clearinghouse for Bilingual Education.

Spady, W.G. 1976. "The Impact of School Resources on Students." In W.H. Sewell, R.M. Hauser, and D.L. Featherman, eds., *Schooling and Achievement in American Society*. New York: Academic.

Spolsky, Bernard. 1972. "The Language Education of Minority Children." In B. Spolsky, ed., *The Language Education of Minority Children*. Rowley: Newbury House.

Stevens, Rosemary, Louis Goodman, and Stephen Mick. 1978. *The Alien Doctors*. New York: Wiley.

Teitelbaum, Michael, and Richard Hiller. 1977. "Bilingual Education: The Legal Mandate." *Harvard Education Review* 47 (May):138-70.

Thomas, John, and Earl Huyck. 1967. "Resettlement of Cuban Refugees in the U.S." Paper presented at the annual meeting of the American Sociological Association, San Francisco.

Thornton, Clarence, and Bruce Eckland. 1980. "High School Contextual Effects for Black and White Students: A Research Note." *Sociology of Education* 53 (October):247-52.

Tienda, Marta. 1981. "Sex, Ethnicity, and Chicano Status Attainment." University of Wisconsin-Madison: Center for Demography and Ecology.

U.S. Bureau of the Census. 1979. *Persons of Spanish Origin in the U.S.: March 1978*. Population Characteristics, series P-20, no. 339.

U.S. Commission on Civil Rights. 1978. *Social Indicators of Equality for Minorities and Women*. Report (August).

U.S. Immigration and Naturalization Service. 1977. *Cubans Arrived in the U.S. by Class of Admission, Jan. 1, 1959-Sept. 30, 1976*. Special reports. Washington: INS Statistical Branch.

Vásquez, Jo Ann. 1974. "Will Bilingual Curricula Solve the Problem of the Low-Achieving Mexican-American Students?" *Bilingual Review* 1:236-42.

Veltman, Calvin. 1979. *"The Assimilation of American Language Minorities: Structure, Pace, and Extent."* Report to the National Center for Education Statistics.

von Maltitz, Frances. 1975. *Living and Learning in Two Languages.* New York: McGraw-Hill.

Weinberg, Meyer. 1977a. *A Chance to Learn.* Cambridge (England): Cambridge University Press.

Wilson, Kenneth. 1979. "The Effects of Integration and Class on Black Education Attainment." *Sociology of Education* 52 (April):84-98.

Wilson, Kenneth, and Alejandro Portes. 1980. "Immigrant Enclaves: Labor Experiences of Cubans in Miami." *American Journal of Sociology* 86:295-319.

7

Jobs and Employment for Hispanics

George J. Borjas

This chapter has as its fundamental premise the thesis that the systematic study of labor market characteristics of Hispanics will contribute both to our knowledge of the economic development of Hispanics in the United States, and to our more general knowledge about adjustment mechanisms of the national labor market. Empirical work has been done in the areas of the economic progress of Hispanic immigrants, Hispanic/non-Hispanic wage differentials, human capital accumulation and labor supply. This work forms the base for the present discussion. Differences within the Hispanic population with regard to economic progress are observed, as well as differentials in the accumulation of human capital such as educational attainment. George J. Borjas points out that in general Hispanics face less discrimination than Blacks, but suffer from low wages due to lower levels of human capital investment. Future research and policies must address such issues if the economic status of the Hispanic population is to be significantly improved. While the importance of differences in human capital accumulation rates as a factor in wage differentials between Hispanic groups themselves and between Hispanics and non-Hispanics seems quite clear, the reasons for the differences have yet to be fully discovered. Finally, this chapter points to the need for examining the ways in which policies providing increased educational opportunities for Hispanics could be designed and implemented.

The last two decades have seen an explosion of research on the importance of race and sex as determinants of labor market outcomes. This research has, to a very large extent, concentrated on documenting the labor market experiences of Blacks and women in the U.S. labor market. It has been found that Blacks and women have significantly lower wage rates than White men of similar skills (Freeman, 1974; Lloyd and Neimi, 1979). The interpretation of this finding has been the subject of heated debate, and

147

little consensus exists on whether these wage differentials measure discrimination or unobserved productivity differences among the various groups.

This voluminous literature is remarkable for its nearly total disinterest in the economic status of other minority groups in the U.S. economy. Recently, however, this omission has been addressed by a few social scientists who recognized the socioeconomic and political implications of the emergence of the Hispanic minority in the United States. This recent literature shows that the systematic study of Hispanic labor market characteristics yields important new insights not only about the economic development of Hispanics in the United States, but also about the adjustment mechanisms of labor markets.

The Hispanic population contains a large number of immigrants. In the 1976 Survey of Income and Education (a large intercensal data set which oversampled Hispanics) over a third of all individuals of Hispanic origin are foreign-born. Clearly any study of recent immigration in the United States must explicitly analyze the size, reasons, and consequences of the large Hispanic immigration. More importantly, the study of the immigration and assimilation experience of Hispanics can be expected to yield insights on such diverse topics as the importance of language acquisition in the labor market; the accumulation of human capital investments by "new" labor market entrants (i.e., the immigrants); and the importance of the reason for the immigration (i.e., "economic" immigrants versus political refugees) as a determinant of success in the U.S. labor market.

The study of Hispanics should help to clarify the importance of intergenerational mobility as a determinant of labor market outcomes. For example, the 1970 Census indicates that about 45 percent of all Mexican-origin individuals had foreign-born parents. This empirical fact raises a multitude of possibilities for empirical research on the transmission of human capital from the immigrant parents to the native-born children. This type of analysis can serve as an important addition to the developing literature on the intergenerational properties of income distribution (Becker, 1981).

The study of Hispanics provides important insights into the role of nationality in determining labor market success. There are five major nationality groups in the Hispanic population: Mexicans, Puerto Ricans, Cubans, Central and South Americans, and "other" Hispanics. The heterogeneity in labor market characteristics among the five groups is remarkable. For example, the various groups tend to be located in different geographic regions; the labor force participation rates vary strikingly among the five groups; and average earnings has a large variance across the groups (Borjas, 1982). These empirical facts suggest that nationality may be an important factor in determining labor market success of Hispanic individuals. Informal evidence indicates that national background may have played an important role in determining the economic development of some non-Hispanic groups in the United States. Therefore, the analysis of the Hispanic population provides a unique opportunity to isolate the factors responsible for the importance of nationality as a determinant of the group's success in the U.S. labor market.

Further, careful analysis of the Hispanic population provides important results on how the labor market adjusts to large shifts in the supply (both in numbers and in terms of skills) of workers. For instance, the growth of the Hispanic population has been so fast (due both to high birth and immigration rates) that it has been "blamed" for various changes currently taking place in some labor markets. An important research question, therefore, is the impact of Hispanics on the local labor market. This type of analysis would shed light on how Hispanics affect the earnings, unemployment, and occupational characteristics of other groups in the population. More importantly, such studies would deal largely with a fundamental question in economics: how do labor markets work? The systematic study of Hispanics therefore provides significant insights into the adjustment mechanisms in modern labor markets.

In summary, not only is the study of Hispanics in the labor market interesting per se, but it is also an important endeavor because it can be expected to shed light both on important research questions and on significant policy issues.

Most of the literature on Hispanic individuals in the U.S. labor market is quite recent and is based on two data sets: the 1970 Public Use Samples of the U.S. Census, and the 1976 Survey of Income and Education. The four major topics in the literature are: the economic progress of immigrants; Hispanic/non-Hispanic wage differentials; human capital accumulation; and labor supply.

Economic Progress of Hispanic Immigrants

One of the important issues about immigration is the question of how immigrants fare in the U.S. labor market. Chiswick (1978) sparked a renewed interest in the question by providing a framework for the analysis of the assimilation process. He found that most immigrant groups faced relatively low wage rates immediately after arriving in the United States, but as time elapsed the groups' wage rate increased rapidly so that within fifteen-twenty years the wage rate of immigrants was actually above the wage rate of native Whites.

The question of how Hispanic immigrants adjust to the labor market has been recently addressed by Borjas (1982). His analysis estimates the "standardized" wage differential between the most recent immigrants (those arriving after 1970) and immigrants who arrived prior to 1970. These wage differentials have been adjusted for differences in schooling, labor force experience, and other observable socioeconomic characteristics. The empirical evidence indicates that the wage rate of male Hispanic immigrants who arrived in the United States in 1970-76 is 8.2 percent lower than the wage of Hispanics who immigrated in 1965-69; 19 percent lower than for 1960-64 immigrants; 21 percent lower than for 1950-59 immigrants; and 38 percent lower than for immigrants who arrived prior to 1950. Chiswick (1978, 1981) interprets these results within the context of a human capital model: over time the immigrants learn and adjust to the U.S. labor market, hence accumulating skills valued by American firms (e.g. language) and are rewarded for this higher productivity through a higher wage rate.

Borjas reveals a much more significant finding: the rewards of the assimilation process are not shared equally by all Hispanic groups. The estimated wage growth paths for each of the five Hispanic groups reveal the dramatic heterogeneity among the groups. For example, male Mexican immigrants do not have statistically significant higher wage rates than the most recent immigrants until about fifteen years after the immigration. Puerto Rican migrants must wait over twenty-five years before the assimilation experience has a significant effect in their wage rates. The results for both Cubans and Central/South Americans are somewhat similar: these groups exhibit a steady growth in their wage level as the assimilation process takes place.

The main implication of these results is that male Hispanic immigrants cannot be analyzed as a single group. Indeed the variation within the Hispanic population may be greater than the wage differences existing between Hispanics and non-Hispanics. A more substantive implication is that simple stories of the human capital accumulation process for immigrants will not be adequate unless we also know why some groups wish to accumulate more human capital than others. Further research, therefore, must pay close attention to the reason for the immigration and to the incentives these immigrants face when entering the United States in order to explain these intra-Hispanic differences.

Hispanic/Non-Hispanic Wage Differentials

An important related question tackled by several studies (Chiswick, 1981; Gwartney and Long, 1978; Reimers, 1981; Tienda, 1981) is the extent of wage differences between Hispanics and non-Hispanics. The study by Reimers (1981) is based on the 1976 Survey of Income and Education and provides an extensive analysis of the data set. Her study calculates the average percentage wage differentials between Hispanics and White non-

Hispanics for each of the various Hispanic groups and tabulated separately for males and females. These estimates reveal, for example, that male Mexicans earn 30 percent less than non-Hispanic White males, while female Mexicans earn about 20 percent less than non-Hispanic White females.

These observed wage differentials may be due to several factors. For example, part of these wage gaps may be a result of differences in educational attainment and other forms of observable human capital variables. Labor economists have traditionally used regression analysis to decompose these observed wage differentials into two parts: that due to differences in observable socioeconomic characteristics, and an unexplained residual. The latter portion may be due to unobserved differences in skills, motivation, etc., among the various groups or may also reflect the presence of labor market discrimination against particular groups.

For the largest group of Hispanics, the Mexicans, the Reimers (1981) study found that once the researcher controls for observed differences in socioeconomic characteristics the wage differential nearly vanishes. In the male sample it drops from 30 percent to about 5 percent; while in the female sample it falls from 20 percent to nearly zero. In the Puerto Rican sample the same result holds for females, but in the case of males a sizable unexplained differential between 9.5 and 17.2 percent remains. In the Cuban sample, the standardization for skills leads to the result that Cubans earn about 6-13 percent more than non-Hispanic Whites. The results for Central/South Americans are different: in the male sample a sizable unexplained differential remains after controlling for skill differences.

These statistics indicate that for a large proportion of Hispanics there are only minor standardized wage differences between Hispanics and non-Hispanic Whites. The results show that some Hispanic groups (Cubans, Mexican females, and Puerto Rican females) do as well as or better than the respective groups in the White non-Hispanic population. The policy implication of these results is very clear: Hispanics do not generally face the same extent of discrimination (as defined by the unexplained wage residual) as Blacks. Instead their relatively low wage in the labor market is due mostly to differences in human capital investments. Presumably policymakers should focus on these differences if their objective is to improve the economic status of the Hispanic population.

Human Capital Accumulation

Since human capital differences are a major (if not the major) source of Hispanic/non-Hispanic wage differentials, it is important to review the empirical evidence on these differences. For example, the Reimers (1981) study reveals that in the 1976 Survey of Income and Education the mean educational attainment for male non-Hispanic Whites was 12.4 years; for Mexican males it was 9.4 years; for Puerto Rican males it was 9.8 years; for Cuban males it was 11.3 years; for Central/South Americans it was 11.8 years; and it was 11.0 years for "other" Hispanics.

These differences translate into substantial wage differentials. Consider, for example, the 3-year difference between Mexican and White non-Hispanic males. If the rate of return to a year of education is 5 percent, the educational gap indicates a 15 percent wage differential between the two groups. If the rate of return to a year of education were 10 percent, a 30 percent wage differential would arise. In other words, the differences in educational attainment (and presumably other forms of human capital investments) are responsible for creating large wage differentials among the various groups.

The literature, however, has not seriously studied the reasons for the differences in human capital variables. A study by Borjas (1982) analyzed the extent to which male Hispanic immigrants differed in their propensity to acquire schooling after the immigration. This kind of investment is presumably crucial for the economic progress of the immigrant in the U.S. labor market. The study found that regardless of the year of immigration, Cuban immigrants had invested more in U.S. schooling than all other Hispanic immigrant groups. For instance, Borjas (1982) found that a Cuban who immigrated in 1965-69 had by 1976 obtained 2.1 more years of U.S. education than a Mexican immigrant who arrived at the same time (and had similar levels of educational attainment at the time of immigration). If the rate of return to education was 5 percent, this difference in investment behavior is translated into a 10 percent wage differential between the average Cuban and Mexican immigrant by 1976. Borjas (1982) interprets these results by considering the incentive structure facing the various immigrant groups as they arrive in the United States. Regardless of the interpretation, however, the empirical analysis reveals convincingly the importance of differences in the rate of human capital accumulation as a determinant of intra-Hispanic (and Hispanic/non-Hispanic) wage differentials (Carliner, 1976).

Labor Supply

Clearly an important component of economic welfare is the extent of work supplied to the market by Hispanics. Most of the labor market studies have concentrated on analyzing the determination of wage rates and have generally ignored the labor supply of Hispanics. The papers by Borjas (1981) and Carliner (1980) provide initial glimpses into the labor supply characteristics of Hispanics in the U.S. labor market. The brief analysis contained in the Carliner paper reveals that recent Hispanic immigrants must go through a period of adjustment as they learn the "tricks of the trade" in the U.S. labor market. It is not surprising, therefore, that immediately after immigration individuals tend to work fewer hours.

Borjas (1981) expands this analysis by studying the differences in labor supply among the various Hispanic and non-Hispanic groups in the population. Several interesting findings emerge from his data. For example, there is a large variance in the labor supply of the five Hispanic immigrant groups. Puerto Ricans have labor force participation rates 6-8 percentage points lower than the other groups, and those who do work supply about 5 percent fewer hours to the labor market. Second, a comparison of the Hispanic immigrant with the Hispanic native population indicates that native Hispanics have substantially lower labor supply than Hispanic immigrants. For example, in the Mexican samples this result is revealed by a 10 percentage point difference in annual hours of work, while in the Puerto Rican samples the result is given by a 10 percentage point difference in the labor force participation rate.

These results show the promise of extending the study of Hispanics in the labor market to characteristics other than wage rates. In the long run what is needed is a full accounting of employment contract differences among the various Hispanic and non-Hispanic groups.

The studies surveyed in the previous section have yielded some insight on important questions concerning the economic development of Hispanics in the U.S. labor market. As with all research, these insights have been obtained at the cost of narrowing down the focus of analysis to questions with relatively simple methods of solution. Thus the studies have ignored many important issues which are crucial if the goal is to develop a broad view of how Hispanics have fared in the United States.

The Role of Language Acquisition

Empirical studies trying to determine whether bilingualism "pays" in the labor market have often reached inconclusive results (Tienda and Neidert, 1981). The problem is that the measured consequences of language acquisition on labor market outcomes are affected by changes in model specification and sample definitions. That is, whether knowing English leads to labor market success depends on the regression model being analyzed, the sample being considered, and even the definition of knowing English. There are at least two reasons for this sensitivity. First, it is not clear what the proper theoretical concept of language acquisition skills should be since the usefulness of such skills is likely to vary across jobs and occupations. Second, the theoretical mechanism (or model) by which language can be expected to affect labor market outcomes has not been explicitly set out. Unless such conceptual work is conducted, it is unlikely that we will learn more about the role of language in the labor market from further repetitions of the empirical analysis. Moreover, it should be clear that these issues have important policy implications considering the political battles currently being waged over the role of bilingual education in the nation's public school system.

The Impact of Hispanics in the Labor Market

One question of particular importance is the effect that the emergence of the Hispanic minority has had on the surrounding labor market. For instance, it is often alleged in the popular media that Hispanics (or immigrants) have "taken jobs away" from Blacks or other groups in the labor market, thus hampering the economic development of these groups. These discussions implicitly assume that Black and Hispanic labor are substitutable inputs in the production process, so that firms can easily interchange the two types of workers. Despite the potential importance of these issues, published studies (Grant and Hamermesh, 1981) which analyze the substitutability of various groups usually ignored the Hispanic population. A preliminary study of labor market competition among the Black, Hispanic, and non-Hispanic White population (Borjas, 1983) found no evidence that Hispanics had a negative impact on the earnings of the other two groups. It is clear that the practical importance of this question will lead to extensive research in the future.

The Neighborhood Effect

Since Hispanics tend to concentrate in a relatively small number of labor markets, important questions arise as to how Hispanic enclaves or neighborhoods help or hamper the progress of Hispanics currently entering those labor markets. For example, it can be argued that Hispanics are helped by the existence of strong community ties and the information networks that these close-knit communities tend to create. On the other hand, the supply of Hispanics is increased, and if employers (for whatever reason) view Hispanics as a distinct input, this will lead to a drop in the Hispanic wage. The importance of these neighborhood effects has been analyzed in the Cuban community by Wilson and Portes (1980), and in descriptive sociological literature by Piore (1979). This important research question, however, deserves much more systematic work.

Unemployment

Even though Department of Labor statistics invariably indicate that Hispanics have higher unemployment rates than the non-Hispanic White population, there has been no serious work trying to determine the source of these differences. The literature on Hispanic economic development should be expanded to study questions such as: what factors account for the higher unemployment rates of Hispanics? What is the role of nationality? Does the immigration and assimilation experience affect unemployment propensities? Is the higher unemployment rate of Hispanics due to higher incidence (i.e., a higher probability of getting unemployed) or to longer duration of unemployment spells?

To what extent do the children of Hispanic immigrants retain the progress made by their parents? This important question has received only the most preliminary analysis. For example, Chiswick (1981) suggests that second generation Mexicans do relatively well in the labor market. Very little, however, is known about this type of economic mobility for the other nationality groups which compose the Hispanic population.

Public Policy Issues

These research questions are of interest not only for scientific reasons, but also because they deal with some of the most important labor market problems of the day. These policy problems can be seen as two related questions.

First, *how can the government alleviate the disadvantaged economic status of the Hispanic population?* A number of studies (briefly reviewed in this chapter) point to the low educational attainment of Hispanics, and *not* to labor market discrimination, as the main culprit behind the relatively low wage of Hispanics. Policymakers, therefore, should concentrate their efforts on programs and policies which open up educational opportunities to Hispanics since this is the main barrier preventing the majority of Hispanics from achieving income parity with non-Hispanic Whites. Additionally, research needs to be done as to the reasons why there are differential human capital investments among different Hispanic groups. Policies to encourage such investment and to provide incentives to engage in such activities ought to be devised and tested. A useful development would be the further explication of the nature of human capital extant in the various Hispanic groups within the country. What can they build on? What are the human capital strengths of Hispanics in the United States today? Documenting these would be very useful for policy considerations.

Second, *should the doors be closed to further Hispanic immigration?* The basis for an informed answer to this important political question must lie in a comparison of the costs and benefits associated with alternative immigration policies. Perhaps the cost most worrisome to policymakers is the impact that the Hispanic immigrant has on other disadvantaged groups in the labor market. Although research addressing this fundamental problem is still in its preliminary stages, it is becoming increasingly clear that Hispanics have *not* had a major negative impact on the earnings of such groups as Blacks. Hence discussions of the immigration issue must revolve around alternative costs of selected immigration policies. How can immigration policies provide incentives to Hispanics for the accumulation and reinvestment of human capital? How can such reinvestment be stimulated from one generation to the next? Answers to these questions would provide useful insights for those responsible for policy formulation and development.

References

Becker, Gary S. 1957. *The Economics of Discrimination.* Chicago: University of Chicago Press.

———. 1981. *A Treatise on the Family.* Cambridge: Harvard University Press.

Borjas, George J. 1981. "The Labor Supply of Male Hispanic Immigrants in the United States." Mimeo. (November).

———. 1982. "The Earnings of Male Hispanic Immigrants in the United States." *Industrial and Labor Relations Review* (April).

———. 1983. "The Substitutability of Black, Hispanic, and White Labor." *Economic Inquiry* (January).

Carliner, Geoffrey. 1976. "Return to Education for Blacks, Anglos, and Five Spanish Groups." *Journal of Human Resources* (Spring):172-84.

———. 1980. "Wages, Earnings, and Hours of First, Second, and Third Generation American Males." *Economic Inquiry* (January):87-102.

Chiswick, Barry R. 1978. "The Effects of Americanization on the Earnings of Foreign Born Men." *Journal of Political Economy* (October):897-922.

———. 1980. "An Analysis of the Economic Progress and Impact of Immigrants." Final report to U.S. Department of Labor (June).

Freeman, Richard B. 1974. "Labor Market Discrimination: Analysis, Findings, and Problems." In *Frontiers in Quantitative Economics,* vol. 3, ed. M. Intriligator and D. Kendrick. Amsterdam: North Holland.

Grant, James H., and Daniel S. Hamermesh. 1981. "Labor Market Competition among Youths, White Women, and Others." *Review of Economics and Statistics* (August):354-60.

Gwartney, James D., and James E. Long. 1978. "The Relative Earnings of Blacks and Other Minorities." *Industrial and Labor Relations Review* (April).

Lloyd, Cynthia B., and Beth T. Niemi. 1979. *The Economics of Sex Differentials.* New York: Columbia University Press.

Piore, Michael J. 1979. *Birds of Passage: Migrant Labor and Industrial Societies.* New York: Cambridge University Press.

Reimers, Cordelia. 1981. "Why Are Hispanic Americans' Incomes so Low? An Analysis of the Family Income and Earnings of the Major Hispanic Origin Groups in the U.S." Final report to U.S. Department of Labor.

Tienda, Marta. 1981. "Nationality and Income Attainment among Native Immigrant Hispanics in the U.S." In *Hispanic Origin Workers in the U.S. Labor*

Market, ed. Marta Tienda. Final report to U.S. Department of Labor (October).

Tienda, Marta, and Lisa J. Neidert. 1981. "Language, Education and the Socioeconomic Achievement of Hispanic Origin Men." In *Hispanic Origin Workers in the U.S. Labor Market*, ed. Marta Tienda. Final report to U.S. Department of Labor (October).

Wilson, Kenneth L., and Alejandro Portes. 1980. "Immigrant Enclaves: An Analysis of the Labor Market Experiences of Cubans in Miami." *American Journal of Sociology* 86 (September):295-309.

8

Hispanics and Health Care

Aida L. Giachello

*In the last two decades there has been an increasing interest in His-
panic health care issues. Unfortunately, knowledge of Hispanic health
care remains limited. Hispanics have been omitted until recently from
national and state data sources, and when included have been treated
as a homogeneous group. In this chapter Aida L. Giachello reviews
the literature to determine what is known and what is absent in our
understanding of health care and access to health care among Hispanics. An analytic framework is provided which breaks down health
care into predisposing, enabling, and need factors. Giachello argues
that Hispanics have lower utilization of health services as compared
to other racial and ethnic groups in the United States. For example,
even though the Hispanic population is characteristically young,
which might indicate less need for medical services, Hispanic women
are less likely to receive prenatal care during the first trimester of
pregnancy than non-Hispanic women. Hispanics lack a regular
source of health care in large part because a large segment of the
population is not eligible for government medical programs or covered
by private insurance. Giachello notes that too often in the literature
ethnicity and cultural explanations are posited as the reasons for low
utilization of health care services when social class explanations are
more persuasive. The former blames the victim while the latter
blames the system. In the final section of the chapter Giachello makes
recommendations for improving the research on Hispanic health care
and service delivery.*

In the last two decades there has been an increasing interest in Hispanic
health issues, but our knowledge about their health beliefs, health status,
and health behavior, and how they vary among the different Hispanic
subgroups, is still very limited. The main purpose of this paper is to describe the state of the art in regard to health care among Hispanics in the
United States, and to examine the many factors affecting their access to the

medical care system. In doing so, current health issues are discussed, and a series of suggestions for future research and public policy are presented.

Access implies ease of entry to the health care system. The framework for the study of access developed by Andersen (1968) and expanded by Aday and Andersen (1975) is followed here for analysis. The access framework involves a set of interrelated components. It takes into consideration the socioeconomic, demographic, and cultural characteristics of the population at risk, the structural characteristics of the health delivery system, the actual utilization of health services, and consumer evaluation of medical care received.

In the application of this access model the characteristics of the Hispanic population are classified into predisposing, enabling, and need factors. Predisposing factors describe the biological or social "given" characteristics which can either facilitate or inhibit individuals from using the medical care system (Aday et al., 1980). Those factors that are examined here include age, sex, education, consumer knowledge, occupation, language, cultural factors, and family structure. Enabling factors describe the resources available to Hispanic individuals and families for the use of health services, as well as system characteristics which can either encourage or discourage the use of medical services. The enabling factors that will be discussed in this chapter are: conveniences and type of regular source of medical care, type and extent of health insurance coverage, and geographic location. Need factors refer to illness indicators. They are the strongest predictors of health services use. They include such factors as self-perceived health status, worry levels about health, and morbidity and mortality information.

The components in reference to the characteristics of the health care delivery system that are of interest here include accessibility and availability of health facilities, manpower composition, and the organization of health services. Finally, the outcome component describes the level and pattern of use of health services by Hispanics, and the attitudes toward the medical care system of those Hispanics who have experienced a contact with it.

Characteristics of the Hispanic Population

Hispanic age structure is an important predisposing factor in the assessment of health services needs and access to care. Hispanics are one of the youngest populations in the United States, with a median age of 23. The age composition of the Hispanic population needs to be taken into account because the health status and pattern of health service utilization vary among different age groups. In addition, an understanding of the age factor gives the researchers and health services providers an indication of the types of health services most needed (e.g. family planning, prenatal and pediatric care, etc.) (Giachello et al., 1983). Studies which have reported findings related to age indicate that older Hispanic people are more traditional in their health beliefs and health practices (Edgerton and Karnon, 1971; Welch et al., 1973).

The sex distribution of the Hispanic population can also be considered a predisposing factor because numerous studies for the total United States population indicate that health needs and health services utilization vary by sex. Hispanic sex composition varies by the different subgroups. For example, in 1980 Puerto Rican females represented the majority of the Puerto Rican population in the United States (54 percent), while there are a slightly higher number of Mexican males (51 percent) than Mexican females (49 percent) (U.S. Census Bureau, 1981b).

Health services research on Hispanics has overlooked sex differences in health behavior and health services utilization. The few studies done in this area have indicated that Hispanic men do not readily accept the notion that they are ill and therefore will not visit the physician in the same proportions. More studies are needed in this area to explore possible differences in health behavior by sex within the Hispanic population.

Education is a factor which presents a special health care barrier among Hispanics. The Hispanic population has the lowest levels of education of any ethnic group in the United States. Madsen (1964) and Farge (1975) found that traditional health beliefs and the practice of folk medicine varied inversely with social class (education being one of the dimensions of social class). Suchman (1964) in his study of sociomedical variables among different ethnic groups found that low education was associated with the traditional or "parochial" type of orientation. Welch et al. (1973) found that Mexican-Americans with low education had high levels of distrust of modern medicine and doctors; and that age, sex, education, and income were powerful factors in explaining utilization of health services.

Urdaneta (1973) in her study on "Fertility and the Pill in a Texas Barrio" found that the lack of participation of Mexican-Americans in family planning clinics was due not to cultural factors (i.e., machismo, Catholicism, etc.), but to conditions of poverty and lack of education. She stated that Mexican-Americans with little or no education frequently feel embarrassed at their inabililty to read the clinic forms or provide the required information (e.g. spouse income), and are thereby discouraged from obtaining medical services.

McLemore (1963) found that years of education were related to willingness to be hospitalized. For example, Mexican-Americans with little or no education were averse to hospitalization. Another study (Andersen et al., 1981b) found that low education, among other factors, was related to low utilization of medical and dental services and low rates of preventive exams among Hispanics in the southwestern United States.

A factor which can facilitate or inhibit access to medical care among Hispanics is the level of consumer knowledge about health resources and medical services. According to Welch et al. (1973), the knowledge of health resources is related to the individual's sociodemographic and economic characteristics. Knowledge about health services resources is also believed to be linked with the permanence of an individual in a particular community. However, Andersen et al. (1981a) did not find any relationship between short length of residence among Hispanics in the Southwestern states and their pattern of utilization of health services.

Occupation is a predisposing factor related to low access to care among Hispanics. The majority of the Hispanic population (47 percent) occupy blue-collar jobs compared to one-third for the non-Hispanic population (U.S. Bureau of the Census, 1979). They are heavily represented in the operative low-paying occupations (i.e., factory jobs). These jobs have few fringe benefits, which therefore suggests that Hispanics' low occupational status seems to be related to the fact that Hispanics have no or limited health insurance coverage, which is usually provided through the place of work (Andersen et al., 1981b).

A great deal of the literature on Hispanics' physical and mental health indicates that language is a major barrier to access and appropriate utilization of health services. Language presents a problem when the population to be served is mainly Spanish-speaking. Edgerton and Karno (1971) state that the language barrier may very well be linked to other barriers depending on whether the individual is bilingual or mainly monolingual either in Spanish or English. For example, Hispanics who are only Spanish-speaking tend to have less education, lower income, are older and seem to be more attached to their culture. According to Edgerton and Karno (1971), Hispanic monolinguals in English express their acculturation and are essentially indistinguishable from other Americans in their health attitudes and behavior. However, recent national survey data do not provide evidence that language per se is a barrier in seeking medical care among the Hispanic population in the Southwestern states (Andersen et al., 1981b). These findings were borne out in East Los Angeles as well (Moll, 1976).

Cultural Factors

The sociocultural predisposition of Hispanics toward medical care has been frequently proposed as an explanation for low access to medical care. A great deal of the literature on Hispanics has been devoted to exploring these factors. Early studies stressed the existence of a Hispanic health subculture that consists of a different set of health beliefs and practices. The Hispanic health subculture has been described as one with a holistic view of health and illness in which good health means that a person is behaving according to his conscience, to God's mandate, and according to the norms and customs of his group: church, family, and local community (Gregory, 1978). There seems to be no separation between the psychological and total well-being of the individual according to this view.

Illness has then been perceived as the result of the following causes: (1) psychological states, such as embarrassment, envy, anger, fear, fright, excessive worry, turmoil in the family, improper behavior, or violations of moral or ethical codes; (2) environmental or natural conditions such as bad air, germs, dust, excess of cold or heat, bad food, or poverty; and (3) supernatural causes, such as malevolent spirits, bad luck, witchcraft, living enemies (believed to cause harm out of vengeance or envy).

As part of the Hispanic health subculture a hot and cold classification of diseases has frequently been described (Harwood, 1971; Gregory, 1978). The Hot and Cold Theory of Disease, as it is often called, reflects the Mediterranean influence carried to Latin American countries by way of colonial Spain. It is derived from Hippocratic ideas concerning bodily humors and associated with fire, earth, water, and air. According to this theory, health is a "temperate" condition or a balanced state avoiding any excesses of hot or cold elements. Illness is caused by extremes of hot, cold, wet, and dry conditions which upset the body humors. Food and medication (including home remedies) are classified as hot, cold, or an intermediate category ("cool"). Cold-classified illness (e.g. "cold" which is believed to be caused by a chill which may occur when a person moves from heated to unheated surroundings) are treated with hot medication (e.g. penicillin is classified as a hot substance because it may cause rash or diarrhea, which are hot diseases), and hot food (e.g. chicken soup, hot tea, but not orange juice or fruit or any other cold remedies frequently recommended by health providers). Hot illnesses are treated with cool or cold substances. It is therefore recommended that health providers should be knowledgeable of this folk classification of illness as a means of better understanding Hispanic lack of compliance with medical treatment (Harwood, 1971).

Other folk diseases frequently described in studies done in Spanish communities are *mal de ojo* (evil eye), *susto* (fright, soul loss), *empacho* (upset stomach) and *mollera caída* (fallen fontanelle). According to Clark (1959) and Rubel (1960) women and children are considered weaker in the Hispanic culture and therefore more susceptible to these kinds of folk illnesses. *Mal de ojo* may occur when a child is admired by an adult who may be jealous of the parent. The symptoms are usually high fever, headaches and, in the case of a child, excessive crying. *Susto* occurs when a person has been exposed to a traumatic experience (e.g. a marital argument, a car accident, etc.). Psychologically speaking, the person is in the early stage of a "nervous breakdown."

Empacho may occur when the person is psychologically stressed during or right after eating (as a result of bad news received, etc.). The person describes feeling a "ball in the stomach" and stomach pains.

In the case of *mollera caída*, the victim is an infant. It involves the dislodging of the fontanelle from its usual position at the top of the infant's head. Restlessness and loose bowels are some of the symptoms. According to Rubel (1960) this illness produces a blockage of the oral passages; therefore, it may even cause the death of the infant if it is not treated.

Other traditional health practices frequently described in ethnographic studies include the use of herbs, teas, and other home remedies and over-the-counter (OTC) medication to treat childhood diseases, discomfort during pregnancy, and acute and chronic illnesses. Recent empirical studies indicate that these traditional health practices are still utilized by Hispanics (Welch et al., 1973; Andersen et al., 1981b). Andersen et al. found that 21 percent of the Hispanic population in the Southwestern states of the United States use herbs and other home remedies to treat episodes of illness. This is almost twice the percent reported by the total U.S. population. In addition, the same study found one-third of all Hispanics believed that illness can be better treated by home remedies than by prescribed medicine, compared to 24 percent for the total U.S. population (Andersen et al., 1981b).

The use of lay persons such as *curanderos* (faith healers) for health advice and folk treatments has received much attention in the Hispanic health and mental health literature (Madsen, 1964; Rubel, 1960; Kiev, 1968; Clark, 1959; Samora, 1961; and others). Folk practitioners have been postulated to be a major alternative resource to the use of established health and mental health resources by Hispanics.

Different types of folk practitioners or *curanderos* described are: the herbalist, the "general practitioner," and the *espiritista*. The herbalist is the simplest form of *curandero*. It refers to persons who prepare various home remedies with the use of herbs, for curing members of the family that suffer from internal and external injuries.

Another type of *curandero* is the folk healer, who can usually be compared to the general practitioner in a medical setting. This type of *curandero* deals chiefly with physical ailments which have an apparent physical manifestation, such as sprain, dislocation, fractures, and fevers. The *espiritistas* (spiritualists, healers) are the highest-ranking *curanderos* (Ayala, 1972). They not only have knowledge about how to treat physical ailments and folk diseases, but they are also perceived to have the power to communicate with spirits.

Espiritistas are the chief folk resource for dealing with emotional problems. They relieve the individual of guilt feelings by blaming external forces for the person's behavior and problems. They establish a strong positive rapport and mutual trust with the client. The client has faith in their capacity to cure, and the *espiritistas* have high expectations of client improvement. The absence of fees (or the low fee) for their services has been cited as a strong motivating force to seek their services.

Other studies on Hispanic health and mental health have presented data indicating that the amount of practice of folk medicine and folk practitioners is related to certain variables such as age, attachment to ethnic group, occupation, income, education, place of birth, length of time in the United States, etc. (Newsom, 1974). It is frequently mentioned that older poor people, born in Mexico with very little education, tend to be more tradition-oriented, more attached to the ethnic group, and therefore more actively involved in folk practices.

However, this model is too simplistic to explain the diversity of behavior of the Hispanic population. Few studies have presented empirical data about numbers of *curanderos* and *espiritistas*, where they are located, their sociodemographic characteristics, and the kinds of clients they serve. Other studies claim that folk practitioners have virtually disappeared (Martínez and Martin, 1966); and their salience as a health resources alternative has been questioned in the work of Edgerton, Karno, and Fernández (1970) in Los Angeles. In addition, the access study by Andersen et. al. (1981b) did not find evidence of the use of *curanderos* among the Hispanic population in the Southwestern United States. Others assert that use of such practitioners does not necessarily preclude Hispanics' seeking care through the regular health care system as well (Quesada and Heller, 1977).

The Hispanic health subculture has attracted the attention of many researchers, especially anthropologists. Weaver (1976), Farge (1975), and Salazar (1978) in their review of the literature on Hispanic health indicate that there have been three generations of researchers. The first generation of researchers were the founders of the theory of a Hispanic health subculture (Saunders, 1954). They were concerned about gathering data (usually by participant observation) about Hispanic health beliefs, attitudes, and behavior and their implications for utilization of medical care. A series of generalizations and stereotypes were developed about Hispanics' culture and personalities (Farge, 1975).

The second generation of researchers on Hispanic health conducted a series of community studies, primarily in the late 1950s and in the 1960s

(Clark, 1959; Madsen, 1964; Rubel, 1966; among others). They also focused on ethnic factors and continued the generalizations and stereotypes about the Hispanic population. They studied Hispanic folk diseases, folk medicine, and folk practitioners.

The limitations of the first and second generation of researchers are related to sample selection. They primarily conducted case studies and the subjects interviewed were those who sharply delineated the phenomena being studied. The researchers, especially those who were participant observers, relied on their subjective perceptions and interpretation of the situation. In addition, little attention was given to quantitative or statistical data in their reports.

According to Weaver (1976), Farge (1975), and Salazar (1978), the third generation of researchers began conducting epidemiological and sociological studies in the late 1960s and during the 1970s. These researchers used more systematic survey techniques. The "new" research agenda was to focus on Hispanic demographic and socioeconomic characteristics, especially as it affected health services utilization, and to move away from studying cultural factors. However, currently the question exists as to what is the stronger determinant of Hispanic health behavior, ethnicity or social class. This issue will be discussed further.

Family Structure

Reliance on the family has frequently been propsed as an explanation for low utilization of health services among Hispanics. Hispanic families have been frequently described as a group which is highly integrated, with strong ties, and possessing most of the attributes of the classical extended family system. The family has been perceived as providing a source of social support to Hispanics in the United States. Even if the family system may be temporarily disrupted due to migration, family members tend to reunite within a short period of time.

Sena-Rivera (1979) in his trigenerational study of Mexican families in the Midwest found that relatives often live in the same household or a relatively short distance from one another (in the same building, in the same block, or within less than one mile away). The high degree of interdependency among the different members of the network for personal services (i.e., babysitting and emotional support such as giving advice) have also been described. Family members are seen to be dependable and reliable; there is a sense of duty toward each other and they appear to be willing to give, often with the idea that they themselves might be in a position of needing family help in the future.

According to Sena-Rivera (1979), there is a particular household which serves as the nucleus or the center of the network, and members tend to get together in that particular household. Sena-Rivera describes this network as the "modified-extended family system". This type of family structure may vary among the different Hispanic groups depending on the degree of acculturation and assimilation and their socioeconomic status.

Keefe, Padilla, and Carlos (1976) provide empirical data on the nature of the support system among Mexican-Americans (U.S.-born). They have developed an "extended family integration scale" based on proximity of relatives' households, frequency of contacts, and exchange of aid among family members. They found that White families in their sample were unintegrated, while Mexican-American families were highly integrated on this scale. What is more, their findings remained statistically significant regardless of occupational levels, years of education, or length of residence.

Research on Hispanic mental health has studied the Hispanic family extensively. The underlying assumption has been that the Hispanic family structure has functioned to protect an individual under stress from further mental deterioration (Ramírez, 1978). Ramírez studied the role of the family in help-seeking behavior among Mexican-Americans in Detroit. He found that the majority of the Mexican-Americans in his sample talked to at least two family members and/or friends about their personal or emotional problems (79 percent). Fewer consulted professionals (21 percent), and those who consulted family and friends found them more helpful, compared to those who consulted professionals. However, Aday et al. (1980) and Andersen et al. (1981) found that Hispanics, primarily Mexican-Americans from the Southwest, were not more likely to seek lay health advice from relatives than are members of the majority White population.

The effect of the family on health services utilization among Hispanics has also been studied. Hoppe and Heller (1975) and Nall and Speigelberg (1967) found that the close-knit relationship between family members during illness had a negative effect on the utilization of medical services. High familial integration with the family network will lead individuals to first seek help (curative measures) within the family except when illness is very serious.

Compadres (godparents), friends, and neighbors are also consulted early for home treatment advice, and to help the individual decide whether to seek medical care (Moustafa and Weiss, 1968). Only after all possible resources have been exhausted by the individual and/or family is the professional physician contacted.

Integration into the ethnic community has also been proposed as a deterrent to health services utilization. Suchman (1964) found that highly cohesive groups (i.e., Puerto Ricans, Irish) not only use services less, but were more likely to have traditional health attitudes, low knowledge levels about diseases, skepticism toward professional medical care, and dependency on family during illnesses than those who were not members of such groups. In general, the form of social organization appeared to be more important than ethnicity and social class in relation to the sociomedical variables studied.

Others have found that ethnic factors were not necessarily associated with the above characteristics. Ethnic factors can either encourage or discourage utilization of medical services, depending on the value system that may prevail among the ethnic groups in relation to health (Gertsen et al., 1975).

In addition to predisposing factors this section will discuss a series of enabling factors which may serve as potential barriers to access and utilization of medical care among the Hispanic population. These factors are family income, convenience and type of regular source of care, and type and extent of health insurance, among others (Aday et. al., 1980).

Hispanic median family income is one-third lower compared to the median family income of the non-Hispanic population (U.S. Census Bureau, 1980). With this lower income Hispanic families have to support a larger family size. In addition, the cost of medical services has been frequently cited as an important barrier affecting the access to medical care among Hispanics. Governmental programs such as Medicaid and Medicare have made medical services accessible and available to the poor and to the elderly; however, "working poor Hispanics," who are the largest segment of the Hispanic population, are not eligible for these programs and cannot afford the rising cost of medical services (i.e., they are "medically indigent").

In sum, recent studies have indicated that Hispanics' low socioeconomic status (low income, low occupational status, and low education) has served as a barrier to medical care utilization (Welch et al., 1973; Moustafa and Weiss, 1968; Roberts and Lee, 1980; Andersen et al., 1981b).

Utilization of Health Care

Having a regular source of medical care is an enabling factor, as it is considered a good predictor of health services utilization. However, studies on Hispanic health indicate that Hispanics are less likely to have a regular source of care. Aday et al. (1980), in a national survey on access to medical care, have found that Hispanics in the Southwestern states were less likely to have a regular source of medical care compared to any other racial and ethnic group in the United States. The percent of Hispanics without a regular source of care was 17 percent compared to 12 percent for the total U.S. population (Aday et al., 1980). The percent without a regular source of care increases among Hispanics below the poverty level (20 percent compared to 13 percent for White non-Hispanics) (Aday et al., 1980).

Roberts and Lee (1980) in their study of medical use by Mexican-Americans in Alameda County, California, found similar results. In addition, a national health survey conducted by the National Center for Health Services Research found that minority groups (primarily Hispanics and Blacks) without a regular source of care were less likely to visit the doctor, therefore diminishing treatment opportunities for these populations (Bernstein and Berk, 1981).

Other studies (Aler, 1978; Bernstein and Berk, 1981) also indicate that, for these groups, when a regular source of care is reported, public health facilities and hospital outpatient clinics are the usual source of medical care. For example, one study found that elderly Hispanics were as likely as elderly Blacks to use as a regular source of health care the hospital outpatient clinics (22 percent) compared to 7 percent among aged Whites (Bernstein and Berk, 1981).

Despite this, other studies have found that Hispanics are as likely as Whites to indicate preferences for private physicians (Weaver, 1978). Factors affecting the choice of medical facilities are related to income, doctor's ethnic background (i.e., doctor's ability to speak Spanish), and the individual's immigration status (Stern and Giachello, 1977). However, when Hispanics and Blacks reported a physician's office as their regular source of care, they were most likely not to have medical services available outside office hours (i.e., evening hours, weekend hours) (NCHSR, 1982).

The lack of health insurance also presents special barriers to Hispanics entering the health care system. Andersen et al., (1981b) in the nationwide study on access to medical care in the United States, found that the Hispanic population in the Southwest had the lowest percentage of health insurance coverage of any racial or ethnic group studied. This percentage (65 percent) was also lower than that of the total U.S. population (88 percent). When adjustments were made for socioeconomic factors, the percentage with health insurance increased but still remained considerably lower than for other groups (Andersen et al., 1981b). Studies examining medical expenditures also reveal that Hispanics are more likely to pay for medical expenses out-of-pocket (Welch et al., 1973).

Inconveniences in obtaining health care refer to the problems that people have in the process of obtaining health services. Some of the indicators of inconveniences are traveling time to a medical facility, waiting time in the doctor's office, and time spent with doctor (Aday et al., 1980). According to the study on access to medical care, 55 percent of the Hispanics living in the Southwestern United States spent 15 minutes or less traveling to seek medical care compared to 48 percent for the total population. Apparently traveling time to a medical facility is not a serious inconvenience for Hispanics living in this region.

Sixty-five percent of the Hispanic population in this same survey waited thirty minutes or less in the doctor's office. This percentage is basically the same compared to the total U.S. population (64 percent). Waiting in a doctor's office can be affected by a variety of factors such as the individual's socioeconomic status (limiting his choices of sources of care), nature and stage of illness to be treated, having or not a doctor's appointment, and the characteristics of the health delivery system (i.e., number of health providers available, etc.) which were not taken into account during the analysis.

Regarding time spent with the doctor, 28 percent of the Hispanics in the Southwestern states spent 15 minutes or less with their physicians. More Hispanics had short visits than any other group studied (Aday et al., 1980).

Besides the above inconveniences, there is very little known about other factors which may serve as barriers to receiving medical services. There is very little data on babysitting arrangements (in view of the large average Hispanic family size), waiting time for appointments, and inconveniences in taking time off from work and/or losing pay for time taken off to see the doctor. These and other factors need to be explored to gain a more complete picture of the kinds of inconveniences facing Hispanics in obtaining medical services.

Geographic location of the regular source of care has frequently been proposed in the Hispanic mental health literature as a factor affecting access to medical care among Hispanics, particularly because health facilities are not located in Hispanic barrios (Edgerton and Karno, 1971; Torrey, 1972; and others). However, studies (Beiweiss et al., 1977; Aday et al., 1980) indicate that traveling time to a medical facility appeared not to be a problem among the Hispanic population in the Southwest.

In sum, Hispanics' low family income, low health insurance coverage, lack of a regular source of medical care, and inconveniences—including geographic isolation—are some of the enabling factors affecting access to medical care.

Health Care Needs

In addition to predisposing and enabling factors, need or illness levels of the Hispanic population need to be taken into account in the analysis of their access to medical care. Medical needs are the strongest predictors of health services utilization. Aday et al., (1980) identified a series of need measures, including self-perceived needs and medical needs evaluated by physicians. The self-perceived measures of needs include: individuals' general evaluations of health status, the amount of worry or pain they have experienced, symptoms of illness during the year, disability days (beds days and restricted activity days), and episodes of illness which may have caused three or more days of disability with considerable pain or worry. Medical needs evaluated by physicians include physicians' severity rating of conditions and symptoms experienced in the year (Aday et al., 1980).

Data on self-perceived health status obtained from the Health Interview Survey during 1976-77 indicated that Hispanics and Blacks were more likely than Whites to perceive their health as poor or fair (U.S. DHHS, 1980). This same study indicated that Hispanics reported less restricted activity days per year than Whites and Blacks, which may be due to the fact that some restriction of activities is "prescribed" by medical care contacts who are seen less often by Hispanics. In addition, the survey indicated that the number of restricted days varies by income. Hispanics with less than $10,000 a year reported 21 days compared to 26 and 25 days for Whites and Blacks, respectively. Hispanics with $10,000 or more of yearly income also reported slightly fewer restricted days (12), compared to Whites (14) and Blacks (15) (U.S. DHHS, 1980). A national survey supported these findings. It examined the Hispanic population of the Southwestern states and found that Hispanics reported slightly fewer mean disability days per year (7), compared to the total U.S. population (10 days) (Andersen et al., 1981b). Morbidity and mortality data on Hispanics is fragmented, subject to substantial reporting errors, limited to local areas, or is outdated, so that it is difficult to provide a comprehensive, accurate profile of the overall health status of Hispanics.

Characteristics of the Medical Care System

In addition to the characteristics of the Hispanic population, there are several structural aspects of the health delivery system associated with low access to medical care among Hispanics. One aspect has to do with cultural factors; the other is related to health manpower composition.

It is a common belief that provision of health care for Hispanics is frequently ineffective because providers of services do not understand the Hispanic culture and are not sensitive to its members' needs. This has frequently been "called the culture conflict perspective" (Torrey, 1972; Schensul, 1975b). This perspective tends to assume that the American or White culture is in conflict with Hispanic culture. However, there is limited empirical data to support this.

The Hispanic health literature that addresses structural characteristics of the health delivery system states that language barriers and class and culture disparities between client and providers are discouraging features of health care services and facilities (Keefe, Padilla, and Carlos, 1976). According to Schepers (1971), these factors have implications for services delivery. Referring to mental health services, he states that interpretation of psychological factors based on the dominant American cultural framework may lead to possible diagnostic errors. For example, Hispanics with spiritualist beliefs may be construed as psychotics.

Language presents a cultural barrier when the population to be served is mainly Spanish-speaking. However, there are also other situations in which the communication between health providers and clients tends to fail. For example, a frequent failure in communication occurs when too many technical words or too much medical terminology is used to explain health problems and the treatment to be followed (Quesada and Heller, 1977). This tends to be a problem not only for the Hispanic population, but also for other racial and ethnic groups, as well as for the low-educated population. Related to this issue is the reluctance of Hispanics to admit confusion about medical instructions they have been given or to ask "foolish" questions.

A frequent failure in communication between Hispanics and health providers is produced by the lack of rapport between patient and physician, or the impersonal relationship between health providers and patients. the Hispanic may tend to view the physician as the "authority," the relationship involving a high degree of "paternalistic dependency." When this type of relationship does not occur, a social distance between doctors and patients is created. At times this is accentuated by the assignment of different doctors to patients for different appointments. This tends to occur more often in neighborhood and hospital clinics.

The attempt by health providers to impose their middle-class values and attitudes toward health and illness on Hispanic patients, plus their possible prejudice and discrimination against Hispanic patients, may maintain and reinforce this social distance between patient and health providers (Quesada and Heller, 1977). This social distance then worsens because Hispanic people and health providers are often victims of stereotypes about each other's personalities and health behavior. Non-Hispanic physicians often regard Hispanics as superstitious, present-oriented, and uninterested in preventive exams; they wait too long to seek care and do not follow medical treatment (Gregory, 1978). Hispanics, on the other hand, may perceive doctors as being money-oriented because of their high fees for services, not interested in their patients' welfare, etc. However, Farge (1975) found that these stereotypes diminished with an increase of socioeconomic status among the Hispanic population.

Other discouraging characteristics of the health delivery system are the long waiting time in the doctor's office for a brief visit with the physician or nurse, and the bias of the clinics to treat well babies while turning down sick children.

It is frequently mentioned in the literature that cultural barriers can be overcome by recruiting bilingual and/or bicultural staff. But according to Vásquez (1974), Ruiz (1972), and Phillipus (1971), cultural barriers in the health setting are not solved by simply recruiting bilinugal personnel. There is also a need for health providers to get more involved in community affairs affecting their "catchment area" population as a means of becoming more acquainted with clients' community problems. In-service training is also recommended for health providers to develop cultural awareness.

But even more important, Treviño (1979) provides empirical data which indicates that in the case of mental health centers, these services become highly utilized if Hispanics also are employed as administrators or in other decision-making positions within these agencies. To occupy a position of "power" facilitates changes in agency policies (i.e., recruitment, services, delivery policies) aimed at making services more relevant and accessible to the Hispanic population.

As a result of some of the barriers to access to care imposed by the structural characteristics of the health delivery system, Schensul et al. (1975) state that the emergency room is increasingly becoming the point of entry to the medical care system. He states that it is a faster way of "getting into the system" than waiting days and weeks for an appointment. It is open twenty-four hours a day, seven days a week, making it more accessible, and, until recently, most visits to the emergency room were covered by health insurance, benefiting those Hispanics with such coverage.

Another perspective to the culture conflict explanation is reflected in a study by Moll (1976) in an East Los Angeles mental health facility. This study found that Hispanic consumers preferred English over Spanish for the therapeutic process. This contrasts sharply with the perceptions of the bilingual staff. In addition, providers perceived bilingual and bicultural staff to be extremely important in the therapeutic relationship while Hispanic clients were less concerned about these two factors. This finding may have been biased by the bilingual/monolingual status of the study population.

Other studies (Schensul et al., 1975; Farge, 1975) had similar results. These findings do not necessarily mean that there are no cultural conflicts in health or mental health settings, but perhaps that users of these services consider ethnic factors to be of less importance.

Health Manpower

The health literature on Hispanics documents the concern about the lack of health professionals serving the Hispanic population (Quesada and

Heller, 1977; Bruhn, 1974; Bruhn and Rowden, 1974, and others). Quesada and Heller (1977) found that in Texas, counties with the highest concentration of Mexican-Americans had "fewer patient-care physicians" equivalents than the State of Texas ratio of physicians to the general population. He added that some of these counties had no physicians or practicing dentists at all (Quesada and Heller, 1977). Apparently, the health manpower shortage occurs more frequently in rural areas where Mexican-Americans have a higher percentage of young people with little education (Quesada and Heller, 1977).

Morales (1970), studying the mental health problems in East Los Angeles, stated that the problem is not a shortage of mental health professionals but a maldistribution of these professionals. His implied recommendation to improve this situation is to motivate Non-Hispanic personnel to practice their profession in the geographic area where the needs are greatest.

There are few Hispanic professionals in the health care field, although increasing numbers of Hispanics occupy positions as health care technicians. In 1970, 37.2 percent of the so-called allied medical services, or technicians' jobs (Enos and Sultan, 1977), were held by Hispanics. Lay midwives and dental laboratory technicians had the highest representation of Hispanics. Only 16.5 percent of the Hispanic population were employed in "professional" jobs in the health field, of which 3.7 percent were M.D.s (U.S. DHEW, 1977). However, no increase is expected in the number of Hispanic physicians in the near future. National statistics on total school enrollment in medical schools in the United States reveal that Mexican-Americans comprised 1.6 percent, Puerto Ricans 1.9 percent, and other Hispanic groups 1.5 percent, while Blacks comprised 5.6 percent (*JAMA*, 1983). In 1981, the representation of Hispanics in postgraduate training in medicine was the same: Mexican-Americans 1 percent, Puerto Ricans 1.8 percent, other Hispanics 2.1 percent; Blacks represented 5.2 percent (*JAMA*, 1983).

Health of the Population

Proof of access per se is ultimately reflected in the utilization of health services by the Hispanic population. Recent empirical data documents that Hispanics have lower utilization of health services compared to other racial and ethnic groups in the United States. For example, national data from the Health Interview Survey, 1976-77, indicate that Hispanics made slightly fewer visits to a physician than did Whites or Blacks. The number of visits per person per year was 4.2 for Hispanics, 4.6 for Blacks, and 5.0 for Whites. The number of physician visits is slightly more for the three racial/ethnic groups with earnings of less than $10,000 a year, and slightly less for those earning $10,000 or more a year (U.S. DHHS, 1980).

The low utilization of health services among Hispanics is again reflected by the low percentage of persons who reported at least one visit to the physician during the year prior to the Health Interview Survey. Sixty-nine percent of the Hispanic population reported at least one physician visit compared to 76 percent for Whites and 74 percent for Blacks (U.S. DHHS, 1980).

The same survey also found that Hispanics as well as Blacks were least likely to report a dental visit in the year prior to the interview. The percentage with a dental visit was 34 for both groups. The percentage was lower for persons earning less than $10,000 a year. Hispanics in this income category reported 28 percent, compared to 31 percent for Blacks and 39 percent for Whites. On the other hand, the percentage with dental visits increased for those with incomes of $10,000 or more a year: 41 percent for Hispanics, 40 percent for Blacks, and 59 percent for Whites (U.S. DHHS, 1980).

Regardless of income, Hispanics reported fewer days in the hospital per year (9 days compared to 10 for Blacks and 11 for Whites). The number of hospital days was slightly higher for the 3 groups earning less than $10,000 a year (U.S. DHHS, 1980). Hospital use rates are, to a considerable extent, a function of the age and severity of conditions of the individuals admitted.

Similar results on Hispanics' low utilization of health services have been obtained from earlier studies conducted by Moustafa and Weiss (1968) in San Antonio, Texas; Galvin and Fan (1975) in the Los Angeles Metropolitan Area; Roberts and Lee (1980) in Alameda County, California; and Andersen et al. (1981b) in the Southwestern states, among others. In addition, Andersen et al. (1981) found that the Hispanic population in the Southwest reported substantially fewer preventive exams in the absence of illness, compared to the total U.S. population. These researchers concluded that the low utilization of medical services (reflected in low medical and dental visits) was related more to socioeconomic and enabling factors than to need factors which should not be predictors of health service utilization. The lack of insurance coverage appears to be a particularly significant barrier to the use of physicians' services.

Data for 1975 from the National Institute of Mental Health also documents low utilization of mental health services among the Hispanic population. According to the findings, Hispanics were less likely to receive outpatient and inpatient psychiatric services compared to Whites and Blacks. In addition, Hispanics had the lowest admission rates to state and county inpatient psychiatric facilities as well as to private and nonpublic mental health hospitals. However, when inpatient services were needed,

Hispanics were more likely to be admitted to public mental hospitals, comprising 10 percent of total admissions. Hispanic females had a higher age-adjusted admission rate for inpatient psychiatric services than Hispanic males (U.S. DHHS, 1980).

Hispanics who received outpatient psychiatric services were younger than Whites of non-Hispanic origin. Hispanic females were older with a median age of 31 compared to 25 for Hispanic males. Finally, Hispanics who were hospitalized in private mental hospitals had shorter stays than Whites and Blacks (12 days compared to 19 days for Blacks and 21 days for Whites) (U.S. DHHS, 1980).

Underutilization of health services is also reflected in the area of prenatal care and family planning. Hispanic women are considerably less likely to receive prenatal care during the first trimester of pregnancy than non-Hispanic women (NCHS, 1981). Puerto Rican mothers have the least amount of prenatal care, with less than half receiving prenatal care within the first three months of pregnancy and 10 percent receiving none. The variations in the month in which prenatal care begins among Hispanic women are related to education, age, and number of previous children (NCHS, 1981).

Data from the National Survey of Family Growth for 1973 and 1976 (also collected by NCHS) indicated that White married women were most likely to report family planning visits (59 percent for Whites, compared to 51 percent for Hispanics and 46 percent for Blacks). Among Hispanic married women, the percent of family planning visits varies by age. The percent of family planning visits among Hispanic married teens was less (42 percent) than the percent of family planning visits among all Hispanic women in the sample (51 percent) (NCHS, 1979).

In regard to specific birth control methods used, the survey indicated that Hispanic as well as Black and White married women reported a slightly lower use of birth control pills in 1976 compared to 1973. Hispanics were most likely to use intrauterine devices (IUD) for both years compared to Black and White married women (NCHS, 1978).

In sum, the nationwide empirical data presented in this section documents that low access to medical care as evidenced by the utilization of health services is still a reality for the Hispanic population.

Consumer satisfaction with medical care refers to the "attitudes toward the medical care system of those who have experienced contact with it" (Aday et al., 1980). It is an important dimension because it may determine subsequent utilization of health services. Empirical data on Hispanic levels of satisfaction with the delivery of health services is limited. However, data from the 1976 access study indicate that Hispanics from the Southwest were the most dissatisfied with the cost of medical care during their last physician visit. The percentage of dissatisfaction with this indicator was slightly above that for the total U.S. population (39 percent versus 37 percent, respectively). Dissatisfaction with appointment and office waiting time rank second with 32 percent of the Southwest Hispanics expressing dissatisfaction with these indicators. This percentage is substantially higher than the 16 and 28 percent dissatisfied with appointment and office waiting time, respectively, for the total U.S. population. Dissatisfaction with the interaction with providers (measured by the information provided by M.D.—24 percent, and time spent with M.D.—23 percent) ranked third. These percentages of dissatisfaction were higher compared to the total U.S. population (18 and 16 percent, respectively). When adjustments were made for socioeconomic factors, needs and previous experience with the health care system, dissatisfaction with cost of care, and time spent with physician appeared to be associated more with socioeconomic variables than with level of need and experience (Andersen et al., 1981b).

Current Health Issues

So far an attempt has been made to review the current status of Hispanic health following the theoretical model on access developed by Andersen (1968) and expanded by Aday and Andersen (1975). Based on this literature review there are three important issues of current concern that need further elaboration: limitation of health data, issues related to ethnicity versus social class, and use of the formal medical care system versus self-care in health.

Despite the numerous studies reviewed here, the limited health data on Hispanics is still a problem and an area of current concern. More information is needed to identify and document Hispanic health needs, to set health policies, and to plan and develop meaningful health services for Hispanics.

There are a number of reasons for the limited health information available on Hispanics. Some have to do with governmental data organization and classification practices. First, there have been several inadequacies in the collection of Hispanic data. Hispanics have been merged into categories such as "White," "non-White," "others," "racial and ethnic minorities," etc. This practice has made it difficult to obtain accurate data not only for Hispanics, but for other racial and ethnic groups as well.

Second, in major national or state data sources, Hispanic items have been omitted until very recently. For example, the National Center for Health Statistics did not incorporate Hispanic items in their Health Interview Survey until 1976 (NCHSR, 1980). At present there are still states which do not include Hispanic items in their state forms, records and/or in their data gathering; or they rely on different Hispanic identifiers (i.e., place of birth, Spanish surname list, etc.). Some states are becoming aware of this problem and are in the process of making changes, most frequently in birth and death certificates. Still, interstate comparability of health data is an almost impossible task, and repeated errors have been identified in states with ethnic and Hispanic identifiers in vital statistics records (Treviño, 1982; Powell-Griner and Streck, 1982).

Third, where data on Hispanics data is available, it gives the impression that it refers to a homogeneous group. The data is rarely broken down into different Hispanic ethnic groups (Cubans, Mexicans, Puerto Ricans, etc.); or further broken down into sex, education, and the like.

Fourth, most studies on Hispanic health have been limited in scope in terms of their content and sample size. They are often based on non-probability samples in local areas. These local areas are usually the Southwestern states. Few studies focus on Hispanics in other states, despite the increasing number of Hispanics concentrated in some of them. Most of the studies have focused exclusively on the Mexican-American population. At times inappropriate generalizations to other Hispanic groups have been made based on those findings (perhaps because there is no other "similar" data available to measure Cubans' and Puerto Ricans' health).

Fifth, large surveys which do contain Hispanic data are based on national probability samples, in which Hispanics are sampled according to their proportion to the total population, resulting in small numbers of Hispanics in the sample. This practice makes it difficult to conduct detailed analysis and make valid generalizations about this group.

Sixth, due to the small proportion of Hispanics (6 percent) to the total population, it has been difficult to justify allocation of resources for large-scale surveys of this group or for oversampling of Hispanics.

In spite of these shortcomings, some progress is being made. In 1977 the Office of Management and Budget (OMB) directed federal agencies to follow a set of race and ethnic standards in their statistical activities (NCHSR, 1980). The National Center for Health Statistics (NCHS) has been given legislative mandate under the Public Health Services Act (PL 95-623) to collect and publish health data on this and other groups (Blacks, elderly, etc.). Also, from 1977 to 1980 the Department of Health and Human Services (DHHS) created a Hispanic initiative with a series of goals, one of them stressing the regular collection and publication of data on the socioeconomic and health conditions of Hispanics (NCHRS, 1980). As a result, funds were allocated for a special Survey on Hispanic Health and Nutrition (known as Hispanic HANES), which is currently underway. In addition, states and administrative agencies are revising relevant documents to incorporate Hispanic items.

Another positive move is the U.S. Census Bureau's incorporation of an item on Hispanic origin in the 1980 Census. For the first time, all Americans during the 1980 census were asked if they were of Spanish/Hispanic origin. The count of the Hispanic population from the Census is based on this item. As a result, a wide variety of data on Hispanics are now available. This step by the U.S. Census Bureau has solved some methodological issues related to the definition of the Hispanic population (Giachello et al., 1983).

Although more information on Hispanic health is expected in the near future, with government budget cuts the dissemination of this information to the public is less comprehensive than originally planned.

Despite this progress, more empirical data is needed on predisposing, enabling, and need factors, such as demographic, socioeconomic, and cultural characteristics related to Hispanic health care behavior, organizational characteristics of the health delivery system; and use of health services by Hispanics. This data is needed for the different Hispanic subgroups.

Ethnicity and Social Class

A common theme in the Hispanic health literature concerns ethnic factors as determinants of health behavior. Hispanics are viewed as an ethnic group that can be distinguished by socially selected cultural characteristics (Wilson, 1976). Some of the cultural traits which provide a mark or a sign of ethnic membership are names, language, accents, mannerisms, dress, gestures, typical facial expressions, food habits, religious practices, and various types of behavioral characteristics.

The ethnic perspective in health stresses that the culture of a group plays an important role in determining thoughts, actions, and feelings about illness (Saunders, 1954). Many studies of Hispanic health have contributed a significant body of knowledge about the existence of a Hispanic health subculture. These studies have emphasized, directly or indirectly, that ethnicity is an important variable in health delivery and medical care. The Hispanic health subculture, as well as other cultural traits, are reinforced by the continued communication of Hispanics with family in their native countries and by the continued flow of Hispanics into the United States. Therefore, ethnicity is, and should be, considered an important variable in health care. In addition, countless studies present empirical data which indicate that different health indicators such as birth rate, mortality rate, and the rate of incidence of certain diseases, and the like, vary with ethnic identification.

Although ethnicity is an important variable, it is not the only important one to be considered. Considerable research indicates that a new reference group (in this case American society) may serve to bring about conformity to new norms despite contrary and well-established practices and attitudes. The data from the Mother-Infant Research Study (Stern and Giachello, 1977) in the Mexican community on Chicago's West Side indicates that recently arrived pregnant Mexican women (primarily from rural areas in Mexico) were willing to receive prenatal care and to have their babies delivered in a U.S. hospital, even though their babies from previous pregnancies had been delivered in the home with the help of a midwife. According to the authors, these women sought prenatal care because they had been told that otherwise no one would deliver their babies. Another striking finding of this study was the overwhelming number of recently arrived Mexican women who were bottle-feeding their children while the majority of them had breast-fed their babies in Mexico.

Organizational characteristics of the medical care system are partly responsible for the decision to bottle-feed an infant among Mexican women, as suggested by the Mother-Infant Research study. Standard hospital procedures sometimes require relatively long periods of time before mother and infant are reunited after the delivery. During this time the staff often bottle-feed the infant (Jellifer and Jellifer, 1971). These examples suggest that in most cases Hispanics accommodate themselves, sometimes reluctantly, to American medical care practices. It appears that the situation in which the individual finds himself does much to determine which of his heterogeneous attitudes and behaviors about health will be brought into play.

The problem with ethnicity is that it has been overused as the sole explanation for all types of behaviors among Hispanics. Socioeconomic and demographic characteristics of the Hispanic population and other factors such as recency of arrival, types of health problems, knowledge of health resources, past experience with the health care system, all need to be taken into consideration as well.

In recent years attention has been given to some of these factors, and social class is joining ethnicity as an explanatory variable. The social class perspective in health tends to assume that socioeconomic factors are the strongest determinant of health behavior. The acceptance of the social class perspective implies to some degree that the importance of ethnicity in health is declining. However, it may not necessarily mean that it is disappearing because, even when socioeconomic factors have been equalized, differences between Hispanics and other groups still remain (Andersen et al., 1981b). A problem in attempting hypothetically to separate both perspectives is related to the fact that ethnicity and class tend to converge in the United States empirically, they go together. As a result, Blacks and Hispanics tend to predominate in the lower class, making it difficult to distinguish what kinds of health behavior is related to socioeconomic factors and which is culturally determined.

The question is unresolved as to which of these perspectives can better predict or at least describe Hispanic health behavior. It will probably be several years before an adequate theoretical model can be developed that can accurately describe the diversity of health behavior among Hispanic groups. Part of the problem is that large-scale surveys based on probability data have not been able to provide empirical findings documenting the existence of a Hispanic health subculture. The problems seem to be related to methodological issues. Perhaps surveys are not the most proper means of identifying ethnic factors among Hispanics, or perhaps the instruments used are not sensitive enough to pick up these factors.

It is my position that cultural and social class factors are both important in determining Hispanic health behavior. For the initial entry or access to the formal medical care system, studies indicate that social class factors (e.g. income, education, health insurance coverage, etc.) appear to be the strongest determinants (Andersen et al., 1981b; Aday and Andersen, 1984). But once the person is in, language barriers, and other cultural differences between clients and providers, and the organization of health services (e.g., long waiting time to see the doctor) are factors which discourage further utilization of these services.

Other health behavior such as the use of home remedies, folk practitioners, and the like, are primarily determined by Hispanic cultural values and beliefs which vary by their level of acculturation and assimilation to this country. Those Hispanics who engage in such health-related behavior are also the poorest, the ones who experience the most social discrimination and isolation, and the ones with the most serious barriers in obtaining medical services. To some degree social class factors reinforce the preservation of some traditional health behavior among Hispanics. There are other identifiable forces in the preservation of this behavior: (1) Hispanic commitment to tradition; (2) continued communication with relatives and friends from their countries of origin; and (3) continued immigration of Hispanics to the United States. But for Hispanics to seek formal medical services rather than their traditional and cultural health behavior, the former must first be proven to be more useful (Giachello et al., 1982a).

The purpose of most Hispanic health studies has been to search for factors (socioeconomic, demographic, or cultural) that may explain Hispanics' low utilization of health services. Methods to increase the exposure of Hispanics to medical technology and treatment have been the recommendations of these researchers. Therefore, most social scientists have overemphasized the salience of medical care institutions to Hispanics without considering the possibility that the formal medical care system may not satisfy all their health needs. In addition, high cost of care and long waiting time for medical services, among other factors, discourage Hispanics' use of medical care.

Social scientists apparently have given little attention to the emerging social movement which discourages the use of medical services at the primary care level and encourages the acquisition of health knowledge and self-care skills for health maintenance and for prevention and treatment of illness. Participants of this movement have been described as members of the middle class (Fleming and Andersen, 1976). Apparently this segment of the population has become increasingly dissatisfied with the quality of care delivered by medical professionals, often believing that people are better off if they stay away from technology and professionals. In addition, increasing cost in medical care becomes an issue of great concern when consumers feel they are not getting the kind of medical services needed and expected.

There are other motivational factors behind the self-care movement which are beyond the scope of this chapter and will not be discussed here. The point is that self-care activities as well as the use of the formal medical care system should be studied. The formal medical system is one of a variety of health resources available to Hispanics. In addition to asking why Hispanics do not use the formal medical care system, researchers should ask what services and resources Hispanics use and/or have available to solve their diverse health problems. Researchers should identify all the helping resources available, instead of centering the Hispanic health problem-solving behavior solely on the formal medical care institutions.

Self-care can be perceived as a health resource to Hispanics which can either supplement, substitute for, or provide an alternative to the formal medical care system. Although self-care has been described as a middle-class movement, traditional self-care activity is a common practice in Hispanic communities (Giachello and Andersen, 1981). It is a traditional health behavior deeply entrenched in Hispanic culture. Self-care among Hispanics is reinforced in this country because medical services are limited to Hispanics due to problems of accessibility, availability, and relevancy. In addition, it has been argued that the Hispanic family has played an important role in transmitting traditional health knowledge to its members and reinforcing traditional health practices. However, recent empirical findings in the self-care field have not been able to provide support for these arguments (Giachello et al., 1982a,b; Andersen et al., 1981a). Furthermore, self-care for health maintenance and health promotion (i.e., exercise, weight control) is practically nonexistent among Hispanics in the United States (Giachello, 1983).

The idea here is not to "oversell" self-care as the main mode of treatment or one that will solve all Hispanic health needs. There are those who may argue that a lack of quality control in self-treatment may result in more serious illness; or that Hispanics may be "blamed" for their illness because of evidence indicating that a great deal of illness is related to lifestyle and bad personal health habits (Surgeon General's Report, 1979).

However, Hispanics' engaging in self-care activities does not imply that their illnesses are primarily related to their health habits and lifestyles. They may be caused primarily by structural conditions in society which are beyond their control. These conditions include poverty and environmental and occupational hazards, among others. During the 1970s, Hispanics have struggled for equitable access to medical care and for services relevant to their needs. These efforts should be continued. There are health problems which are only appropriate for the formal medical care system to treat. The researcher's task is to identify and study the variety of health resources available to Hispanics and relate the needs of the group to the most effective utilization of these alternative resources.

Recommendations for Future Research

This section attempts to provide a series of suggestions for health services research relevant to Hispanics. The suggestions presented here also follow Aday and Andersen's (1975) theoretical framework on access to medical care. Therefore, research suggestions are largely based on Hispanic characteristics, those of the health delivery system, and outcome factors. The first twelve recommendations are based on what we need to know about the characteristics of the Hispanic population before we can implement policy and program changes.

A profile of users and nonusers of health facilities is much needed. This profile should include information on socioeconomic, demographic, and cultural characteristics (e.g., health beliefs and knowledge, language use, family resources, etc.); types of services sought and for what health conditions; past experiences with the health care system; and the relationship between family size, family composition, and health services use, etc.

Research on the health needs of high-risk groups such as infants, youth, the elderly, individuals with chronic health conditions, and individuals living in extreme poverty are very much needed.

There is also a need to study the relationship between health status and having or not having a regular source of health care or insurance. We may find that a person without a regular source of care, for example, may be in better health; or that Hispanics without a regular source of care and health insurance have a higher incidence of untreated illness.

More empirical data is needed to document Hispanics' self-care practices in the presence or absence of illnesss (use of home remedies, frequent exercise), and the use of lay health practitioners (*curanderos* and *espiritistas*). We need to find out for what problems these resources are used, and if they are used simultaneously or as a substitution for the formal health care system.

More research is also needed to determine to what extent health problems are taken care of by the family (i.e., parents), and for what conditions and reasons (because of problems in seeking care, lack of family resources, etc.).

There is a great need to study Hispanic health finances and medical expenditures. We need to investigate whether Hispanics pay for medical care mostly out-of-pocket; what proportion of annual family income goes to medical care; whether health facilities have special problems in getting Hispanics to assume responsibility for their medical bills; what is the relationship between the type of health facilities used by Hispanics and payment policies of such facilities (e.g. charge for services based on a sliding fee scale, monthly payment plan versus total sum of medical cost in one payment).

There is a need to study how Hispanics are linked to a regular source of medical care—what factors affect preferences, is the illegal status of some Hispanics a factor? Are public health facilities overutilized compared to private settings? Are Hispanics using the hospital emergency room in increasing numbers?

We need to know more about Hispanics' problems in obtaining medical care from regular sources (appointment waiting time, babysitting arrangements, etc.).

Data on Hispanic health practices, health maintenance, and prevention of illness is also needed. Are these practices based on traditional or on contemporary health knowledge?

Are Hispanic patients less likely to comply with medical treatment regimens than other groups? What are the factors involved in low or high compliance rates?

More local and nationwide studies are needed to obtain accurate and updated information about the health status of Hispanics. This should include life expectancy, incidence and frequency of illnesses, causes of death, disability days related to illness, etc. This information should be obtained and analyzed not only for the total Hispanic population, but for the major Hispanic subgroups such as Mexican, Puerto Rican, and Cuban. Health status should be correlated with Hispanic socioeconomic and demographic characteristics, as well as health services utilization.

Evaluative research is needed to ascertain the degree to which medical service affects the health status of the Hispanic population.

In addition, we need to know more about the structural characteristics of the health delivery system in order to determine which of these results in making health care less accessible to Hispanics. The following five recommendations address these questions.

More research is needed on consumer and provider perceptions of the need for bilingual and bicultural staff in health and mental health services provisions, as well as on other factors related to the "cultural disparity" between Anglos and Hispanics.

We need to find out what has greater impact on the utilization of health services by the Hispanic population: the characteristics of health providers, those of the administrators, or the overall characteristics of the health facility (location, kind of services available, etc.).

How do health providers view Hispanics as patients, and vice versa, is an area that needs further exploration.

What steps have been or can be taken in health facilities to make services relevant to Hispanics? Can community nurse's aides help in this process? What changes by health facilities have taken place or need to take place to make services more attractive to the Hispanic population? Who has been more successful in linking their services to Hispanics: public health facilities or private doctors in the community? What have been the procedures followed to link prospective Hispanic clients with health facilities?

What are health facilities doing to increase health knowledge among their Hispanic clients and to improve compliance among this group?

Finally, we need to know more about utilization of health care among Hispanics as well as their satisfaction with such care.

More data on Hispanic utilization patterns should be gathered. Data can come from carefully conducted household surveys or from units comprising the medical care system itself. An enumeration of the frequency and pattern of use of relevant medical facilities, together with the underlying reasons why people use these facilities, will tell us how the group is currently receiving its medical services.

More research is needed documenting whether Hispanics come to physicians with more serious illnesses than other groups.

More empirical data is needed to document Hispanics' level of satisfaction with services received. Do their levels of satisfaction vary by type of health facility?

Public Policy Issues

As we have seen throughout this chapter, access to medical care continues to be difficult for Hispanics. While a series of social programs implemented in the 1960s and 1970s (Medicaid and Medicare, Migrant Health Center, Rural Health Initiative) did increase the availability of health services to minority groups (Ahern, 1979), recent studies indicate that differences still exist in the sources, patterns, and quality of health care received by these groups compared to Whites (Aday et al., 1980; Aday and Anderson, 1984). Louis Harris's (Aday and Anderson, 1984) study found that one-fifth of Hispanic adults had particularly serious problems in obtaining care when they needed. They tend to have no insurance coverage and no regular source of medical care, among other problems. Hispanics and other minorities are now being substantially affected by federal reductions in the areas of physical and mental health, maternal and infant care, Medicaid and Medicare programs, among others. These factors, combined with the rapid inflation in medical care cost in recent years and financial barriers resulting from high unemployment and inflation, are undoing much of the progress made by the poor and by minority groups in the last decade, leading to further inequalities in access and utilization of health services. For the remainder of this decade we have an ambitious agenda, that is, to bring the equity we seek. Some policy suggestions are as follows:

- The federal government should make long-term commitments to provide more grants to states and localities to take care of the health needs of special interest groups such as the poor, minority groups, and the elderly. These commitments can also be reflected in better coordination of services between federal, state, and local agencies, and by providing technical assistance to Hispanic groups in need of aid in program development and implementation, proposal writing, and the like.
- At the federal, state, and local levels Hispanics should be involved in the planning of health services to ensure that their health and social needs are taken into consideration, as well as a fair share of the resources that will be made available.
- At the local level, special efforts should be made to identify Hispanics without a regular source of care and link them with existing resources, as having a regular source of care is an important determinant of health services use when medical care is needed. Outreach efforts, particularly in rural areas, among migrant workers, and in areas with high density of Hispanics should be pursued. A massive campaign, particularly in Hispanic neighborhoods, can be effective in informing the community of the health resources available. The use of local media, as well as the involvement of community groups (e.g., churches) have proven to be effective in informing the residents.
- Due to Hispanics' low levels of health insurance, comprehensive financing of health services, such as an insurance plan targetted to this group, or a third-party initiative, appear to be proper in increasing their access

to formal health care and in reducing some of the inequalities for this group.

- Other improvements to increase access to medical care for Hispanics depend on more long-term social and structural changes such as an increase in income and educational levels.
- As a means of making health services more available and relevant to Hispanics:
  - More comprehensive health and mental health clinics should be located within the Hispanic communities. Despite some improvements in this area a lot more needs to be done.
  - The hours and days of services should be flexible and should be established according to the needs of the community.
  - Bilingual and bicultural professionals and paraprofessionals should be recruited, particularly in those medical settings which provide health services to a high percentage of Hispanics. Special efforts should be made for bilingual and bicultural clients to receive services from health providers with bilingual and bicultural capabilities. Hispanics should be recruited not only as direct service providers, but also in administrative and policy-making positions.
  - State and local officials should make special efforts in obtaining a better distribution of health manpower in rural areas, where many Hispanics live, and in neighborhoods where there is a health manpower shortage.
  - Due to the shortage of Hispanics in health professions, Hispanic students should be motivated to enter health professional schools as early as possible. Information on financial aid, admissions requirements and so forth, should be made available to potential students while they are still in high school. Financial and moral support should be provided to potential students in gaining entrance to health professional schools, as well as in completing their health careers. Furthermore, medical schools should revise their admission criteria to allow more Hispanic students into their programs. It is imperative that financial aid be made available to these students.
  - Administrators of health facilities should examine culturally insensitive policies and procedures and should institute action for change. For example, in a study of health facilities in New York, it was found that 40 percent of the hospital patients were Hispanic, yet Hispanic dishes were not included on the hospital menus, and Hispanics often refused to eat standard hospital meals. As a result of the examination of these policies and practices, Hispanic food was included as a regular part of the menu.
  - In-service training programs should be designed and implemented in health facilities serving a large number of Hispanic clients. They should be geared toward developing cultural awareness among health

providers about Hispanics' health beliefs and behavior. These types of activities can improve communication and understanding of Hispanic culture. Cultural orientation manuals for incoming staff should also be made available.

Other health policies for consideration are as follows:

- The federal government should issue a mandate that either Hispanic identifier or ethnic origin questions should be included in all vital statistics records. State and local governments should cooperate and coordinate efforts toward this end.
- Due to a series of inadequacies in reporting health and vital statistics for Hispanics in this country (Treviño, 1982; Powell-Griner, 1982, clear and consistent guidelines and directives should be issued by state and local departments of health. Persons involved in filling out vital and health statistics records (hospital personnel, funeral directors, etc.) should participate in ongoing training programs designed to improve the recording system.
- In the area of maternal and child care, steps should be taken by state and local health department officials to set as priority maternal and child services to Hispanic women. Approximately one-third of the Hispanic population is below the age of fifteen. The need for family planning services and prenatal care and pediatric services for the newborn will definitely increase. Maternal and infant care is one of the areas most affected by federal cuts. Therefore, we are concerned that an increasing number of Hispanic women and infants may not receive the necessary prenatal and postnatal care.
- More attention and resources need to be allocated in the areas of prevention of illness and health education programs for Hispanics. A common belief among health providers is that prevention and the development of health education programs for Hispanics is an almost impossible task because "they simply don't care." However, recent studies have documented that Hispanics are more likely than Whites to participate in health education programs, particularly in the area of child care and family planning (Giachello et al., 1982; Giachello, 1983).

References

Aday, Lu Ann, and Ronald Andersen. 1975. *Development of Indices of Access to Medical Care.* Ann Arbor: Health Administration Press.
_____. 1984. "National Profile on Access to Medical Care: Where Do We Stand?" *American Journal of Public Health.* (Forthcoming).

Aday, Lu Ann, Ronald Andersen, and Gretchen V. Fleming. 1980. *Health Care in the U.S.: Equitable for Whom?* Beverly Hills: Sage.

Ahern, Mary C. 1979. "Health Care in Rural America." *Agriculture Information Bulletin*, no. 429. U.S. Department of Agriculture, Economics, Statistics, and Cooperative Services.

Aler, Jose O. 1978. "Puerto Ricans and Health: Findings from New York City." Hispanic Research Center. Monograph no. 1, Fordham University, New York.

American Public Health Association. 1974. *Minority Health Chart Book.* Washington: U.S. Government Printing Office.

Andersen, Ronald. 1968. "A Behavioral Model of Families' Use of Health Services." Center for Health Administration Studies: University of Chicago, Research Series 25.

Andersen, Ronald, Gretchen V. Fleming, Aida L. Giachello, Patricia Andrade, and Brenda Spencer. 1981a. "Self-Care Practices and Attitudes in the U.S.: Analysis of National Data." Report submitted to the National Center for Health Services Research.

Andersen, Ronald, Sandra Z. Lewis, Aida L. Giachello, Lu Ann Aday, and Grace Chiu. 1981b. "Access to Medical Care among the Hispanic Population of the Southwestern United States." *Journal of Health and Social Behavior* 22 (March):78-89.

Ayala, Philip. 1972. "Folk Practices, Folk Medicine, and Curanderismo in the Lower West Side of Chicago." Manuscript.

Bernstein, Amy, and Marc Berk. 1981. "Perceived Health Status and Selected Indicators of Access to Care among the Minority Aged." Paper presented at the annual meeting of American Public Health Association, Montreal.

Bleiweis, Phyllis R., Richard C. Reynolds, Louis D. Cohen, and Neil A. Butler. 1977. "Health Care Characteristics of Migrant Agricultural Workers on Three Northern Florida Counties." *Journal of Community Health* 3 (Fall):32-43.

Bradshaw, Benjamin S., and Edwin Fonner. 1977. "Mortality of Mexican Americans, 1969-71." Paper presented at the Conference on Demography of Racial and Ethnic Groups, Austin, Tex.

Buch, Maria M. 1971. "The Afro-Cuban Cult as a Social Support System." Paper presented at the 30th annual meeting of the Society for Applied Anthropology, Miami.

Buechley, Robert, John E. Dunn, George Linden, and Lester Breslow. 1957. "Excess Lung Cancer Mortality Rates among Mexican Women in California." *Cancer* 10 (January-February):63-66.

Buell, Philip, Winifred Mendez, and John E. Dunn. 1968. "Cancer of the Lung among Mexican Immigrant Women in California." *Cancer* 22 (July):186-92.

Bruhn, John G. 1974. "Health Manpower Needs among Mexican-Americans in Texas." *Texas Reports on Biology and Medicine* 32 (Fall-Winter):633-47.

Bruhn, John G., and David W. Rowden. 1974. "Health Manpower and Educational Needs among Mexican-Americans in Texas." In "Barriers to Medical Care among Texas Chicanos." A project of the Southwest Medical Sociology ad Hoc Committee. Manuscript.

Clark, Margaret. 1959. *Health in the Mexican-American Culture.* Berkeley: University of California Press.

Edgerton, Robert B., Marvin Karno, and L. Fernández. 1970. "Curanderismo in the Metropolis: The diminishing role of folk psychiatry among Los Angeles Mexican-Americans." *American Journal Psychotherapy* 24:124-34.

Edgerton, Robert B., and Marvin Karno. 1971. "Mexican-American Bilingualism and the Perception of Mental Illness." *Archives of General Psychiatry* 40 (March):286-90.

Ellis, John M. 1959. "Mortality Differences for a Spanish-Surname Population Group." Southwestern Social Sciences Quarterly 39:314-21.

_____. 1977. *The Sociology of Health Care: Social, Economic, and Political Perspectives.* New York: Praeger.

Enos, Darryl D., and Paul Sultan. 1962. "Spanish Surname Mortality Differences in San Antonio, Texas." *Journal of Health and Human Behavior* 3:125-27.

Farge, Emile. 1975. *La Vida Chicana: Health Care Attitudes and Behavior of Houston Chicanos.* Houston: R. E. Research Associates.

Fleming, Gretchen V., and Ronald M. Andersen. 1976. *Health Beliefs of the U.S. Population: Implications for Self-Care.* Chicago: Center for Health Administration Studies (CHAS), University of Chicago.

Galvin, Michael, and Margaret Fan. 1975. "The Utilization of Physician Services in Los Angeles County, 1973." *Journal of Health and Social Behavior* 16 (March):74-94.

Gertsen, R., M.R. Klauber, M.R. Rindflesh, R.L. Kane, and R. Gray. 1975. "A Re-Examination of Suchman's Views on Social Factors in Health Care Utilization." *Journal of Health and Social Behavior* 16:226-37.

Giachello, Aida L. 1983. Self-Care Practices in Three U.S. Central City Areas." Paper presented at the American Public Health Association Meetings, Dallas, Tex.

Giachello, Aida L., and Ronald M. Andersen. 1981. "Self-Care among the Hispanic Population in the United States." Paper presented at the Spring Institute, University of Chicago.

Giachello, Aida L., Gretchen V. Fleming, and Ronald Andersen. 1982a. "Self-Care Practices among Racial and Ethnic Groups in the U.S.: Analysis of National Data." Paper presented at the International Sociological Association meetings, Mexico City.

_____. 1982b. "Self-Care Practices and Attitudes in the U.S." Final report. Submitted to NCHSR, DHHS under contract #R01HS 04106-02 (November).

Giachello, Aida L., Ralph Bell, Lu Ann Aday, and Ronald Andersen. 1983. "Uses of the 1980 Census for Hispanic Health Services Research." *American Journal of Public Health* 73 (March):266-74.

Gregory, David D. 1978. "Transcultural Medicine: Treating Hispanic Patients." *Behavioral Medicine* (February):22-29.

Gurnack, Anne M. 1979. "Access to Health Care in a West Dallas Mexican-American Community." Paper presented at the Hispanic Health Services Research Conference, Albuquerque. N.M. Manuscript.

Harwood, Alan. 1971. "The Hot-Cold Theory of Disease." *Journal of the American Medical Association* (JAMA) 216 (May):1153-58.

Hoppoe, Sue K., and Peter L. Heller. 1975. "Alienation, Familism and the Utilization of Health Services by Mexican-Americans." *Journal of Health and Social Behavior* 16 (September):304-14.

Jelliffer, Derrick B., and Patrice E.F. Jelliffer. 1971. "An Overview." *American Journal of Clinical Nutrition* 24 (August).

Journal of the American Medical Association. 1983. (JAMA).

Keefe, S., A.M. Padilla, and M.E. Carlos. 1976. "A Comparison of Mexican-Americans and Anglo Americans in Two Cultures." In J. M. Herrera, ed., *The Chicano Community: Psychological Theories and Practices.* New Haven: Yale University Press.

Kiev, A. 1968. *Curanderismo: Mexican-American Folk Psychiatry.* New York: Free Press.

Lee, Eun S., Robert E. Roberts, and Darwin R. Labarthe. 1976. "Excess and Deficit Lung Cancer Mortality in Three Ethnic Groups in Texas." *Cancer* 38:2551-56.

Louis Harris and Associates. 1983. "Updated Report on Access to Health Care for the American People." Princeton: Robert Wood Johnson Foundation.

Lubchansky, Issac, Gladys Egri, and Janet Stokes. 1970. "Puerto Rican Spiritualists View Mental Illness: The Faith Healers as Paraprofessionals." *American Journal of Psychiatry* 127 (September):312-29.

McLemore, Dale S. 1963. "Ethnic Attitudes toward Hospitalization: An Illustrative Comparison of Anglos and Mexican-Americans." *Southwestern Social Science Quarterly* 43 (March):341-46.

Madsen, Williams. 1964. *Mexican Americans in South Texas.* New York: Rinehart Winston.

Martínez, Cervando, and Harry W. Martin. 1966. "Folk Diseases among Urban Mexican-Americans: Etiology, Symptoms, and Treatment" *Journal of the American Medical Association* (JAMA) 196:147-60.

Moll, L.C., S. Rueda, R. Reza, J. Herrera, and L. P. Vázquez. 1976. "Mental Health services in East Los Angeles: An Urban Case Study." In M. Miranda, ed., *Psychotherapy with the Spanish-Speaking: Issues in Research and Service Delivery.* Los Angeles: Spanish-Speaking Mental Health Research Center, University of California.

Morales, Armando. 1970. "Mental and Public Health Issues: The Case of the Mexican-American in Los Angeles." *El Grito* 3 (Winter):3-11.

Moustafa, A. Taher, and Gertrud Weiss. 1968. "Health Status and Practices of Mexican-Americans." *In Mexican-American Study Project: Advance Report II.* Los Angeles: Graduate School of Business Administration, University of California.

Nall, Frank C. II, and Joseph Spielberg. 1967. "Social and Cultural Factors in the Responses of Mexican-Americans to Medical Treatment." *Journal of Health and Social Behavior* 8 (December):299-308.

National Center for Health Services Research. 1980. *Hispanic Health Services Research Conference-Proceeding Publications.* DHHS Publication no. (PHS) 80-3288. Washington: U.S. Government Printing Office.

———. 1982. *Usual Sources of Medical Care and Their Characteristics.* DHHS Publication no. (PHS) 82-3324. Washington: U.S. Government Printing Office.

National Center for Health Statistics. 1978. "Contraceptive Utilization in the U.S., 1973-76." *Advance Data*, no. 36 (August).

———. 1979. "Hispanic Health and Nutrition Examination Survey: Supporting Statement for Preliminary Plans." Manuscript.

———. 1981. "Births of Hispanic Parentage, 1978." *Monthly Vital Statistics Report* 29 (March Supplement).

———. 1979. "Use of Family Planning Services by currently Married Women 15-44 Years of Age, 1973 and 1976." *Advanced Data*, no. 45 (August).

Newsom, Rollo. 1974. "Curanderism: Barriers to Gateway or Health Care." In *Barriers to Medical Care among Texas Chicanos.* A Project of the Southwest Medical Sociology ad Hoc Committee.

Phillipus, M.J. 1971. "Successful and Unsuccessful Approaches to Mental Health Services for an Urban Hispano-American Population." *American Journal of Public Health* 61:820-30.

Powell-Griner, Eve, and Dan Streck. 1982. "A Closer Examination of Neonatal Mortality Rates among Texas Spanish-Surnamed Population." *American Journal of Public Heath* 72 (September):993-99.

Quesada, Gustavo M., and Peter L. Heller. 1977. "Sociocultural Barriers to Medical Care among Mexican-Americans in Texas: A Summary Report of Research Conducted by the Southwest Medical Sociology ad Hoc Committee." *Medical Care* 15 (May Supplement):93-101.

Ramírez, Oscar. 1978. "The Role of *la Familia* in Chicano Mental Health Help-Seeking: Preliminary Research Results." Paper presented at the Coalition of Spanish-Speaking Mental Health Organizations (COSSMHO), National Hispanic Conference on Families, Houston, Tex.

Roberts, R.E., and E.S. Lee. 1980. "Medical Care Use by Mexican-Americans: Evidence from the Human Population Laboratory Studies." *Medical Care* 18 (March):266-81.

Rogler, L.H., and A.B. Holingshead. 1961. "The Puerto Rican Spiritualist as a Psychiatrist." *American Journal of Sociology* 7:17-21.

Rubel, A.J. 1960. "Concepts of Disease in the Mexican-American Culture." *American Anthropologist* 62:795-814.

———. 1966. *Across the Tracks: Mexican-Americans in a Texas City.* Austin: University of Texas Press.

Ruiz, Pedro. 1972. "The Indigenous Nonprofessional: The Primary Therapist in a Mental Health Program." Paper presented at the annual conference of the Society for Applied Anthropology, Canada. Manuscript.

Salazar, Jaime. 1978. "Mexican-American Illness Attitudes." Health Research Services Association, Los Angeles. Manuscript.
Samora, Julián. 1961. "Concepts of Health and Disease among Spanish-Americans." *American Catholic Sociological Review* 22 (Winter) 314-23.
Saunders, Lyle. 1954. *Cultural Differences and Medical Care: The Case of the Spanish-Speaking People of the Southwest.* New York: Russell Sage.
Schensul, Steve, and Mary Bakszysz. 1975. "The Role of Applied Research in the Development of Health Services in a Chicano Community in Chicago." In *Topias and Utopias in Health.* The Hague: Mouton.
Schensul, S., Philip Ayala, and J. Bymel. 1975. "Cultural and Community Factors in Health Services Delivery: A Case from the Chicago Chicano Community." Paper presented at the American Anthropological Association meeting.
Schepers, Emile. 1971. "Comparison of Folk and Professional diagnoses Using the Hypothetical Case Study Method." Paper presented at the Florida State Psychiatry Institute.
Sena-Rivera, Jaime. 1979. "Extended Kinship in the United States: Competing Models and the Case of *la Familia Chicana.*" *Journal of Marriage and the Family* (February):121-29.
Slesinger, D.P., and E. Cautley. 1981. "Medical Utilization Patterns of Hispanic Migrant Farmworkers in Wisconsin." *Public Health Reports* 96 (May-June):255-63.
Stern, Gwen, and Aida L. Giachello. 1977. "Applied Research: The Mother-Infant Project." Paper presented at the Medical Anthropological meetings, New York.
Suchman, E.A. 1964. "Socio-Medical Variations among Ethnic Groups." *American Journal of Sociology* 70 (November):319-33.
Surgeon General's Report. 1979. *Healthy People: Surgeon General's Report on Health Promotion and Disease Prevention.* HEW (P.H.S.) 79-5501. Washington: U.S. Government Printing Office.
Sussman, Marvin B. 1959. "The Isolated Family: Fact or Fiction?" *Social Problems* 6 (Spring):333-40.
Teller, C., and S. Clyburn. 1974. "Trends in Infant Mortality." *Texas Business Review* 48 (October):240-46.
Thoma, Madeline. 1977. "The Effects of a Cultural Awareness Program on the Delivery of Health Care." *Health and Social Work* 2 (August).
Torrey, E. 1972."The Irrelevancy of Traditional Mental Health Services for Urban Mexican-Americans." Paper presented at the 47th annual meeting of the American Anthropsychiatric Association.
Treviño, Fernando. 1979. "Community Mental Health Center Staff's Patterns and Their Impact on Hispanics Use of Services." Paper presented at the Hispanic Health Services Research Conference.
———. 1982. "Vital Health Statistics for the U.S. Hispanic population." *American Journal of Public Health* 72 (September): 979-81.
Urdaneta, Maria. 1973. "Fertility and the Pill in a Texas Barrio." Paper presented at the Fourth International Conference on Anthropology and Ethnography.

U.S. Bureau of the Census. 1981. *1980 Census of the population: Supplementary Report.* Series PC(80) 51-1. Washington: U.S. Government Printing Office.

———. 1980. *Current Population Reports.* Population Characteristics, series p. 20, no. 354, "Persons of Spanish Origin in the United States: March, 1979." Washington: U.S. Government Printing Office.

———. 1981a. "Medium Income and Poverty Status of Families in the U.S., 1980." Advance data, Consumer Income Series, p. 60, no. 127, Washington: D.C.: U.S. Government Printing Office.

———. 1981b. *Current Population Reports.* Population Characteristics, series P. 20, no. 361, "Persons of Spanish Origin in the U.S., March, 1980." Advance report. Washington: U.S. Government Printing Office.

U.S. Department of Health, Education, and Welfare (DHEW). 1977. Health of the Disadvantaged. HEW Publ. no. (HRA) 77-68. Washington: U.S. Government Printing Office.

U.S. Department of Health and Human Services. 1980. *Health of the Disadvantaged, Chart Book II.* Publication no. (HRA) 80-633. Washington: U.S. Government Printing Office.

———. 1979. *Healthy People.* General Surgeon Report. Washington: U.S. Government Printing Office.

Vázquez, Albert. 1974. "The Effects of a Change in the Cultural Orientation of Community Mental Health." Manuscript.

Weaver, Jerry L. 1976. *National Health Policy and the Underserved: Ethnic Minorities, Women, and the Elderly.* St. Louis: Mosby.

———. 1978. "Mexican Health Care Behavior: A Critical Review of the Literature." *Social Sciences Quarterly* 50 (no. 1):85-102.

Welch, S., J. Comer, and H. Steinman. 1973. "Some Social and Attitudinal Correlates of Health Care among Mexican-Americans." *Journal of Health and Social Behavior* 14:205-13.

Wilensky, Gail, and Daniel Walden. 1981. "Minority, Poverty, and the Uninsured." Paper presented at the annual meeting of the American Public Health Association, California.

Wilson, W. 1976. *Power, Racism, and Privilege: Race Relations in a Theoretical and Historical Perspective.* New York: Macmillan.

9

Hispanics and the Social Service System

Carmen Rivera-Martínez

One of the prinicpal challenges facing the complex social service sys-
tem in the United States is the immense diversity of the groups which
the system and its agencies seek to serve. Nowhere is this more true
than with regard to the various groups that make up the larger group
referred to as "Hispanic." Rivera-Martinez, in this chapter, discusses
the nature of this challenge and suggests approaches and concrete
work that needs to be done. The social needs of Hispanics are framed
in the context of their educational condition, poverty, language and
cultural differences and the overall condition of the social service sys-
tem. The author points to the issues of access to the system and
communication problems within the system as typical of the diffi-
culties facing Hispanics. The diversity of Hispanic family styles is
described and materials are presented showing how this characteristic
is both a treasured richness for Hispanic cultures and a problem for
those trying to function within the United States social service bu-
reaucracies. One section is devoted to a treatment of the emergence of
what the author terms "natural helping networks," which are informal
ways in which members of Hispanic communities provide services
and support for one another. The churches within these communities
are also part of this system and their role is described. Sections also
contain material on child welfare policies and the rise of Hispanic
social service agencies and the influences which these factors have on
the life of the communities. Finally, four specific policy recommenda-
tions are offered for future consideration.

The Hispanic population presents a challenge to the social service delivery system of the United States. The complex and heterogeneous characteristics of the Hispanic population as well as its diverse history provide the
elements of this challenge: many Hispanics are racially different from the
White majority society, which may result in discrimination and denial of
opportunites; geographic proximity to the homeland, which may cause the
individual to keep options open and not make a permanent commitment

to the American culture and values; easy travel back and forth to the homeland (with the exception of Cuban and Central and South American political refugees), providing constant nurturing of culture and language; for some groups (Puerto Ricans and some Mexican-Americans) the right to demand services as monolingual Spanish-speaking American citizens by birth. The heterogeneity of the Hispanic population requires differences in approach and design of social service programs for the different Hispanic subgroups.

Hispanics are near the bottom of the American socioeconomic structure, consequently, they are near the top in terms of need. Hispanics are young, tend to have large families and low educational levels compared with the majority population, so that a high proportion of Hispanics are overrepresented among those who depend on the social welfare system. Given these conditions, programs and services offered by the social service delivery system to provide avenues for access to mainstream society are of critical importance for Hispanics.

The social service system in the United States is composed of a series of organized efforts to ensure a basic standard of physical, emotional, and mental well-being of the members of society. These efforts are characterized by the existence of services and programs created or supported by public or private agencies and organizations to prevent social problems or to protect individuals and society. Ultimately, the purpose of the social service delivery system is to provide access to all individuals and groups to the mainstream of society (NASW, 1977).

Within this general mission the social service delivery system has been assisting immigrant groups to adapt to American society and to achieve higher standards of living. Hispanics, one of the last immigrant groups arriving in the United States, need the social service system as much as previous immigrant groups did. Here we will examine the needs of the Hispanic population vis à vis the social service delivery system and how this system is responding to or meeting those needs.

It is recognized that the social service delivery system has serious problems which limit its ability to provide the services it should to all members of American society. Kamerman and Kahn (1976:440) have described the social service system as having "limited provisions for access, fragmentation of service provisions, duplication of services, discontinuities in service and care, inequities, inadequacies, and unresponsiveness in service provision and delivery." These problems in the social service delivery system are magnified in terms of the ability of the system to provide and enhance opportunities for access to mainstream society to the Hispanic population in the United States.

Characteristics of the System

Several characteristics contribute to the effectiveness of service delivery. These include accessibility, adequacy of communication, and right to benefits and services. Accessibility refers to the "arrangements by which the social service delivery system assures that the consumers are informed about the availability of rights, benefits, and services; assures that those persons eligible for services obtained them; refer the consumers to appropriate offices and services and get them there physically if necessary; and most importantly assures that the service providers are responsive to the needs of beneficiaries" (Kamerman and Kahn, 1976:436). Among the elements affecting the access of Hispanics to the social service system are adequacy of communication strategies from service providers, knowledge among Hispanics of their rights to services, language barriers, and cultural differences. In addition, the presence of natural helping networks in Hispanic communities is an important aspect that needs to be understood as it relates to issues of access.

To make use of the system, the individual must know the type of services available and where to go to obtain them. The social service system has not been as effective as other systems in the dissemination of information about its services. In some cases even the existence of agencies and programs are known only to very specialized groups. This lack of communication may constitute a major barrier to Hispanics who may lack linguistic skills or knowledge of social and institutional behavior and be easily confused by the labyrinth of programs offered by public and private agencies.

Dissemination of information about social services targeted to the Hispanic population is essential to provide access. This dissemination could take the form of: participation in radio and TV programs in the Hispanic media, obtaining press coverage about programs and services, and establishing store front agencies and community outreach programs. While the responsibility of informing the community about available services belongs to the service providers, not all agencies actively recruit clientele. Some social service agencies may wish to discourage easy access to their services because inadequate staffing and resources prevent them from serving their current caseload. Another potential barrier to dissemination of information is that agencies operating in changing neighborhoods may not have identified Hispanics as being a new source of clients. The agency must first recognize and then adjust to needs of the Hispanic population. This process may take several years before the agency revises its services and makes them relevant to Hispanics.

Another factor affecting the level of utilization of social services by Hispanic communities in the United States is the issue of rights to benefits and services. Many Hispanics still are treated as second-class citizens in many parts of the country. Individuals that have experienced denial of services and opportunities due to their race, language, or national origin would tend to be reluctant to voice their concerns or demand their rights for fear of persecution and retribution (Aragón de Valdés and Gallegos, 1982). Recent immigrants in particular have fear of deportation. Hispanics perceive the welfare bureaucracy as those who take their children to courts and jails and deny their welfare checks.

Recent Hispanic immigrants often bring similar negative experiences vis à vis social services provided by the government or the private sector in their native countries. Central and South American immigrants tend to bring with them fear and mistrust of institutions, given the denial of civil rights going on in many of their countries. Most come from countries where social welfare systems are minimal or nonexistent. Those who have experience using social services in their country find that those social service systems in no way resemble that in the United States. In some of these countries there are no such services as income guarantees or a publicly supported child welfare system. Social services in some of these countries are still limited to philanthropic activities supported by the few and restricted to strictly defined populations among children, the elderly, the emotionally disturbed, and the poor.

An important aspect of the issue of access to information about rights and privileges relates to the needs of the undocumented Hispanic alien. Although studies show that undocumented aliens make little use of the welfare system (Bustamente, 1977; Villalpaudo, 1980), they do make use of needed health and other emergency services. Often undocumented aliens who need these services find themselves having to lie in order to benefit or forego the assistance altogether. On the other hand, social service providers are in the dilemma of denying services to this population, thus becoming an extension of the law enforcement system, jeopardizing issues of confidentiality and privacy, or providing services to this clientele and causing discontent and posssibly reprisals from other systems in the society. Some agencies, confronted with this dilemma, have resorted to not asking questions about legal status unless it is an absolute requirement of the programs. The burden of responsibility is then placed on the individual client.

Language and Cultural Barriers

Linguistic differences between Hispanics and social service providers limit the possibility of effective communication between them. Language retention patterns among Hispanics are very high. Among the poor who live in the barrio, many are monolingual, while many others are Spanish-language-dominant (Durán, 1983). The highest incidence of Spanish monolingualism is among adults who are over forty-four years old (Estrada, 1980). Thus agencies which provide services to the elderly have a particular need to inform users about services available in Spanish and to provide Spanish-speaking staff.

The social service system attempting to serve this population has been slow in responding to this reality. Unfortunately, data that shows nationwide evidence of the availability of bilingual staff in the social service system does not exist. For example, in a survey conducted by the National Association of Social Workers (1982) among its membership in the United States, only 1.8 percent reported being of Hispanic origin. This number does not indicate whether these persons are bilingual. On the other hand, some non-Hispanic social workers are bilingual, but no one knows how many. It is impossible to know if the Hispanic social workers serve Hispanic clients or how many of the bilingual non-Hispanic social workers are doing so.

Another indication of the slow response of the social service system to the Hispanic population is apparent in the training of social service professionals. For instance, only four schools of social work have specific curricula oriented toward understanding the problems confronting the Hispanic population. Furthermore, Hispanic social work students comprise only 4.5 percent of all social work master's students in 1982. It is difficult to determine whether schools of social work are actively recruiting Hispanic students. While the percentage of Hispanic social work students is low, those students enrolled full-time tend to receive financial assistance. In 1982, approximately 71.5 percent of Hispanic master's students received aid compared with 40 percent of White students (Rubin, 1983). Unfortunately, the magnitude of the aid is unknown. While it appears that schools of social work are providing some assistance to Hispanic social work students, it remains unclear whether Hispanics are actively recruited into the profession. Thus it is likely that services to Hispanics will continue to be provided by mostly non-Hispanic professional staff.

Information regarding availability of bilingual staff could be obtained by agencies' reports of language resources among their staff. This type of report is very limited and tends to be produced mostly at the request of funding sources. Unfortunately, at this point most of the information available is based on impressionistic evidence collected in conversations and exchanges with relevant parties. It seems that bilingual staff in many social service agencies are concentrated in clerical and paraprofessional positions. This staff is often utilized as translators during interviews, counseling, and even psychological evaluations (Samuda, 1975). The implications of this situation are very serious, since translation errors have been know to cause extremely serious consequences. One case documented by Travelers and Immigrants Aid in Chicago involved a recent Cuban refugee from the Mariel boat lift. In this instance when the immigration officials were interviewing through an interpreter, the person was asked whether he had ever been accused of child molesting. The translator used a literal translation and asked whether the person had been accused of *molestar a un niño* (annoying a child) instead of the correct *perversión de menores* (contributing to the perversion of a minor). The refugee answered that every once in a while he had done so, but meant that he had annoyed children, not "molested" them. Consequently, he was denied entry and was placed with other alleged criminals until the confusion was clarified.

Information and referral in social service agencies involves those activities which help individuals find their way among the different types of services and agencies available in their communities. Information and referrals services need to make an assessment of the nature of the problem or the request and determine what is the appropriate system or subsystem that should deal with it. Communication skills are of the essence in an effective information and referral system. In cities with large concentrations of Hispanics the social service system is involving bilingual professionals at this level of service. However, beyond information and referral, very few agencies have the kind of bilingual personnel needed to implement programs. Hispanic agency executives complain that non-Hispanic agencies limit their services to Hispanic clients to sending them to Hispanic agencies (United Way of Chicago, 1982).

Cultural Differences: The Family

Cultural differences between users and providers of services affects the accessibility of social services to the Hispanic population. The difference between Hispanic culture and majority society culture have been documented elsewhere (Ramírez and Castañeda, 1974; Fitzpatrick, 1971; Green, 1982; Mizio and Delaney, 1981). However, some authors argue that many of the observed characteristics ascribed to Mexican or Puerto Rican culture disappear when controls for education and socioeconomic class are introduced (Laoza, 1980; Hess, 1970). Another factor that needs to be added to an understanding of cultural differences between Hispanic and majority society is length of stay in the United States. It is possible that a third-generation Hispanic will feel more affinity to majority society than to a first-generation Hispanic of the same socioeconomic and educational level. Thus educational level, social class, and length of residency in the United States combine to complicate issues of cultural differences among Hispanics and non-Hispanics.

The Hispanic family needs to be included in any discussion about cultural differences between Hispanics and non-Hispanics. The Mexican family has been described as traditional, hierarchical, with ascribed sex and status roles (Aragón de Valdés and Gallegos, 1982). The Puerto Rican family is described in very similar terms:

> Patriarchal . . . in which roles are clearly defined and carefully monitored. . . . The Puerto Rican family espouses extended family patterns; its elderly are respected and its children are deeply loved. . . . In Puerto Rican culture, the male is seen as innately superior to the female, who is overprotected, has limited freedom and even today, is encumbered by the traditional virginity and machismo cults . . . dependency is encouraged . . . achievement is less important than conformity. In the middle and upper classes there is less emphasis on subordination patterns, but they are still interwoven into the fabric of all Puerto Rican society [Mizio and Delaney 1981:110].

However, some aspects of the majority society culture might be similar to those ascribed to Hispanic families and cultures. For example the machismo/virginity notions might have some commonality with the so-called double standard for male/female behavior among majority society. Subordination and dependency of children to parents, wives to husbands, younger siblings to older siblings might be also found to some extent among non-Hispanic families. The critical aspect of these differences is the degree of conflict Hispanic families may find when majority cultural values are encountered in their use of the social service delivery system.

The social service delivery system follows policies and practices determined by majority society, reflecting contemporary values and culture. Consequently the design of the social service delivery system is based on an ideal family size and structure as well as the type of relationships and roles defined by prevalent cultural values. Accordingly, the contemporary social service delivery system in the United States is based on programs and policies that foster autonomy and independence, achievement and individuality, egalitarianism, and nuclear families. These discontinuities between the reality of the majority of Hispanic families and this "ideal family" create conflict and limit the ability of the social service delivery system to assist Hispanic families.

Almost all governmental policies have an impact on the family. A review of public policies and programs that affect families (Johnson, 1981) found that in 1978 at least 268 programs at the federal level provided direct assistance to individuals and families. Policies and programs enacted for the purpose of assisting families have the potential of affecting some families positively, others negatively, and some might not be affected at all. Hispanic families participating in a variety of programs and services are due to be affected by these policies in a direct manner.

Many have speculated that the dramatic changes in the number of female headed households among Puerto Rican families might be an example of the negative impact of social policies directed to help families. In this instance, 15.3 percent of the Puerto Rican households were female headed in 1960; this number increased to 24.1 percent in 1970 and to 38.2 percent according to the 1980 Census (Cooney and Colon, 1978; U.S. Bureau of the Census, 1983). This explosive growth in the number of female-headed households among the Puerto Rican population has not been studied adequately, so that we lack a reasonable explanation for it. This phenomenon parallels that of the population as a whole in the United States.

Analysis of the statistics about the number of female-headed families among the Puerto Rican population in the United States are complicated by the fact that in 1980, only 11.5 percent of the Puerto Rican families in the island had similar characteristics (U.S. Bureau of the Census, 1983). Thus it might be that the migratory experience has a negative effect on the Puerto Rican family. There may be a need for supportive social services to these families to address the impact of the migration experience. Specifically, social services to Puerto Rican families need to take into consideration the cultural stresses under which a great majority of these families live. Moreover, recently arrived Puerto Rican families may need to be served in a manner that will enhance the chances of maintaining two-parent households and prevent further deterioration of the family.

Natural Help Networks

Another aspect of the Hispanic culture that requires attention by the social service delivery system is the presence of natural support networks. The concept of natural support networks in Hispanic communities has been amply documented in the literature (Cafferty et al., 1981; Angel and Tienda, 1981; Delgado and Humm-Delgado, 1982; de Valdés and Gallegos, 1982). It could be argued that the natural support system in Hispanic communities takes place at different levels: the family, the neighborhood, and the church.

Hispanic families tend to be organized around a multigenerational household with other satellite households relating to it. The multigenerational household is likely to be formed by at least one elderly parent, a married child with a spouse, and their children. Children of the elderly parent become a satellite household by keeping in close contact with this nucleus and seeking and giving help as needed. *Compadres*, people that have been added to the family constellation by virtue of being godparents at baptism, weddings, or birthdays, are also part of the satellite households. Any member of these support networks might belong to several support networks, given that each spouse might have relatives within close proximity.

These constellations of households form a network of support and resources. This support system is likely to be the most efficient utilization of the resources of the group. They can share resources by lending, bartering, or buying from each other as needed. Poor families are forced to share limited resources to maximize their income opportunities. It is common for these families to lend the best shoes and the best coat to that member who is trying to secure a job. Exchange of services such as baby sitting and small maintenance work are obtained through the network (Green, 1982; Mizio and Delaney, 1981).

Hispanic families, like Black families, have to maintain a family support system to meet basic survival needs: food, shelter, and clothing. The extended family and the natural support network among Hispanic families is considered an economic necessity for its members (Angel and Tienda, 1981). By pooling everybody's resources the individuals involved in this network increase their noncash income potential.

The social service delivery system tends to focus on household units instead of kinship systems. The household is defined as a group of people sharing a common residence (U.S. Bureau of the Census, 1982). By not understanding and utilizing the kinship system as part of the design and implementation of social services and programs, an important resource for addressing needs is lost.

At another level, the neighborhood also functions as a natural support system. Some Hispanic neighborhoods are organized replicating homeland geographic distributions. In a Puerto Rican barrio, people immediately ask newcomers which is their hometown. The bonding among *compueblanos* is formed by sharing memories of far away places and people. The most widely known social groups among Puerto Ricans are formed and named after home towns: Hijos de Ciales or Hijos de Aibonito. Interestingly, many of these clubs' names start with "Hijos de" (children of), which immediately elicits images of eternal bonding to the homeland. The formation of networks around country of origin or hometowns is so strong that rivalries between neighboring towns or states are also transposed to the United States. On one occasion it was heard of a young Puerto Rican female from San Lorenzo, by then living in the Westtown community of Chicago, that most of the small entrepreneurs in the community were from her hometown and that other Puerto Ricans in the community were jealous of their accomplishments. These comments, of course, were made with due pride on her part, she being from San Lorenzo.

This example also indicates that small entrepreneurs in the community, together with the social clubs, form a network of support to the members of the community. Small entrepreneurs are able to advise other members of the community wishing to establish their own businesses. In addition they become the first alternative for loans and other forms of economic relief, if formal financial assistance is not available. Small entrepreneurs are also asked to become leaders when community needs demand the formation of some action group.

The literature on natural support systems also mentions the presence of folk healers as part of this support network (Giachello, 1984). Folk healers have been identified as individuals with knowledge of herbs and other forms of healing who dispense their services in mostly informal ways. The folk healer is different from the *espiritista* in that the former is mostly concerned with physical manifestations of illness and the latter with emotional or spiritual phenomena. The folk healer normally does not engage in practices that might harm a person on behalf of another. The *espiritista*, on the other hand, might be asked by the client to harm enemies or to attract someone who is resisting a relationship. Both the folk healer and the *espiritista* are perceived as people with power who can be asked for help in case of need. The social service system needs to recognize the uniqueness of these networks of support and should attempt to integrate the strength of these communites in a model for service.

The Catholic churches in Mexican barrios and the Catholic and Protestant churches in Puerto Rican communities are another source of support for Hispanics in the United States. The Catholic tradition of the Mexican population includes a mix of European Catholic worship and elements of Indian religions. The richness produced by this combination makes the Catholic church in Mexican communities a strong center of community action. Puerto Ricans bring with them extensive exposure to Protestantism mostly in the form of Revivalist or Pentecostal movements. Some authorities have remarked that Puerto Ricans do not have as strong a sense of church as other Hispanic groups (Fitzpatrick, 1971). This statement notwithstanding, the small Protestant churches dispersed in Puerto Rican barrios in the United States are important forces in the shaping of community life.

Reliance on the natural support system among Hispanics serves to minimize the need to contact formal resources or outside institutions. Unfortunately, this reliance on the natural support system is frequently interpreted by professionals as personal or social deficits of the individual client. Several examples might serve to illustrate this point. Clients who come with other members of the family when visiting a social service agency might be labeled as dependent and insecure by workers. Parents who leave their children with grandparents or other relatives in order for them to try to find work in another area might be accused of child abandonment. People who attempt to receive medical care through a folk healer or an *espiritista* might be considered mentally ill.

Social service providers need to recognize that the natural support systems respond to historical, sociopolitical, and economic realities affecting the Hispanic population. In order to meet the needs presented by this population, understanding of these systems is needed.

In addition, besides the general concerns regarding access for all Hispanic groups in the United States, special consideration should be given to the problems of particular population groups. It is particularly important to understand the problems affecting Hispanic children and Hispanic women using the social service system, and indicate options for improving programs and services for these populations.

Children

Child welfare services represent the cornerstone of the social service system. Assistance to orphans and abandoned and poor children provided the impetus for the establishment of many child welfare agencies in existence today. Services have enlarged considerably to include foster care, adoption, prevention of child abuse and neglect, and more recently the development of parenting programs. These child welfare agencies are important elements in the development of opportunities for families and children of immigrants. With a large proportion of children in their population, Hispanics are an important group to benefit from these services. The distribution of services and resources within the child welfare system is significantly different among groups based on race and income.

Stehno (1982) argues that the services offered to minority children in the mental health, child welfare, welfare, and juvenile justice systems are discriminatory. Minority youth and White youth are treated differently in all four systems. Data from the U.S. Bureau of the Census, the National Center for Juvenile Justice, the National Institute for Mental Health, the Law Enforcement Assistance Administration, and the Children's Defense Fund found a consistent pattern of discrimination and differential treatment based on race: a disproportionate number of Black, American Indian, and Hispanic (compared to White) children are placed outside the home; a higher proportion of Black youth are processed through the juvenile justice system for criminal behavior than as status offenders; a greater proportion of minority children are placed in less desirable placement; most minority children in the social service system are served through the public sector rather than in private sector agencies; and lastly, minority youth are less likely to receive therapy of in-home services before being admitted to mental health hospitals or placed outside the home. Stehno's analysis indicates that even though poverty is a mediating variable affecting the differential treatment of children and youth in the social service delivery system, racial discrimination accounts for a portion of the differential treatment.

Similarly, Gruber (1980) presented evidence of the racially biased distribution of children and mental health patients among types of social service institutions. In his study, more affluent and White clients are passed "upward" to more desirable types of programs or interventions (community-based programs, psychotherapy, etc.) and the poor and minority child is passed "downward" to more coercive and controlling institutions. He utilizes the concept of "status rationing" to refer to the process by which social esteem, honor, and merit are allocated among institutions. Gruber contends that clients have a value for the institutions based on: (1) the perceived probability of success or good outcome where the higher the social status of the client the higher the perceived probability of success; (2) the anticipated financial drain to the organization from such items as time and personnel costs, which vary inversely with the perceived probability of success; and (3) the honor deflected from client to staff, personnel, and the organization where the higher the social status of the clientele, the greater the honor, while the lower the status of the clientele, the greater the "stigma by association." Hispanics are among the poorest of all groups in American society, and they are stigmatized because of their poverty. The contention, stated by Hispanic social service providers, that Hispanic clients are more likely to be referred out of non-Hispanic agencies might be in part explained by Gruber's hypothesis.

Services to Hispanic children need to take into consideration the fact that the parents are an integral component of any efforts to serve children. Enhancing the parents' ability to be effective parents in American society might be an appropriate approach for working with these children. Hispanic parents, who are stuggling with their own issues of adaptation to a new language and culture, are subjected to additional stress in trying to educate a child to function effectively in a society they themselves do not fully understand. Social service institutions should orient themselves to this reality and should examine their programs and practices vis-à-vis the congruence between the parents' goals, objectives, and parenting practices and the goals, objectives, and practices of their programs. It could be argued that the higher the congruence between parents' and children's goals, the higher the probability of success.

One example of the right to involve parents in the decision making process regarding children's welfare took place in Illinois. The Burgos Consent Decree between the State of Illinois and the Illinois Department of Children and Family Services (DCFS) established the right of Hispanic parents to demand appropriate foster care facilities for their children. The parents affirmed that their children were placed in English monolingual homes and that this placement affected the ability of the family to be reconstructed after the children were returned to them. The court ruled in favor of the parents and the department was ordered to find culturally and linguistically appropriate homes for nonmajority children. Child welfare agencies were forced to engage in active recruitment and training of Hispanic foster parents to meet the court order. In 1982 the DCFS was taken to court again by a non-Hispanic family which had a Hispanic infant as a foster child and challenged the Burgos Decree by expressing their desire to adopt the child. DCFS took the position of supporting the Burgos decision. Eventually the court reaffirmed the Burgos Consent Decree. This ruling continues to reflect the continuing conflict of assimilation into majority society and relation of native culture which contributes to problems in providing social services to Hispanic children.

The Supreme Court in 1984 overturned the Burgos decision as it applies to the adoption of children. It is likely that in coming years there will be a distinction drawn between the guidelines for foster care, involving children who are likely to be returning to their natural parents, and for adoption, where children are being placed in a more permanent setting. The conflict concerning the "impact on assimilation" will undoubtedly continue to be central to cases of this type.

Hispanic Women

There are important differences among Hispanic women which have important implications for the delivery of social services to the group. As previously mentioned, the percentage of female-headed households among Puerto Rican families is 40 percent while for Mexican families it is 16 percent (U.S. Department of Commerce, 1983). An important implication of these figures is that female-headed households tend to be poorer than male-headed households or two-parent households. Specifically, 51.3 percent of the Hispanic female-headed households were below the poverty level as compared to 10.3 percent for all families in 1980 (Giachello et al., 1981). In terms of income, Hispanic female-headed households earned approximately 50 percent less than the median income for all families and two-thirds less than the median income for families with a working wife.

The social service delivery system attempting to serve Hispanic women should take into extra consideration the tremendous economic deprivation in which these women try to function as mothers and as active members of society. Services for this population should focus on strategies and programs geared to alleviate some of their basic needs. Concrete services such as assistance in securing their right to participate and benefit from programs, and help in securing food, clothing, and adequate shelter are essential.

Social service programs predicated on counseling models or intervention therapies focusing on enhancing relationships have limited appeal for women living under conditions of extreme poverty.

Rubenstein and Bloch (1978:74) reported that in their study of fifty minority female clients in a private social service agency, clients' and workers' perception of the nature of the problems differed. Workers tended to give more emphasis to intrapersonal and interpersonal factors to explain clients' problems while "clients tended to emphasize their lack of resources and interpersonal factors as contributing to their problems. Clients rarely spoke of their own behavior as contributing to their problems."

Hispanic Social Service Agencies

The programs offered through the social service system vary greatly and reflect the fact that the social service system is almost a "catch all" phrase that includes those societal activities that are not in the arena of education, health, housing, employment, or income maintenance. Within these services are found: child welfare programs, community centers, settlement houses and group programs, refugee programs and special programs for migrants and American Indians, community mental health programs, programs for the retarded, and community development programs, among others (Kamerman, 1976).

Support for social service programs comes both from the public sector (local, state, and federal governments) and the private sector (mostly in the form of grants from philanthropic institutions, corporate and family foundations, as well as United Way or other forms of individual giving). Community-based efforts are a special form of private social services which we wish to analyze separately from other forms of private sector social services. The rationale for this distinction rests on the understanding that indigenous communities empower themselves via the creation and nurturing of their own institutions. An analysis of Hispanics in the social service system needs to include how Hispanics are gearing their resources to accomplish their goals.

The establishment and nurturing of indigenous organizations and institutions signals that a particular community or group has some stability and has the leadership needed to initiate those efforts. Mexican and Puerto Rican organizations have existed for several decades now. Among the oldest Mexican organizations are LULAC (League of United Latin American Citizens) and the GI Forum founded after World War II. These two organizations have grown from regional Southwestern groups into institutions which have state chapters in several cities in different regions in the

United States. Puerto Rican organizations are younger and tend to be concentrated in the Eastern Seaboard states. ASPIRA of America and the National Puerto Rican Forum seem to be the most successful of the Puerto Rican organizations which have an impact outside of their original founding state.

Both Mexican and Puerto Rican organizations have legal advocacy organizations. These organizations are appropriately called MALDEF (Mexican American Legal Defense and Education Fund) and PRLDEF (Puerto Rican Legal Defense and Education Fund). These two organizations have been actively engaged in legal issues such as the right to bilingual education, affirmative action, housing rights, etc. One important area of activity of the legal advocacy organizations is their pressuring law schools to increase the number of Hispanic students and faculty.

Most of the national Mexican, Puerto Rican, or Hispanic organizations are focused on issues of education (ASPIRA, MALDEF, PRLDEF, National Chicano Council on Higher Education, Hispanic Council on Higher Education, National Association for Bilingual Education, among others) political power (National Council on La Raza, LULAC, Southwest Voter Registration Project), or employment (SER, Jobs for Progress, National Puerto Rican Forum).

COSSHMO, the National Coalition of Hispanic Mental Health and Human Service Organizations, represents the major effort at organizing Hispanics in the social service system. COSSHMO offers advocacy services, seminars, conferences, and networking services. Most of the membership at COSSHMO represents Mexican or Chicano community agencies, so that the appeal of the organization to all Hispanics is somewhat limited.

Hispanics are creating and developing new agencies in the communities where they live. Most are social organizations that served White immigrants for many decades and that due to changes in the composition of the neighborhood population now find themselves serving Hispanic immigrants. These agencies suffer through upheavals and tension while the old and new immigrants establish working relationships that allow for maintenance of the facility and continuation of the services. On some occasions the transition from old to new immigrant groups does not occur, and agencies are known to collapse in the ensuing battle for control (Cafferty et al., 1981).

Successful transitions occur when the older immigrant group and Hispanics are able to orchestrate a natural process of change. Of course the first sign of change is in the nature of the clientele, where after a few years almost all seem to be Hispanic; by then, staff positions are being filled with Hispanic clerical staff, paraprofessionals, and later on professionals. In most cases the board of directors of the agency begins to recognize the need for Hispanic representation on the board and starts to include them. Still, control might rest on a non-Hispanic executive director and a majority non-Hispanic board. Normally several years might pass under these conditions until such a point that the board feels they are ready to transfer administrative leadership to a Hispanic person. This process takes place not without pain for everybody involved, but results in the community keeping the funding resources that make these types of agencies possible. Examples of the process abound in many cities with a large concentration of Hispanics.

While the agencies become more responsive to the needs of the Hispanic population there remains the issue of dissemination of information. For Hispanics, a productive method of disseminating information about available services is participation of agencies in community forums such as schools, churches, and grass-roots organizations. Furthermore, the staff of social service organizations should be encouraged to be active in community affairs to build the trust neccesary for effective dispensation of services.

Public Policy Issues

Although very little information is available on Hispanics and the social service system in the United States, some preliminary recommendations are appropriate:

- Hispanics cannot be served as a homogeneous population. Their diversity of cultures, different histories, and different patterns of assimilation must be understood and acknowledged.
- Recognition and support of natural help networks is particularly important to the Hispanic population. Especially, a development of public/private partnership involving the churches should be encouraged since they provide social services and natural networking within the Hispanic community.
- Schools of social work need to develop a curriculum which addresses cultural values and specific needs of Hispanics and to recruit and train Hispanic social workers. In addition, staff of agencies serving Hispanic communities should receive Spanish-language training.
- Much more information is needed to design social policies and programs to serve Hispanics. Schools of social work and other institutions should take the lead in designing research which will define the reality of the Hispanic experience.

References

Angel, R., and M. Tienda. 1982. "Determinants of Extended Household Structure: Cultural Pattern or Economic Need?" *American Journal of Sociology* 87:1360-83.

Baca-Zinn, M. 1979. "Chicano Family Research: Conceptual Distortions and Alternative Directions." *Journal of Ethnic Studies* 7:59-71.

Baron, Augustine. 1979. *The Utilization of Mental Health Services by Mexican-Americans: A Critical Analysis.* San Francisco: R. & E. Research Associates.

Bustamente, Jorge A. 1977. "Undocumented Immigration from Mexico: Research Report." *International Migration Review* 11 (no. 2): 149-77.

Cafferty, P.S.J., W. McCready, and C. Rivera-Martínez. 1981. "A Pilot Study of Social Service Providers and Hispanic Assimilation." Chicago: Technical report to the Ford Foundation and the Taylor Institute.

Cameron, J.D., and E. Talavera. 1976. "Advocacy Program for Spanish-Speaking People." *Social Casework* 57 (July): 427-31.

Cole, J., and M. Pilisuk. 1976. "Differences in the Provision of Mental Health Services by Race." *American Journal of Orthopsychiatry* 46 (July):510-25.

Cooney, R.S., and A. Colon. 1980. "Work and Family: The Recent Struggle of Puerto Rican Females." In C. Rodrígues, V. Sánchez Korrol, and J. D. Alers, eds. *The Puerto Rican Struggle: Essays on Survival in the United States* New York: Puerto Rican Migration Research Consortium.

Delgado, M. 1979. "A Grass Root Model for a Needs Assessment in Hispanic Communities." *Child Welfare* 58:571-76.

Delgado, M., and D. Humm-Delgado. 1982. "Natural Support Systems: Source of Strength in Hispanic Communities." *Social Work* 27 (January).

de Váldez, Aragon T., and J. Gallegos. 1982. "The *Chicano Familia* in Social Work." In James W. Green, ed., *Cultural Awareness in the Human Services.* Englewood Cliffs, N.J.: Prentice-Hall.

Durán, R.P. 1983. *Hispanics' Education and Background.* New York: College Entrance Examination Board.

Estrada, Leopardo F. 1980. "Language and Political Consciousness among the Spanish-Speaking in the U.S." In D.J.R. Bruckner, ed., *Politics and Language: Spanish and English in the United States.* Chicago: Center for Policy Studies, University of Chicago.

Fishman, R.G. 1979. "Notes on Culture as a Variable in Providing Human Services in Social Service Agencies." *Human Organizations* 38 (Summer):189, 192.

Fitzpatrick, J. 1971. *Puerto Rican Americans: The Meaning of Migration to the Mainland.* Englewood Cliffs, N.J.: Prenctice-Hall.

Giachello, Aida L. 1984. "Hispanics and Health Care." In Pastora San Juan Cafferty and William C. McCready, eds., *Hispanics in the United States: A New Social Agenda.* New Brunswick, N.J.: Transaction.

Giachello, A.L., S. Puente, and P. Andrade. 1981. *Profile: Hispanas Revealing the Mosaic.* Chicago: Illinois Hispanic Women's Conference.

Green, James W., ed. 1982. *Cultural Awareness in the Human Services.* Englewood Cliffs, N.J.: Prentice-Hall.

Gruber, M. 1980. "Inequality in the Social Services." *Social Service Review* 54 (March):59-75.

Hess, R. 1970. "Social Class and Ethnic Influences upon Socialization." In P. Mussen, ed., *Carmichael's Manual of Child Psychology*. New York: Wiley.

Hesse, K.A.F. 1976. "Paraprofessionals as a Referral Link in the Mental Health Delivery System." *Community Mental Health Journal* 12 (Fall):252-58.

Institute for Social Research Newsletter. 1982. "Maintaining a Group Culture." East Lansing: The University of Michigan, Institute for Social Research.

Jenkins, S. 1980. "The Ethnic Agency Defined." *Social Service Review* 54 (June):249-61.

Johnson, S. 1981. "Interim Conclusions of the Family Impact Seminar." In J. Tropman, M. Dluhy, and R. Lind, eds., *New Strategic Perspectives on Social Policy*. New York: Pergamon.

Kamerman, S. 1983. "The New Mixed Economy of Welfare: Public and Private." *Social Work* 28 (January-February):5-11.

Kamerman, S.B., and A. Kahn. 1976. *Social Services in the United States*. Philadelphia: Temple University Press.

Laosa, L. 1980. "Maternal Teaching Strategies in Chicano and Anglo-American Families: The Influence of Culture and Education on Maternal Behavior." *Child Development* 51:759-65.

Maldonado, L. 1979. "Internal Colonialism and Triangulation: A Research Example." *Social Service Review* 53 (September):464-73.

Martínez, Marco A. 1985. *"Hispanic Identity: Toward a Model of Socialization for Hispanic Identity: The Case of Mexican-Americans*. Chapter 4 in this volume.

Mizio, E., and A. Delaney. 1981. *Training for Service Delivery to Minority Clients*. New York: Family Service Association of America.

National Association of Social Workers (NASW). 1977. *Encyclopedia of Social Work*, 17th ed. New York: NASW.

_____. 1982. "Social Work and People of Color." Special Issue 27 (January).

National Commission for Employment Policy. 1982. *"Hispanics and Jobs: Barriers to Progress."* Report no. 14. Washington.

Olmstead, K. 1983. "The Influence of Minority Social Work Students on an Agency's Service Methods." *Social Work* 28 (July-August).

Ozawa, M. 1983. "Income Security: The Case of Nonwhite Children." *Social Work* 28 (September-October):347-53.

Ramírez, M., and A. Castañeda. 1974. *Cultural Democracy, Bicognitive Development, and Education*. New York: Academic Press.

Rodríguez, O. 1982. "Methodological and Conceptual Criteria for the Study of the Utilization of Services by Hispanics." Paper presented at the 1982 meeting of the Society for the Study of Social Problems.

Rubenstein, H., and M. Bloch. 1978. "Helping Clients Who Are Poor: Workers and Client Perceptions of Problems, Activities and Outcomes." *Social Service Review* 52 (March):69-82.

Rubin, Allan. 1983. *Statistics on Social Work Education in the United States, 1983*. New York: Council on Social Work Education.

Samuda, R.J. 1975. *Psychological Testing of American Minorities*. New York: Dodd, Mead.

Scott, J.I., and M. Delgado. 1979. "Planning Mental Health Programs for Hispanic Communities." *Social Casework* 60:451-56.

Stehno, S. 1982. "Differential Treatment of Minority Children in Service Systems." *Social Work* 27 (January):39-46.

U.S. Department of Commerce, Bureau of the Census. 1982. *Provisional Estimates of Social, Economic, and Housing Characteristics*. PHC 80-51-1. Washington: U.S. Government Printing Office (March).

———. 1982. *Supplementary Report: Persons of Spanish Origin by States, 1980*. PC 80 Si-7 (August).

———. 1983. *Conditions of Hispanics in America Today*. Washington: U.S. Government Printing Office.

United Way of Chicago. 1982. "Reports of the Ad Hoc Committee on Hispanic Concern." Chicago.

Villalpando, Mañuel. 1980. "Facts and Myths about the Illegal Migrant." In Robert S. Landmann, ed., *The Problem of the Undocumented Worker*. Washington: U.S. Government Printing Office.

Watkins, T., and R. González. 1982. "Outreach to Mexican Americans." *Social Work* 27 (January):68-73.

10

Hispanics and the Criminal Justice System

Leo M. Romero and *Luis G. Stelzner*

A recurring theme in many of these chapters is the lack of research on Hispanics in substantive areas of social science. Nowhere is this more apparent than in the criminal justice system, where scholars and others have concluded that the problems of Hispanics are similar to those of Blacks and therefore do not merit investigation. Data bases which might offer information on Hispanics have frequently classified them as "other" and "non-white". In addition, the uniqueness of each Hispanic group makes it problematic to draw inferences to other Hispanic groups. Leo Romero and Luis Stelzner review the literature on Hispanics in the criminal justice system. The bulk of this literature focuses on Mexican-Americans. Romero and Stelzner contend that relations between police and Mexican-Americans are poor, in part because of language problems and civil rights violations. Mexican-Americans appear to have unusually high arrest and incarceration rates. Within the structure of the criminal justice system, Mexican-Americans are underrepresented in the judiciary and bar in every Southwestern state except New Mexico. Romero and Stelzner note that Hispanics have "higher victimization rates than non-Hispanics; but in most cases their rates of reporting crime to the police are lower than for the non-Hispanic population." Aside from a few isolated studies, little research has been conducted on Puerto Ricans, Cubans, and Central and South Americans. In their public policy section, Romero and Stelzner propose a research agenda which covers a broad range of topics such as the attitudes of Hispanic communities on crime, incarceration and guilty verdict rates for Hispanics, and the incidence of juvenile delinquency among Hispanics.

Until quite recently, little attention has been paid to the experiences of Hispanics in the criminal justice system. In a comprehensive review, Trujillo (1974) found only eighteen studies concerning Hispanics and crime from 1900 to 1940. By contrast, Savitz (1973) found over 500 articles on Blacks in the criminal system for the same period. One reason for the small number of empirical studies of Hispanics in the criminal system appears to be the assumption that Hispanic experiences are similar to those of Blacks and thus do not require independent research.

Empirical research has now begun to focus on the different experiences of various minority groups in the criminal system. For example, in a 1969 study of police-minority relations in Denver, Colorado, Bayley and Mendelsohn (1969:v) analyzed Denver's population in terms of three distinct ethnic groups: (1) Whites of non-Mexican-American extraction (2) Blacks and (3) Spanish surnames. These authors recognized that

> these divisions within the community are a result of a combination of cultural and racial factors that create feelings of social difference and group identity. People of Mexican-American heritage, while tending to be Latin in appearance, have in common the Spanish language, an historical tradition, and a sense of cultural uniqueness.

Each Hispanic group is unique and similar experiences cannot be assumed without empirical verification. Sissons (1979) suggested that a concern with Hispanic experiences in the legal system in American society is long overdue.

The 1970 U.S. Census permitted people to classify themselves in one of five Spanish heritage categories: Mexican, Puerto Rican, Cuban, Central and South American, and Hispano. The complexity of the issues surrounding attempts to separate Spanish heritage groups into identifiable groups cannot be minimized (Jaffe et al., 1980:9-20). Most research in the post-World War II period focused on Hispanics in the Southwest. The majority of people of Spanish heritage in the region identified themselves as Mexican-American (or Chicano) or Hispano.

Mandel (1979) discussed the underrepresentation of Hispanics in criminal justice statistics. Before 1980, Hispanics were listed as "White." In addition, most local statistics have ignored Hispanics as a group, so that on the local and national levels almost nothing is known about the arrest statistics of Hispanics. Mandel also noted that specific information on Hispanics is often also lacking in surveys of juvenile delinquency and victimization because ethnicity has usually been considered irrelevant.

In sum, it appears that two major factors have contributed to the lack of data on Mexican-Americans and Hispanics within the criminal justice system: treatment of them as White in census and other data collection, and scholarly perception of their problems as common to those of Blacks and other minorities. Perceived in this way, Mexican-Americans and other

Hispanics have become nonexistent within studies of the criminal justice system.

Mexican-Americans

As far back as 1931, the Wickersham Commission Report analyzed the extent of criminal involvement by foreign-born Americans, their relations with the criminal justice system in general, and public attitudes toward the immigrant population and crime. A large section of the report is devoted to the problem of criminal justice and Mexicans in the United States, specifically in Texas, Illinois, and several California cities. The report discussed relations between Mexicans and the police, disposition of their cases in court, sentencing, and Mexican communities' conception of American justice. The report concluded that Mexicans face heavier police deployment and, compared to other citizens, are more likely to face illegal police practices, language barrier, overt racism, and discrimination in the administration of the law.

Paul Warshuis and Paul Taylor, reporters for the Wickersham Report, showed how law enforcement and the general public viewed Mexicans as lawless and criminal. But Max Handman, another researcher for the report, stated: "there is no evidence to show that the Mexicans run afoul of the law any more than anyone else, and if the complete facts were known they would most likely show that they are less delinquent in Texas than the non-Mexican population of the same community."

By focusing on the foreign-born, the Wickersham Report limited its value with regard to Mexican-Americans born in the United States. Nevertheless, because of the close contact and common experiences between immigrant and native Hispanics, the report's findings are also useful with regard to Mexican-Americans.

Another major government report, on the state level, appeared prior to the Wickersham Report in 1930. Governor Young's Report (1930:205), *Mexicans in California* (1930), included a detailed analysis of the roles of Mexicans in California society at that time and their relationship to crime and the criminal justice system. The authors of the report concluded:

> It is not possible to draw any close comparison of the incidence of crime among the Mexican population as compared to the general population. It would appear to be very high but the comparison is affected by the fact that more men than women have entered the country and the age distribution gives a large proportion of Mexicans in the age groups most commonly found in prison. Police officials generally state greater tendency among arrested Mexicans to plead guilty to charges and the common inability to extended

defense and appeal cases, both undoubtedly increase the apparent crime among Mexicans.

The most recent major governmental report was a study of discrimination against Mexican-Americans by police and court agencies in Arizona, California, Colorado, New Mexico, and Texas. The study was undertaken in 1967-68 by the U.S. Commission on Civil Rights to explore allegations of discrimination against Mexican-Americans by criminal justice agencies in the Southwest. The commission heard testimony from some 500 criminal justice employees and private citizens. The commission studied Mexican-American representation on juries and in personnel positions in the criminal justice system. In addition, it studied the processing of complaints and community relations practices of 793 law enforcement agencies (280 responses). The report documented findings on treatment of Mexican-Americans by police and courts, the language barrier, and employment of Mexican-Americans by criminal justice agencies. A bleak picture was painted of the relationship between Mexican-Americans and Southwestern criminal justice systems. The commission found that Mexican-Americans viewed criminal justice agencies with distrust, fear, and hostility; that they were being subjected to unduly harsh treatment by police; that they were often arrested on insufficient grounds, abused physically and verbally, and subjected to disproportionately severe penalties; that they were being denied proper use of bail and adequate representation by counsel; and that they were substantially underrepresented on grand and petit juries. Mexican-Americans were underrepresented as employees in law enforcement agencies, especially in supervisory positions. The language barrier between Spanish-speaking citizens and English-speaking officials further aggravated the problem. Recommendations for remedying the problems identified in the commission's investigation were directed to Congress, federal agencies, and the states.

It has frequently been said that the decade 1968-78 was one of major advances for Mexican-Americans in the Southwest. A 1980 study by the Texas Advisory Committee to the U.S. Commission on Civil Rights, a follow-up to the 1970 report, indicated that Texas, at all governmental levels, consistently underemployed, underrepresented, underutilized, and underestimated Hispanics. The Texas Advisory Committee reported that while Hispanics were frequently employed in rough equivalence to their percentage of the population, both in terms of responsibility and salary they were almost always concentrated in the lowest levels. Hispanics were represented in very small numbers among those who actually enforced Texas laws. The report found particularly disturbing the underrepresentation of Mexican-Americans in the state's judiciary.

In a separate report published in 1980, the Texas Advisory Committee found that Black and Mexican-American representation in government positions changed little during 1968-78. In fact, Texas did not compare well with other Southern and Southwestern states with respect to percentages of minority employees in state government.

Bondavalli (1981) suggested that Spanish-speaking residents, specifically Mexican-Americans and Puerto Ricans, are frequently faced with socioeconomic and emotional pressures often associated with crime. Their income and educational levels are below average, and their residence in an unfamiliar culture deprives them of familiar cues and controls. The amount of crime in Spanish-speaking communities, however, has not been determined. The author suggested that more data must be collected if significant questions regarding the nature and extent of crime in Spanish-speaking communities are to be answered. The available information suggests that there is need for considerable improvement in the processing of Spanish-speaking defendants because they are often distrustful of law enforcement officials, who, in turn, often misunderstand and sometimes mistreat Hispanic suspects. Police officers should be aware of cultural traits which might have an effect on interaction. Bondavalli also suggested that the non-English-speaking defendant's right to counsel, to confront and cross-examine witnesses, and to a fair trial require the presence of an interpreter. The Supreme Court, however, has not ruled on the rights of non-English-speaking defendants, and several critical areas remain unclear. For example, provision of an interpreter at early stages of the criminal process (arrest, bail setting, preliminary hearings) has rarely been required. In addition, Spanish-speaking defendants who are found guilty present a special problem to correctional officials. Traditional therapy is often difficult to apply to them since the intimacies necessary in therapy are traditionally avoided by Hispanics.

Recent research has focused academic attention on problems faced by Hispanics in the criminal justice system and on the inadequacy of the general research into those problems. The extent and nature of those problems is still very much unanswered by the research to date. Mandel (1979) suggested that a principal factor contributing to the inadequate understanding of the Hispanic experience in the criminal justice system is that the six major sources of criminal justice statistics—arrests, courts, prisoners, juvenile delinquency, crime victimization, and public surveys—have rarely included data on Hispanic background.

La Free (1981) complained that the 1970 U.S. Civil Rights Commission Report on the administration of justice in the Southwest provided little systematic empirical data. The report collected data by conducting interviews with law enforcement personnel and private citizens, by holding hearings in various Southwestern cities, and by mailing questionnaires to law enforcement agencies. The report contains an appendix on the percentage of grand jurors with Spanish surnames in selected California counties and six data tables. Two tables show the distribution of Spanish surname citizens in five Southwestern states; one compares the median level of education for Spanish-surname persons with other persons; and three set forth ethnicity figures of police and state court employees, district attorneys, public prosecutors, and law clerks.

The report was mainly concerned with individual cases of official misbehavior. It is descriptive and does not provide data to determine the frequency, extent, or duration of misconduct, nor does the report include factors for determining how such cases of misconduct toward Hispanics compare to the treatment other citizens receive. Research based on impressionistic or unsystematic accounts is not as useful as solid empirical evidence of the broad experience of Hispanics in the criminal justice system (La Free, 1981).

The Criminal Justice System

In addition to the general research summarized above, substantial literature is developing with regard to the involvement of Mexican-Americans in specific stages of the criminal justice system. Some commentators have suggested that this more focused research has tended to be more objective and systematic than the general material (La Free, 1981).

Available evidence suggests an unusually high arrest and incarceration rate among Mexican-Americans (Mandel, 1979). There is little agreement on the reasons for these phenomena. Prior to 1979 arrest or incarceration statistics on Hispanics were not systematically collected. This precluded accurate understanding of the scope of the problem. Since 1980 all major sources reporting to the FBI Crime Reports have been required to reflect data on Hispanic origin. This improved data base will permit researchers to measure the magnitude of the problem and investigate its causes with greater scientific accuracy.

Sotomayer (1979) cited a Texas study that showed that arrested Hispanic youths faced mostly minor charges but were generally taken to court rather than released to parents or referred to services, despite the prevalence of intact families among Hispanics. Moreover, criminal justice facilities were distant from the population.

Sotomayer further indicated that traditional psychotherapeutic and law enforcement approaches are not effective in dealing with gangs of youths in Hispanic communities. The author recommended that future research efforts should focus on the whole behavioral ecology of communities with high rates of juvenile crime. A firm understanding of crime and juvenile deliquency among Hispanics is lacking, and these problems, according to Sotomayer, are almost never addressed in terms of community crime prevention. Research indicates that gang violence is a learned phenomenon supported by numerous community factors.

Ross (1978) published the results of tests of five hypotheses concerning social and psychological factors in juvenile delinquency dispositions. The five hypotheses were postulated as follows: (1) the higher the socioeconomic status of a juvenile, the less severe the disposition by the court; (2) Whites are less likely than non-Whites, Blacks, and Mexican-Americans to receive a severe disposition from the court; (3) there will be a significant difference in socioeconomic status between juveniles who receive an accelerated psychiatric evaluation during the court processing of their cases and those who do not; (4) Whites are more likely to receive a psychiatric evaluation than non-Whites during the court processing of their cases; and (5) for those who receive accelerated clinical psychiatric evaluations, the higher the socioeconomic status of a juvenile, the less severe the disposition made by the court. Ross considered in his study traffic and miscellaneous misdemeanors, drug and alcohol related crimes, property crimes, sex-related crimes, and violent offenses. Data from the analysis were tabulated and the first, second, and fifth hypotheses were supported, while the third and fourth were not.

Moore (1978) reported that Mexican-Americans who serve sentences in California prisons tend to come from territorially based youth gangs. Of the approximately 200 gangs in Los Angeles, 100 are Chicano, according to Sotomayer. In addition, they tend to have been imprisoned for offenses involving narcotics. A study sponsored by the U.S. Department of Justice Law Enforcement Assistance Administration and published in 1979 appears to confirm that the most profitable illegitimate opportunities among young Chicanos were in the drug market (Horowitz, 1979). Moore stated that lower-class Hispanic youths are located in two different opportunity environments—one legal but often economicaly marginal, the other illegal. The variations in illegitimate means available for obtaining normal success in the immediate milieu affect the form of delinquency.

Prisons

The prisoner subculture research is inadequate; there is a pressing need for new descriptions and conceptualizations. Very few subculture studies have been conducted in the Southwest region of the United States (Jacobs, 1979).

Jails often cause feelings of depression and isolation which may lead to suiqide. Studies indicate that Hispanic Americans, who have strong family cultures, have a disproportionately high jail suicide rate. French and Porter (1978) suggested that jailers recognize an especially high suicide risk among members of certain ethnic groups and drug and alcohol abusers. Blacks, on the other hand, have lower jail suicide rates.

A paper presented at the 110th Congress of Correction of the American Correctional Association summarized the results of a District of Columbia study and a 5-state study on the current status of minority group corrections employees and minority prisoner organizations. The paper generally concluded that as the proportion of minority group members in prison populations has increased, the number of minority group members employed on corrections staffs has lagged.

An American Justice Institute study of the staff and prisoner organizations of certain prisons in Oregon, Minnesota, California, New York, and New Jersey indicated that sanctioned prisoner organizations were usually composed of one race. However, the study was unable to corroborate the existence of either community-based or prison-based illegal gangs. Only one prison in New York had a minority group staffing pattern corresponding to the size of the minority group most represented at the institution. A prison in New Jersey had the second highest number of minority group staff members, followed by the California prison system.

While communication between Black staff members and Black inmates was generally open, Hispanic inmates tended to isolate themselves from all staff, including Hispanic staff members. The American Justice Institute study includes tabular data, a 6-item list of other of the institute's publications, and a chart showing recent prison organization and management studies.

Judges and Attorneys

Very little is known about Mexican-American judges and attorneys. Padilla (1974) described Mexican-American judges and attorneys from five Southwestern states in terms of family background, ethnicity, religion, education, age, and occupation. Of the 59 federal district court judges in the Southwest, only one was Mexican-American. At the state level, only 1 out of 961 judges was Mexican-American. This low representation persisted throughout the court systems of the five states, with the exception of New Mexico where 18 Mexican-American judges constituted 31.6 percent of the state's total judiciary. Mexican-American state judges generally were born and raised in the state where they held office. Local judges, also, tended to preside in localities where they were born. Nearly all these judges attended undergraduate colleges and universities in their home states. Except for the New Mexico judges, most attended law schools in their own states.

One-fourth to one-third of all Mexican-American attorneys were engaged in private practice. Padilla assumed, however, that most of these attorneys would engage in public practice at some point in their lives. Traditionally, Mexican-American attorneys have been viewed as a distinct elite. They have held either state elective office or judicial positions. Many have served as prosecutors. Some were members of old elite families, and many attended out-of-state law schools. Little is known regarding these attorneys' self-perceptions of their ethnic identities. Further research is needed in this area, particularly in view of the influx in recent years of larger numbers of Mexican-Americans into the legal profession.

Victims of Crime

A 1980 U.S. Department of Justice report included some general findings on the impact of criminal victimization on Hispanics, including Mexican-Americans. The study, based on a representative sample of persons aged twelve and over living in approximately 60,000 households across the country, provided a comprehensive collection of statistical estimates on crime characteristics.

Hispanics in the United States generally have higher victimization rates than non-Hispanics; but in most cases, their rates of reporting crime to the police are lower than for the non-Hispanic population. With few exceptions, estimated crime rates in the Hispanic community in recent years have evidenced no significant upward or downward trend. Despite the prevalence of comparatively higher victimization rates for Hispanics, however, the distribution of violent crime within that population is not unlike that among the non-Hispanic majority. As measured by the National Crime Survey during 1973-78, households headed by a Hispanic person had higher than average rates for residential burglaries and larceny as well as for motor vehicle theft. Also, Hispanics experienced relatively more forcible entry burglaries and completed motor vehicles thefts than did non-Hispanics.

Business and property crimes, involving no direct contact between perpetrators and victims, were committed in higher numbers against non-Hispanics. Consideration of sociodemographic variables revealed that Hispanic males were victimized to a higher degree than Hispanic females; young Hispanics between the ages of twelve and nineteen accounted for the largest number of both victims and perpetrators of violent crimes. The report indicates that violent crimes against Hispanics were committed by individuals who were poor, unemployed, and raised in broken homes (i.e., with divorced, separated, or unmarried parents). An important factor in the comparative survey, possibly influencing the accuracy of victimization data, is the higher rate of crime reporting to the police by non-Hispanics than by Hispanics.

Crime, Police, and Civil Liberties

Miranda (1980) compared the attitudes of Mexican-Americans with those of Black and White respondents on the issues of crime, the police, and civil liberties. The study sought to assess attitudes of Mexican-Americans toward the police and compare them with attitudes of White and Black respondents in a National Opinion Research Center (Ennis, 1967) study. Miranda also tested Richard L. Block's major hypothesis, from a 1971 study, concerning fear of crime, fear of the police, support for increased police power, and support for civil liberties in a Mexican-American community. The Miranda study setting was a Mexican barrio in a southern California community with approximately 150,000 inhabitants. A random sample of households yielded 170 completed interviews. The hypothesis that fear of crime is associated with greater support for the police was only moderately supported in the NORC survey of White and Black respondents, but it was strongly supported in the Mexican-American sample. The hypothesis that persons who feared the police most were most likely to support the protection of civil liberties found considerable support in the NORC study among White respondents but not among Black respondents. Seventy percent of the Mexican-Americans who feared the police supported the protection of civil liberties.

Among the three racial-ethnic groups, increases in the crime rate generally led to greater support for increasing police power and limiting civil liberties, while fear of the police seemed to lessen support for police power and to increase support for civil guarantees. Despite these similarities, the groups differed in their degree of support for and fear of the police and in the degree of their fear of crime and advocacy of civil liberties.

The authors of a survey based on interviews with 150 persons released from federal prison, under the National Addict Rehabilitation Act, describe what they viewed as five distinct lifestyles associated with addiction: (1) expressive student, (2) social world alternator, (3) low-rider, (4) barrio addict, and (5) ghetto hustler. The first two come primarily from middle- or upper-class socioeconomic backgrounds, and the last three from working-class or impoverished homes. Barrio addicts are mostly Mexican-American; ghetto addicts are mostly Black; social world alternators are ethnically mixed; and expressive students, who all share some form of intellectual or quasi-intellectual (hippie) counterculture, appear to be the most receptive to rehabilitation and the most reachable through group therapy. Social world alternators are likely to react to rehabilitation programs with both spectacular successes and dramatic failures. Low-riders, barrio addicts, and ghetto hustlers are poorer rehabilitation risks, because they have poorer prospects of achieving a legitimate way of life (Lewis and Glasser, 1978).

The amount of crime in the Hispanic community has not been accurately determined (Bondavalli, 1981). Although ethnicity will probably be properly classified starting in 1980 so as to conform to the FBI Uniform Crime Reports, a firm understanding of crime and delinquency among Hispanics is now lacking (Sotomayer, 1979).

The 1970 U.S. Commission on Civil Rights Report found that Hispanics were at a distinct disadvantage under discretionary decision-making laws. The discretion afforded to the police, prosecution, jury system, and judiciary was particularly injurious to Mexican-Americans. The commission also found that Mexican-Americans were deprived of proper use of bail and of adequate representation by counsel. The language problem also contributed to difficulties in the equitable administration of justice to Mexican-Americans. Given the paucity of statistics on Hispanics, more research should yield answers to questions on Mexican-Americans as well as other Hispanic groups.

Puerto Ricans

The 1976 report of the U.S. Commission on Civil Rights focused on the U.S. mainland Puerto Rican population. Puerto Ricans are the next largest single Hispanic group behind Mexican-Americans (6.7 million persons), with nearly 1.7 million persons of Puerto Rican birth or parentage living on the U.S. mainland. Most of this number came to the mainland after World War II. Puerto Ricans represent less than 1 percent of the continental U.S. population. But in New York City, 10 percent of the residents and 23 percent of the schoolchildren are Puerto Rican. Just across the Hudson River in Hoboken, New Jersey, almost one-fourth of the population is Puerto Rican. Major cities such as Chicago, Philadelphia, Cleveland, Newark, Hartford, and Boston also have large Puerto Rican communities.

The 1976 report confirmed that Puerto Ricans comprise a distinct ethnic group with concerns and priorities that frequently differ from those of other minorities, even other Spanish heritage groups. Puerto Ricans suffer the problems of all those whose language, culture, and/or skin color have caused them to be victims of discrimination.

The incidence of poverty and unemployment for Puerto Ricans is more severe than that of virtually any other ethnic group in the United States. As of March 1975, 11.6 percent of all Americans were below the low-income level, and 32.6 percent of mainland Puerto Ricans were below the poverty level. By contrast, 24 percent of Mexican-Americans and 14.3 percent of Cuban-Americans fell below the poverty level (U.S. Bureau of the Census Report, 1975).

At the same time, while the median income for all U.S. families was $12,836 per year, Puerto Rican families earned only $7,629. Mexican-American families earned $9,498 and Cuban-American and "other Spanish" families had incomes of $11,410. While 14 percent of Cuban-American families and 24 percent of Mexican-American families were poor, nearly one-third, 32.6 percent, of mainland Puerto Rican families lived in poverty. (U.S. Commission on Civil Rights, 1976, Table 19).

The report shows that 17.4 percent of mainland Puerto Rican adults had completed less than five years of school, compared to 3.3 percent of all U.S. adults. More than 62 percent of all U.S. adults were high school graduates, compared to 28.7 percent of Puerto Rican adults. Fifty-one percent of Cuban-Americans and 31 percent of Mexican-Americans completed high school. As these figures demonstrate, the mainland Puerto Rican community is not only far below the U.S. average in important socioeconomic areas, but also below other major Hispanic groups.

Despite the significant economic and social differences among Hispanics reflected by the data, relatively little research has been done on Puerto Rican and other non-Mexican-American Hispanics and their relationship to the criminal justice system. Puerto Rican involvement in the criminal justice system was examined by Sissons (1979) in a study of the official data and available statistics relating to the New York Puerto Rican community in correctional institutions. Because very little data is available on Puerto Ricans in the criminal justice system, Sissons relied on the few correctional institutions which offered the most complete and reliable data. Data from a federal court were also used to determine whether Puerto Rican offenders' involvement in the criminal justice system was different from that of other offenders. The authors suggested that several theoretical approaches to the interaction between Hispanic and other cultural groups have been developed, but none has provided a satisfactory basis for understanding the importance of ethnicity for the Hispanic clients of the courts, the prisons, and the probation and parole systems. Sissons also described the relationships between the extralegal characteristics of offenders and the discretionary judgments of criminal justice professionals.

Prisons

A recent cross-sectional survey that collected both cultural and personal history data from ninety-three Puerto Rican inmates in four New Jersey penal institutions found that the problems of the Puerto Rican offender are part of a larger problem faced by minority groups after immigrating to the

United States (Lee, 1979). Often these immigrants must confront antagonistic, stereotypical attitudes toward both criminal offenders and the racial or ethnic minority.

Programs to serve minorities frequently are based on stereotypes, and therefore often fail to appreciate the inmates' real needs. An in-depth profile of Puerto Rican prisoners indicates that Puerto Ricans as a group exhibit as much diversity as sameness. For example, almost all Puerto Rican prisoners (93 percent) had no criminal history in Puerto Rico and first became addicted to drugs or involved in gang activity in the United States.

Diversity in attitudes among Puerto Rican prisoners was apparent depending on age, length of residence in the United States, place of residence, and previous criminal history. Lee recommended that criminal justice programs acquire more Spanish-speaking persons in the courts, correctional institutions, and in public defender positions.

Cuban-Americans

Despite the fact that Cuban-Americans are the third largest Hispanic group in the United States, there is virtually no literature on the Cuban-American and the criminal justice system. The absence of such research may reflect the fact that there has been relatively little involvement of the Cuban-American in the criminal justice system before the more recent arrivals from Cuba. The earlier immigrants tended to be drawn from the wealthier, the better educated, the more urban, and the higher occupational sectors (Fagan et al., 1968).

A recent study found that the composition of the Cuban flow to the United States has not been stable over time. Almost 600 persons were interviewed in 1973-74 and compared with earlier Cuban emigre samples (Portes et al., 1981). While caution is required in comparing occupational categories across samples, there appeared to be substantial differences between the two groups. Notwithstanding the lower occupational and social status of the 1973-74 respondents, Cuban-Americans still had a relatively higher standard of living than Puerto Ricans and Mexican-Americans. Nevertheless, there would appear to be significant differences within the Cuban-American community. These differences may have dramatically increased with the arrival of the "Mariel" Cubans.

The only study that touches on Cubans and the criminal justice system is Willbanks' (1980). Statistical data and graphs included in this report reflected changes in the ethnic composition of Dade County, Florida, over a 22-year period (1956-78). The report describes the changes in ethnic composition as highly relevant to the changing patterns of violent crime and unnatural death. The increase of violent crime during 1958-78 was paralleled by a dramatic increase in three major local ethnic groups. The population increase for Hispanics, primarily Cubans, was almost 3,000 percent; 258 percent for Blacks, and 85 percent for Whites.

A study of Cuban lawyers analyzed the utilization or underutilization of the education and training brought by Cuban lawyers. It described the adaptation process and how much of their competence was transferable under conditions existing in the United States since January 1, 1959 (Moncarz, 1972). The sample involved forty-eight replies to a questionnaire sent randomly to 100 Cuban lawyers. The study determined that Cuban lawyers found it difficult to obtain jobs in their original professions because their training in Cuba did not prepare them for practice in the American legal system. Seventy-seven percent of the respondents had been unable to practice law and had to take jobs completely unrelated to their profession.

Central and South Americans

Research disclosed no studies concerning Hispanic groups other than Mexican-Americans, Puerto Ricans, and Cuban-Americans and their involvement in the criminal justice system. The research on Hispanics does not focus specifically on Central and South Americans.

Although the 1970 U.S. Census permitted people to classify themselves in one of five Hispanic categories—Mexican, Puerto Rican, Cuban, and Central and South American—the last two classifications and the statistical data gathered from this source are not necessarily true indicators of the existence of other Hispanic groups in the United States. For example, in addition to Puerto Ricans, the 1970 Census found more than half a million other Hispanic people living in the New York metropolitan area, but the true number is much higher. The federal government estimates that more than 1 million illegal aliens reside in New York and that 75 percent are Hispanic (mainly Colombians, Dominicans, Argentinians, Ecuadorians, and citizens of different Central American republics). Many reportedly arrive here illegally and try to pass as Puerto Ricans, who are U.S. citizens by birthright, so that they may get a Social Security card and qualify for better jobs (*New York Times,* 18 August 1974). Without legal status as either citizens or resident aliens, these Hispanics are politically disenfranchised and easy prey as victims of employers, landlords, and crime (Wagenheim, 1975).

Public Policy Issues

A great deal of study remains to be done with regard to Hispanics and the criminal justice system. For example, even the early studies of the

1930s point to disparate treatment of Mexican-Americans throughout the system. More scientific data is required on this subject to complement the generally descriptive or impressionistic works of the past. With regard to Puerto Ricans the research is scanty. Cubans and Central and South Americans have been virtually ignored. Attention should be paid to the diversity among different Hispanic groups in the United States, and even within those groups. Research must be done to determine a number of issues:

- The proportion of Hispanics in crime reports, arrests, prosecutions, dismissals, guilty pleas (including plea bargains), guilty verdicts, executed sentences, incarcerations, probation, etc. The proportion of Hispanics at each stage in the criminal justice system.
- What variables predict case outcomes? Do these variables differ for Hispanics and others? If so, for what processing decisions?
- Has the proportion of Hispanic defendants and crime victims and the determinants of case processing decisions changed over time? If so, in what ways? Have Hispanic defendants received adequate representation by counsel? What proportion of Hispanic defendants suffer inordinately high bail? Does bail differ for Hispanics and other defendants? What variables predict high bail? What proportion of Hispanic defendants are released on their own recognizance? What effect does case seriousness and evidence (e.g. eyewitness and expert testimony) have on this decision? Does this differ for Hispanic defendants and other defendants?
- What is the incidence of juvenile delinquency for Hispanics? To what extent does that incidence differ from that of other ethnic groups? What are the socioeconomic variables that affect the form of Hispanic juvenile delinquency? Does the existence of an illegal opportunity market directly affect the form of delinquency?
- What are the characteristics of Hispanic defendants? How do such characteristics compare to those of other defendants?
- What are the characteristics of Hispanic victims? How do they compare to those of other victims?
- What proportion of grand and petit juries are Hispanic? What are their characteristics compared to other jurors? Has the proportion of Hispanic criminal justice officials (judges, prosecutors, defense counsel, probation and parole officers, police and prison officials) increased? If so, has this affected discretionary decisionmaking? How are the characteristics of Hispanic criminal justice officials related to processing decisions?
- The availability of Spanish-speaking counselors, psychiatrists, etc., in prisons and jails. How do such personnel affect the therapy and rehabilitation of Hispanic inmates? What is the availability of interpreters throughout the criminal process? What effect do the language variables have in processing decisions?

- What are the attitudes of Hispanic communities on crime, the police, and civil liberties? How do Hispanic attitudes compare to those of Black Americans, Whites, and others? What is the relationship between the environmental ecology of Hispanic communities and their attitudes on crime, the police, and civil liberties?
- There is a need for a data base to measure the incidence of police violations of Hispanics' civil rights.

Bibliography

Avena, J. Richard, et al. 1980. *Texas: The State of Civil Rights. Ten Years Later, 1968-1978.* Texas State Advisory Committee to the U.S. Commission on Civil Rights. Washington: U.S. Government Printing Office.

Bayley, David H., and Harold Mendelsohn. 1969. *Minorities and the Police: Confrontations in America.* New York: Free Press. Collier-Macmillan Canada.

Bondavalli, B.J. 1981. "Spanish-Speaking People and the North American Criminal Justice System." In *Race, Crime, and Criminal Justice,* ed. R. L. McNeely and Carl E. Pope. Beverly Hills: Sage.

Bonilla, Rubén, Jr. 1979. "A Symposium on Contemporary Issues in Texas Police-Community Relations." Paper presented to the National Minority Advisory Council, San Antonio, Texas (March 23-24).

Brooke, Edward W. 1978. "An Unequal Society: Brutality, Bias against Hispanics." *Washington Post* (May 18).

Castro, Agenor. 1977. "The Hispanic Inmate in Our Nation's Prison Today." Paper presented to the National Minority Advisory Council, Washington (September).

California State Personnel Board. 1978. *Annual Report on the State of California, Affirmative Action Program, 1977-1978.* Sacramento: State Printing Office.

Ennis, Phillip H. 1967. *Criminal Victimization in the United States: A Report of a National Survey.* Chicago: National Opinion Research Center. (The President's Committee on Law Enforcement and Administration of Justice, Field Surveys II.)

Fagan, Richard, Richard A. Brody, and Thomas O'Leary. 1968. *Cubans in Exile: Disaffection and the Revolution.* Palo Alto: Stanford University Press.

French, L., and J. B. Porter. 1978. "Jail Crises: Causes and Control." *In Police and Criminal Psychology,* ed. William Taylor and Michael Bresswell. Washington: University Press of America.

"Governor Young's Report: California State Department of Industrial Relations, 1930." *Mexicans in California: Report of Governor C.C. Young's Committee.* Sacramento, California.

Horowitz, R., 1979. "Delinquency and the Gang or Masked Intimacy." In *Adult Delinquent Gangs in a Chicano Community: Final Narrative Report.* Washington: U.S. Department of Justice Law Enforcement Assistance Administration.

Jacobs, J.B., 1979. "Race Relations and the Prisoner Subculture." In *Crime and Justice: An Annual Review of Research,* vol. 1, ed. Norval Morris and Michael Torvy. Chicago: University of Chicago Press.

Jaffe, A.J., Ruth M. Cullen, and Thomas D. Boswell. 1980. *The Changing Demography of Spanish Americans.* New York: Academic Press.

La Free, G.D. 1981. *"Official Reactions to Hispanic Defendants and Victims in Three Southwestern Cities."* Research Project, Sociology Department, University of New Mexico.

Lee, R.J. 1979. "Profile of Puerto Rican Prisoners in New Jersey and Its Implications for the Administration of Criminal Justice." Rutgers University, M. A. diss. Rockville, Md.: National Criminal Justice Reference Service, Microfiche Program.

Lewis, V., and D. Glaser. 1978. "Lifestyles among Heroin Users." In *Introduction to Corrections: Selected Readings,* ed. George R. Killinger and Paul F. Cromwell, Jr. St. Paul: West.

McWilliams, Cary. 1968. *North from Mexico: The Spanish-Speaking People of the United States.* New York: Greenwood.

Mandel, Jerry. 1979. "Crime and the Hispanic Community." Paper presented to the National Council of the La Raza Symposium Crimen y Justicia (Crime and Justice for Hispanics), Racine, Wisconsin (June 28-30).

_____. 1979. "Hispanics in the Criminal Justice System: The 'Nonexistent' Problem." *Agenda* (May-June): 16-20.

_____. 1978. "The Social and Criminal Impact of Illegal Narcotics Traffic, including Addiction on Minorities and Minority Community." Paper presented to the National Minority Advisory Council on Criminal Justice, Washington (September).

Miranda, A. 1980. "Fear of Crime and Fear of the Police in a Chicano Community." *Sociology and Social Research* 64 (July).

Moncarz, R. 1972. "Cuban Lawyers: Ten Years Later." In *Cuban Exiles in the United States,* ed. C. E. Cortes. New York: Arno.

Montilla, M.R. 1981. "Status of Minorities in Prison Employment: Limited Progress and Uncertain Effects." In *American Correctional Association: Proceedings,* ed. Barbara Hadley Olsson and Ann Dargis. College Park: American Correctional Association.

Moore, J.W. 1978. *Homeboys: Gangs, Drugs, and Prison in the Barrios of Los Angeles.* Philadelphia: Temple University Press.

Morales, Armando. 1972. *Ando Sangrando* (I Am Bleeding). La Puente, Calif.: Perspective.

National Hispanic Leadership Conference. 1977. "We Mutually Pledge." Dallas: Dallas-Fort Worth Spanish-Speaking Program Coordinator Council. *New York Times.* 18 August 1974.

Padilla, F.V. 1974. "Socialization of Chicano Judges and Attorneys." *Atzlan* 5 (Spring-Fall):261-94.

Portes, Alejandro, Juan M. Clark, and Robert L. Bach. 1980. "The New Wave: A Statistical Profile of Recent Cuban Exiles to the United States." In *Cuban Exiles in the United States,* ed. C. E. Cortes. New York: Arno.

Pompa, Gilbert G. 1976. "Ethnic Conflict Resolution in Correctional Institutions." Paper presented to the Mexican-American Correctional Association from Community Relations Services, U.S. Department of Justice (September 25).

Roos, R.A. 1978. "Social Class, Psychiatric Evaluations and Juvenile Court Dispositions in Delinquency Cases." *Dissertation Supplemental Report.* Rockville, Md.: National Crime Justice Reference Service, Microfiche Program.

Sandoval, Rubén, and Douglas R. Martínez. 1978. "Police Brutality: The New Epidemic." *Agenda: A Journal of Hispanic Issues* 8 (September/October):14-22.

Savitz, L. 1973. "Black Crime." In *Comparative Studies of Blacks and Whites in the United States,* seminar, New York.

Silberman, Charles E. 1978. *Criminal Violence, Criminal Justice.* New York: Random House.

Sissons, P.L. 1979. "The Hispanic Experience of Criminal Justice". Bronx: Fordham University Hispanic Research Center.

Sotomayor, M. 1979. "Juvenile Delinquency: A Community Perspective." *Agenda* 9 (September-October):15-19.

Torres, J.L., and M.R. Stansky. 1978. "New Look at the Hispanic Offender: A Proposal by the Puerto Rican Bar Association of New York for a Study of Hispanic Prisoners." Puerto Rican Bar Association of New York.

Trujillo, Larry D. 1974. "La evolución del bandido 'Al Pachuco': A Critical Examination of Criminological Literature on Chicanos." In *Issues in Criminology* 9 (Fall).

U.S. Bureau of the Census. 1975. "Persons of Spanish Origin," Advance Report, Washington (March).

U.S. Commission on Civil Rights. 1980. "A Report on the Participation of Mexican-Americans, Blacks, and Females in the Political Institutions and Processes in Texas, 1968-1978." *Status of Civil Rights in Texas,* vol. 1. Washington.

———. 1976. "Puerto Ricans in the Continental United States: An Uncertain Future." Washington.

———. 1970. "Mexican-Americans and the Administration of Justice in the Southwest." Washington (March).

U.S. Department of Justice, Bureau of Justice Statistics. 1980. "Hispanic Victim: Advance Report." *National Crime Survey Report.* Washington.

———. 1979. "Prisoners in State and Federal Institutions on December 31, 1979." *Full Report.* Washington.

U.S. Government Printing Office. 1978. *The National Manpower Survey of the Criminal Justice System.* Vol. 3: *Corrections.* Washington.

———. 1978. "Parole in the United States, 1976 and 1977." *Uniform Parole Reports.* Washington.

———. 1978. *State and Local Probation and Parole Systems.* Washington.

———. 1977. "National Prisoner Statistics." *NPS Bulletin.* Washington.

———. 1977. *Source Book of Criminal Justice Statistics.* Washington.

Vásquez, Patricia. 1978. "The Courts: An Hispanic Overview." Paper presented to the National Minority Advisory Council, Atlanta, Georgia (December).

Veloz, Esteban V. 1979. "Hispanic Gangs in Los Angeles." Paper presented to the National Council of the La Raza Symposium Crimen y Justicia (Crime and Justice for Hispanics). Racine, Wisconsin (June 28-30).

Wagenheim, K. 1975. *A Survey of Puerto Ricans on the U.S. Mainland in the 1970s.* New York: Praeger.

Wickersham Report. 1931. P. Taylor. "Crime and the Foreign Born: The Problem of the Mexican in Texas." P. Warnhuis. "Crime and Criminal Justice among Mexicans in Illinois. *Report on Crime and the Foreign Born* vol. 2. National Commission on Law Observance and Enforcement.

Willbanks, W. 1980. "Trends in Violent Death in Southern Metropolitan County: A Study of Dade County (Miami), Florida, 1956-1978." In *Contemporary Character of American Homicides*, ed. Margaret Zahn and Marc Riedel. Rockville, Md.: National Institute of Justice.

11

Political Participation

Ricardo Tostado

In this chapter Ricardo Tostado argues that myths and distortions have clouded the reality of Hispanic political participation. He presents data indicating that the long-held assumption that Hispanics are more interested in national than in local politics is not supported by empirical findings. As has been the case with other ethnic groups, Hispanics have experienced a lag time in electing public officials of Hispanic background. In recent years Hispanics have been effective in electing their candidates where their group constitutes a significant proportion of the electorate. Tostado discusses factors which have been offered as explanations for low Hispanic political participation. These include demographic and cultural variables, as well as structural variables such as voter registration laws and availability of bilingual ballots. Tostado concludes by suggesting that political participation by Hispanics will gradually increase over the years, thereby making Hispanics a more powerful group in the political arena.

This chapter presents a discussion of the data and issues involved in understanding the growing participation of people of Hispanic origin in the political life of the country. We will discuss issues of party identification, voter registration, voter behavior, and the mobilization of political strength, all with an eye toward the policy agenda issues which might be involved. Since 1968, there has been more attention in the political science literature to the involvement of Hispanics in politics and political life. Originally much of this literature concentrated on the way Hispanics voted in national elections, and partly for this reason a mythical finding evolved that held that Hispanics were much more interested in national than in local politics.

Since 1975, due in part to the research conducted by SVERP (Southwest Voter Registration Education Project), the political activity of Chicanos in the Southwest has focused almost exclusively on politics at the local level, with a dual result. Not only has there been a 20 percent increase in the number of Hispanics elected to local posts, but there has also been a reversal of the myth that Hispanic voters were only interested in national politics. It is clear that Hispanics will only progress politically by mobilizing their political strength, just as other immigrant ethnic groups have done during the history of this country. Group after group has taken its turn at being the "swing" group in local and national elections. Each has been in a position where their votes were the difference between victory and defeat for specific candidates and parties. By 1984 it is estimated that Chicanos, for example, will be the swing vote in Texas and California, which means they could determine the outcome of elections in states that have nearly 28 percent of the presidential electoral vote.

Each of the issues we will discuss in the following pages has a bearing on the policy implications and agenda-setting processes that will take place over the next decade. How stable is party identification for Hispanic voters and what are the salient issues for them? What is the registration rate in various regions and what are the factors which can influence it? What are appropriate models for the mobilization of Hispanic political strength and how and where is it likely to occur? What are the appropriate research issues and what kinds of data need to be collected?

There are two central reasons why the available literature on Hispanics and politics is so thin: first, there has been relatively little good survey data on which to base empirical studies; and second, there has been a tendency on the part of professional researchers to dichotomize the population into Black and White, ignoring other minority classifications. Only in recent years have the Bureau of the Census and survey groups begun to deal with the question of how to properly include people of Hispanic origin in their data. Accordingly, because of the regionalization and relatively small size of the Hispanic subgroups, the bulk of the usable political science literature deals with Mexicans, and to a lesser extent Puerto Ricans. There has been little empirical work done on other groups, although this situation will eventually be remedied. Our first topic will be party identification and the presumed conservatism of Hispanic voters.

Party Identification

Party identification has been changing in this country for all groups in the population. The authors of one of the most comprehensive studies of American political participation observed: "Perhaps the most dramatic political change in the American public over the past two decades has been the decline of partisanship" (Nie et al., 1976:47). These authors noted that those identifying "strongly" with a party declined from 37 percent in 1952 to 26 percent in 1974. The 1983 General Social Survey data show that 24 percent of the public in that year so identified themselves. Fewer citizens identify with a party; party affiliation is less a guide to electoral choice; parties have lost power both to attract and hold voters; and affiliation is no longer as likely as it once was to be passed along from parents to their children. It is within this changing context that we will try to understand the party identification of Hispanic voters.

Due to the work of the SVERP we have data concerning the party identification of Mexican-Americans. Although this study is not a representative sample, it does provide an approximation of popular opinion. More than 1,800 respondents were asked to name the party with which they identified in 1980. The respondents in the high-income precincts were 82 percent Democrat and those in the low-income precincts were 91 percent Democrat. If this finding is representative (additional research ought to be done around this question), it means that upper-income Mexican-Americans are not nearly as conservative as common political knowledge would have us believe.

Studies by McClesky and Merrill (1973) and Welch et al. (1973) tend to confirm these 1980 findings with approximately 30 percent of Chicano voters describing themselves as "liberal" and less than 20 percent "conservative." However, in 1980 one-quarter of the Chicano vote went to Reagan, and some observers began to speak of a "conservative shift" among Hispanic voters. It may be too early to determine the future of political identification among Hispanics, but there are clearly several simultaneous interacting trends. Party affiliation as a whole is not as strong within the country as it once was, Hispanics are clearly beginning to exert influence in those local areas where their numbers are great, and there is some social status movement within the Hispanic community that may account for some shifting of affiliation. William Velásquez (1982:19) of the SVERP has summarized the situation:

> Taking into account all of these data it would appear that the 1980 Chicano vote in the Presidential election was an aberration and not the culmination of a Chicano conservative trend. The election, however, has afforded the Republican party an excellent opportunity to make inroads into the Chicano vote. With appropriate public policy initiatives the Republicans can transform a blip in the charts into a trend from the Democratic party into the Republican party. Absent those public policy initiatives, it would appear that the Chicano may return to the tradition of voting Democratic in the next election and that the Republicans have missed an opportunity to cut substantially into the Chicano vote.

One implication of this description is that Hispanic voters, like many ethnic voting populations before them, may simply have a much stronger sense of their own group identity and related issues than of party identification. The salient question for Hispanic voters is likely to be "what are *our* candidates and what are *our* issues," rather than "what is the Democratic Party platform." In this way, Hispanic political identification hearkens back to the ethnic voters of the early part of this century.

Voting Behavior

The examination of Hispanic voting in national elections is both relevant and important to the study of American politics, even though much attention needs to be directed toward the local aspects of Hispanic political activity. Much of the literature on ethnic voting in America has reported the difference in political participation between Black and White Americans. These studies have shown that Blacks are less likely to register and vote than Whites (Wolfinger and Rosenstone, 1980; Wilson, 1960; Milbrath and Goel, 1977; Verba and Nie, 1972). Discrimination and disenfranchisement, youth and poor education have all been offered as reasons for this situation.

Data has consistently shown that Hispanics have voted at lower rates than Whites or Blacks, although the interpretations and explanations differ (Levy and Kramer, 1973; Wolfinger and Rosenstone, 1980; Welch, et al., 1973). Researchers who have used multivariate techniques controlling such factors as income, age, education, sex, occupational status, and other variables, have reached mixed conclusions. Some find that when controls are applied Hispanics vote at about the same rate as the rest of the population (Wolfinger and Rosenstone, 1980), while others have found that even when controls are applied Hispanics vote at lower rates in national (Levy and Kramer, 1973), regional (McClesky and Merrill, 1973), and local elections (Antunes and Gaitz, 1975).

Research by principally Hispanic academics has gone a long way in shedding light on these findings and specifying the ways in which factors can combine to constrain voter behavior, independent of culture. Discrimination, registration methods, purging of voter lists, redistricting, have all contributed to lessened participation (García and de la Garza, 1977). One example of how the processes which limit voter participation work can be seen in an analysis of the political behavior of Puerto Ricans in Puerto Rico and those in New York City (Falcón, 1980). Voter turnout in Puerto Rico over the years has averaged near 80 percent and in 1980 it was 76 percent. In New York City, on the other hand, fewer than one-third of Puerto Ricans of voting age are registered and the turnout is as low as 5 percent in some predominantly Puerto Rican districts. Two key variables appear to account for much of the difference. In Puerto Rico registration is done house-to-house like a census, while in New York it is done by the individual devoid of a social context. Additionally, in Puerto Rico elections are only held every four years and then on holidays with a ceremonial flair, while in New York they are held more frequently and during work days.

If we take into account the eligibility requirement of citizenship in order to vote, the gap between Hispanics and others closes considerably. For example, in 1974, according to the Census Bureau, Hispanic voter participation rates were 22.9 percent, with ineligibles figured into the rate and 31 percent if they were taken out—a difference of 8.1 percent. In 1980, according to the same source, the comparable figures were a 29.9 percent rate of participation with the ineligibles in the calculations and 44.1 percent with them out—a difference of 14.2 percent. With the ineligibles in the rate the comparisons for 1980 were Hispanics participating at 29.9 percent, Whites at 60.9 percent and Blacks at 50.5 percent. With the ineligibles out the Hispanic rate climbs to 44.1 percent, whih represents a closing of more than two-thirds of the gap between Hispanic and Black voter participation. In other words, it is imperative to account for the effect of noncitizens when characterizing the voting behavior of Hispanic groups.

In addition to these factors, many factors which researchers have cited for lower Black voting turnout can also be cited for Hispanics. In the case of Hispanics, however, some additional variables besides history, discrimination, and education become relevant to patterns of voting behavior. The first is language difference. The Census Bureau (1980:64) reports that of the 15.3 million people who reported that they spoke another language, 7.6 million said it was Spanish. Of that number almost one-half (3.5 million) said they had difficulty speaking English. Language difficulties may well affect the chances of many of these people of becoming voters. Despite the sporadic availability of bilingual ballots and voter information materials, inability to understand the candidates and the issues in a broader context may negatively affect voter turnout in many Hispanic areas.

Second is the impact of culture on voting behavior. Many Hispanics have lived under very different social and political systems than those of the United States, and a good number have come here because of some political instability in their own countries. Although these factors must be placed in the situational context previously discussed, they nonetheless can be very important in their own right. Customs and traditions can cause political alienation, indifference, or even hostility to anything even remotely connected with government. If new immigrants experience discrimination and segmentation in the U.S. context, some of these feelings will only intensify over time. Even within the second and third generation there may still be some cultural effects on political behavior, partly due to the greater potential for contact with their country of origin of many Hispanics than for many previous immigrants. There is evidence that Mexicans have been relatively slow to naturalize (Pierce and Hagstron, 1979) and that Puerto Ricans, although they are eligible voters as soon as they arrive in the United States, report a similar affinity for following the affairs of the home-land (Jennings, 1977; Bonilla and Campos, 1981). There is evidence that cultural norms for voting affect people for several generations, even those whose parents were born in the United States (García, 1973). Although we ought not to make too much of the influence of culture on voting, it would be a mistake to ignore it altogether in favor of a purely situational and contextual explanation of behavioral differences.

Third is the effect of geographic concentration on Hispanic voting be-havior. Hispanics are predominantly urban, like many ethnic groups be-fore them, and new arrivals tend to live in barrios, the ethnic enclaves of large urban centers, especially those in the Southwest. However, due to the fact that the "progressive" movement of the early 1900s caught on in the Southwest before most of the Hispanic immigration, the benefits of strong party structures and urban machine politics were not available for the majority of Hispanic immigrants after 1910 (Moore, 1976). California, for example, rewrote its state constitution in 1908, led by reformist governor Hiram Johnson (McWilliams, 1949). The change in registration laws, two-party ballots, and other electoral changes brought on by the constitution effectively hampered party and urban machine politics, which in the East and Midwest had been one of the most important factors in mobilizing immigrant ethnic groups. Hispanics have not benefited from such arrange-ments. The ability of urban machines to mobilize political resources by doing favors and so on has been unmatched so far by any new governmen-tal structure. The machines realized the needs of immigrants such as food, adequate shelter, jobs, help with governmental bureaucracies, and so forth, and delivered help in return for political support. This arrangement, albeit less than "democratic" sometimes, was effective since it increased the im-migrant groups' ability to mobilize. Hispanics, for the most part, have not had such benefits.

Fourth is the effect of age on Hispanic voting. Hispanics are on the average younger than the general population, and since the young are less likely to vote, this will tend to reduce overall Hispanic voting and the impact of the total Hispanic vote. There is also some evidence to suggest that this relatively young population is more likely to be affected by recent events such as Vietnam and Watergate that have produced feelings of apa-thy, alienation, and withdrawal among youth in general (Abramowitz, 1980).

Many additional factors such as education, income, occupational status, and others will affect Hispanic turnouts, but it seems reasonable to believe that even when these are controlled, Hispanic voting rates will still be behind those of Whites and Blacks in this society for some time to come. The best data with which to examine the question of voter turnout in some detail is the Census Bureau's *Population Report on Voting and Registration.* Although it has weaknesses, it also has the advantage of being the most comprehensive source from which to gain a representative sample of the entire Hispanic population. The bureau surveys of 1976 and 1978 contain sufficient information to control for many of the variables that affect voting, and they provide the base for the bulk of this analysis.

Regarding overall turnout, there are definite differences between Whites, Blacks, and the "Spanish-origin" categories of the census. Hispanics tend to trail both Whites and Blacks by a considerable margin. For example, in 1976 the Hispanic turnout was 37.4 percent, the Black turnout was 52.1 percent, and the White turnout was 64.5 percent. Even taking into account the problem of ineligibility raised earlier, the rates are still very different from each other. Other data, such as those from the election studies at the University of Michigan, confirm these findings. The consistent order of turnout rates betweeen ethnic groups is clear: Hispanics, as a national aggregate, vote at lower rates than either Blacks or Whites.

The findings do not change very much when we control for sex, and it would be unlikely that they would. Hispanic men vote at a slightly higher rate than Hispanic women, and White men vote at a slightly higher rate than White women. Black women tend to vote at a slightly higher rate than Black men, which may be more a function of the distribution of the "head-of-household" category than anything else. Age also plays a role in these data, and one cannot help but notice that 18-24-year-old Hispanics have an especially low voting rate. For example, in 1976 their turnout rate was 11 percent, as compared to 20 percent for Blacks of the same age and 24 percent for Whites. It remains to be seen whether this will change as the cohort grows older, and there need to be some longitudinal studies to follow this process.

When we use a control for geographic context it appears that rural Hispanics vote at a higher rate than urban Hispanics, which does not appear to be the case for Blacks and Whites. In 1978, for example, there was a 6 percent difference in urban/rural Hispanic voting. Historically, much of the Hispanic political influence has come from the rural areas of the Southwest. César Chavez's farmworkers' union, seizing an issue which gained national attention, was formed in the rural areas of California (Steiner, 1970; Castro, 1974). Moore (1976) and McClesky and Merrill (1972) have documented the case of a small Texas town, Crystal City, whose administration was defeated by a third-party Chicano vote called "La Raza Unida" (the united race), and other studies have shown that rural Mexicans in Nebraska were more likely to feel competent at the national level than were urban Hispanics in the same region (Welch et al., 1973). If this is the case, it may be argued that an increase in feelings of competence and efficacy among rural Hispanics may manifest itself in a large national election voter turnout sometime in the not too distant future. This seems contradictory to the conventional wisdom about differences between urban and rural rates of turnout and participation for the country as a whole, but there is evidence from other studies of negative association between urban living and political activity (Nie et al., 1969) which seems also to be the case for rural Hispanics.

One of the contentions of political scientists over the years has been that as educational levels rise so do rates of voting and turnout. To some (Wolfinger and Rosenstone, 1980), education has a great influence in turnout predictability. If we examine the data concerning those who dropped out of high school as compared to those with some college experience, the effects of education differ for the different groups. In 1976 among Whites who did not finish high school the turnout was 48 percent, while for those who had at least some college it was 70 percent. For Blacks the figures for the same period were 43 and 57 percent, and for Hispanics they were 30 and 44 percent. The fact of having had some college was more important to Whites than to either Blacks or Hispanics, probably because of the effects of other variables for those two groups that do not affect the White difference. Also, given the greater number of Black and Hispanic high-school dropouts, it is likely that the overall impact of education on voting is larger for these groups than for Whites as a whole.

Educational levels among Hispanics are rising: for example, there is a larger proportion of high-school graduates among Hispanics 20 to 24 years old (61 percent), than among those 25 years old and older (41 percent). Additionally, studies have shown that some Hispanics, Mexican-Americans for example, receive different educational and political socialization in school than their non-Hispanic counterparts (C. García, 1973; Moore, 1976; Felice, 1973). Among these influences are higher reported rates of discrimination for those children who consider themselves most "Mexican" in language and culture. Another related finding is that Mexican-American youngsters demonstrate a high degree of affect toward the national (U.S.) community, but as their perceptions change with age, C. García notes, disillusionment seems to occur at a rather rapid rate, especially for those of the lower class. Considerably more research needs to be done on the effects of schooling on voter perceptions within the Hispanic community. Blacks who have completed four years of college have a voting rate of 75 percent as compared to Whites of the same status, who have a rate of 80 percent, while Hispanics who have completed four years of college have a rate of 54 percent. The traditional improvement in participation that has been associated with higher educational levels does not seem to work as directly with Hispanics as it does with some of the other groups.

Hispanics have also tended to vote at lower rates across income categories than have Blacks or Whites. In 1978 Whites with incomes over $25,000 had a turnout rate of 61 percent, Blacks in the same group had a rate of 57 percent, and Hispanics making $25,000 or more had a rate of 42 percent. While income does explain some of the differences in voting turnout within each group, it does not explain very much across the groups. For example in 1978, 26 percent of Hispanics who made between $10,000 and $15,000 voted, while 42 percent of those who made more than $25,000 did so. Rising income clearly made a difference within the Hispanic group in terms of voter turnout. However, the differences between Blacks, Whites and Hispanics still remain relatively unchanged by controlling for group incomes.

The differences between Hispanic white-collar workers and the Black and White groups of similar status are also substantial, as one would expect given the effects of income and education already mentioned. White-collar Hispanics reported voting at a rate of 36 percent while Blacks were at 50 percent and Whites at 56. It appears that regardless of which socioeconomic context Hispanics may be in, they do vote less often than Blacks and Whites in similar contexts, when studied at the aggregate level.

Research Priorities and Political Mobilization

These two topics have been combined because they are closely related. While there has been much greater growth within the Hispanic population than in the general U.S. population during the past decade—something on the order of 60 percent as against 9 percent—the Hispanic population is still highly concentrated in a few regions, a fact which has considerable implications for political strategy. More than 60 percent of the U.S. Hispanic population resides in California, New York, and Texas and within those states the majority of the Hispanic population is found in a few congressional districts. Approximately 50 percent of California's Hispanic total are in 13 congressional districts; 50 percent of New York's Hispanics are in 7; and half of Texas's Hispanics are in 5. This concentration of population has implications for how research needs to be done and for the techniques of political mobilization. Resources must be carefully targeted in order to be effective.

Political power is not only the actual power of votes at the polls, but the power a group collects to itself when others perceive them as powerful. Gerald Lamberty (1978:18) observed:

Many Anglo politicians have concluded that it is not worth more than a perfunctory effect to try to gain their [Hispanics'] support. Saul Alinsky's rule that effective political power is not only that which you actually have but also that which the other guy thinks you have, actually works against the Latinos because most believe they have less clout than they actually possess. The Latino's political image is so negative now that a good deal of the anticipated future increase in their power will come from getting Anglos to stop underestimating their current strength.

There are nearly 3 million registered Hispanic voters in the country now, and conservative projections are that there will be another 4 million added during the 1980s. The actual power and the perceived power of Hispanics needs to be documented and explored in such a manner as to not only understand its workings but also to make it visible to those who now feel it can be ignored.

The single most important research priority may well be the creation of a comprehensive data base of the Hispanic population which can be used to do quality political research comparable to the best done anywhere. Data from the census block-level tapes and voter registration data need to be combined so that effective voter registration may be undertaken. This data base would not have the liability of postelection survey data, which appear to be considerably more error-prone for Hispanics than for the general population. Hispanics on surveys tend to overrepresent their registration, voting, and to some extent the candidate they voted for, according to some preliminary research (Velásquez, 1982).

Such a data base would also help settle the question as to the current turnout picture. Some analysts feel that within the last few years the historically low turnout among Hispanics has begun to change quickly. It is impossible to tell whether this is happening without better data than we presently have. Once an aggregate data base is in place we should turn our attention to the kinds of questions we need to begin to ask in polls and surveys. These data will begin to provide the understanding of political processes and relevant issues within the Hispanic communities and would be invaluable to Hispanic political strategists.

Summary and Conclusion

Hispanics in the aggregate have voted less often than Blacks or Whites even when controlling for various socioeconomic status variables in the elections of 1976 and 1978. Those for which we have comprehensive data from the Southwest tend to confirm these findings. It seems reasonable to infer that group affiliation remains a significant factor in the consistently low voter rates among Hispanics. How significant a factor remains a question, but there should be further study to determine why these differences persist.

It may be that culture plays a large role in Hispanic voter turnout. Language, citizenship, and political socialization differences between Hispanics and Whites may have the effect of lowering overall voter turnout. The relative youth of Hispanics is also a factor that depresses aggregate voting rates. In addition, one of the most important variables that must be addressed is the question of citizenship. For example, in the 1978 Census Bureau studies, 5,197 out of 6,788 Hispanic respondents said they did not vote. Of those 5,197 nonvoters, 2,137 (41 percent) responded that they were not U.S. citizens. We can only speculate as to why Hispanics do not become citizens and become eligible to vote. Many Hispanics may not want to become citizens, and even if they did, they may find the procedures to do so very cumbersome and restrictive. Accordingly, the present political status of Hispanics nationwide is not very strong in relationship to their numbers.

The attention Hispanics have received nationally is due to the fact that when they vote as a consistent bloc, they can be the balance of power in several key Southwestern states. The Hispanic population may have been the "swing" vote for John Kennedy in Texas in the 1960 election, when over 94 percent of Hispanics voted for him in a narrow victory over Richard Nixon (Levy and Kramer, 1973:77).

The low voting rates of Hispanics have also been evident in their lack of representation in Congress. Low voting rates have something to do with this as well as a relative scarcity of Hispanic candidates, even in heavily Hispanic-populated Congressional districts and states.

Hispanics are also underrepresented in legislative bodies at the state and local level. In California, for example, Hispanics constitute roughly 17 percent of the population, yet they hold only six out of the 120 seats in the state legislature. Locally, this political underrepresentation is also evident in some areas of the Southwest. In Los Angeles County, where Hispanics are 29 percent of the entire population, there were no Hispanics on the City Council as of 1981, and none on the county's Board of Education; this is an area where Hispanic children constitute 52 percent of the city's school enrollment.

Some have attributed Hispanics' low rate of political representation to "gerrymandering" by local officials who, they argue, set up districts on a partisan level favoring the incumbent party. While it may be true that gerrymandering has occured in many parts of California and other parts of the Southwest, it is not the main reason for Hispanic underrepresentation. The "Snyder Syndrome" may be a better example of what goes on in predominantly Hispanic political districts. The "syndrome," as described by Frank del Olmo, a political writer for the *Los Angeles Times*, is an interesting case study in Hispanic politics.

Arthur Snyder was the white citycouncilman of the predominantly (around 80 percent) Hispanic district in East Los Angeles in 1981. His district sprawls from the East Side barrios northward through some of the lower-middle-class areas of Highland Park and Eagle Rock. For twelve years Hispanic politicians failed to oust Snyder. They failed for some very practical reasons often overlooked by Hispanic politicians and the media alike.

One reason was that Snyder had proven to be an effective councilman. He made sure that potholes and broken streetlights were repaired. He attended community functions, and spoke Spanish sufficiently well to be an effective communicator. Snyder gained just enough support from a sizable portion of the Hispanic vote, then received large voter turnouts from the ethnically mixed, middle-class precincts of Eagle Rock and Highland Park to remain in office. For twelve years his method worked despite regular attempts to unseat him.

In terms of bloc voting, several authors have commented on the lack of ethnic bloc voting for Hispanic candidates by the Hispanic population (Levy and Kramer, 1973; de la Garza, 1977). Ethnicity, in their opinion, was important, but not the overriding concern of Hispanic voters in electing officials. It appears that among the Hispanics who do consistently vote, variables other than ethnicity affect voting choice. In Snyder's case, people probably felt he was doing his job well enough that he should remain in office or, looking at it another way, not enough voters in his district felt he had done his job badly enough to warrant his replacement by another (presumably Hispanic) candidate.

In some areas, however, Hispanics have had greater political influence than in California. In New Mexico, for example, Hispanics have traditionally held political office proportionately to their percentage of the population. New Mexico's Hispanics have traditionally had greater numbers of state representatives in state and local politics than is true for California and other parts of the Southwest. For example, the only Hispanic U.S. senator in recent years, Joseph Montoya, was from New Mexico.

Some have attributed this to greater wealth and a long-standing alliance with whites in New Mexico by Hispanics (Castro, 1974). If this is true, coalition politics with other non-Hispanic groups would be the most effective political strategy for Hispanics given their voting numbers, even if it does not mean the election of a Hispanic candidate at every election.

The recent victory of Henry Cisneros in San Antonio, Texas—the first Hispanic big-city mayor—is an example of coalition politics. According to published reports, Cisneros fashioned a coalition of white businessmen and Hispanics to gain his victory—despite the fact that 52 percent of the city's population is reported by the Census Bureau to be Hispanic (*Chicago Tribune*, 8 April, 1981).

Given this data, it would appear that the future of Hispanic politics is brighter than its past. With large, growing numbers of potential voters, the ethnic factor can be a mobilizing force to elect qualified Hispanic candidates; it will not happen overnight however, and probably will be gradual. As more Hispanics become eligible to vote they will become a great force in regional and national politics. Maybe then the ethnic factor will decrease and other more traditional turnout variables (ideology, party identification, income) will become more relevant. However, the ethnic factor is still a strong one in measuring Hispanic turnout.

Several institutions have made the effort to tap Hispanic culture and translate it into votes. The Catholic Church, a strong symbolic force in Hispanic culture, has only recently begun to try and politically mobilize Hispanics, while the weak party structure of California has long since stopped trying. The UNO (United Neighborhoods Organization), a church-sponsored, citywide association in Los Angeles, has initiated several voter registration drives in the barrios of East Los Angeles in an effort to increase the Hispanic vote. While their efforts at registering voters have been minimally successful, their unconventional political methods—such as staging highly publicized townhall meetings where public officials are invited to hear citizen grievances—have been gaining widespread attention by the media. More importantly however, UNO's efforts show a dramatic shift in direction by the once conservative-dominated Catholic Church (McNamara, 1972).

Efforts by the church and other institutions to increase Hispanic political representation will be far more successful when larger numbers of Hispanics begin to vote. The potential is there, the ethnic factor will remain a large influence on Hispanics in politics for years to come. Ethnic awareness will serve a functional force in the emergence of Hispanics as a strong, viable political force within the existing American political system.

In conclusion, it seems clear that Hispanics as a group have not achieved political equality partly because of their relatively low voting rates. Other related variables include traditional socioeconomic variables as well as the ethnic group's relative youth. Our argument here is that the ethnic factor remains strong for Hispanics. Hispanics have not become acculturated to many of the political norms—especially voting—in enough numbers to have an overall impact relative to their numbers. Many Hispanics, especially new arrivals and first-generation Americans, remain political outcasts, at least to the extent that they do not vote in substantial numbers. With more Hispanics climbing the socioeconomic ladder and dispersing throughout the country, their impact will grow. How much, only time will tell. The ethnic factor, however, will continue to play a large part for Hispanics and the American political system for years to come.

Public Policy Issues

Because of the pragmatic nature of politics, all political issues are in some way public policy issues. We will suggest two sets of issues to be considered within the political framework outline in this chapter: those issues specific to Hispanics, and those which link the Hispanic population to other immigrant groups. Immigrants have historically found themselves in a conflictive position on the issue of political participation. They have either been considered incapable of understanding the democratic process, thereby making their participation undesirable; or they have been thought of as potential corrupters of the process due to their skewing of elections by bloc voting, which also made their participation less than desirable to those in power. The first set of issues involves research questions which need to be answered for Hispanics before their participation can progress to the next stage.

What are the Hispanic voter registration rates in areas where they comprise more than 10 percent of the total population? These data are needed in order for effective registration drives to be mounted and completed.

What are the reliable sources of political information within the various Hispanic communities? All minority groups suffer from the "spokesperson problem." How should credibility be assessed by the larger political community? It is essential that the relevant actors in the public policy debates concerning Hispanics be credible and supported by the population they represent.

What are the voter turnout rates for Hispanic communities and how have they changed from election to election? These data need to be gathered and analyzed, but primarily disseminated, so that the people working in the communities themselves can be better informed as to the situation. In the absence of this information there is a tendency to make decisions on the basis of the conventional wisdom or stereotypes about a group.

How do various Hispanic groups and communities identify themselves by party? Solid data is needed about the changing party identification among the larger Hispanic groups, especially Puerto Ricans and Mexicans, if they are to be effectively represented regarding public policy development.

Which are the "brokerage" institutions within the Hispanic communities that are trusted and influence public opinions and choices? The roles of social service agencies, private small businesses, and churches need to be more fully understood in terms of their mediating function in the development of choices within Hispanic communities.

What are the principal local and national issues which involve Hispanics and which are most salient to them? A sharing of the issues across the various Hispanic communities would result in an increased understanding of their main concerns.

Recent discussions of the immigrant political process (Lieberson, 1980) have observed that most groups experience a lagtime during which their political power catches up to their numbers in the population. In other words, there is an unknown amount of time required to translate people into regular voters. There is no instant correspondence between population strength of a specific group and its ability to successfully run political candidates. The two reasons most often cited for this are that immigrant groups generally have little money and poor local organizations.

The second set of policy issues concerns correcting the perception of Hispanics as uninterested in political affairs or participation. By placing Hispanics in a context of other immigrant groups and articulating the position that there is a commonality of history between them, it may be possible to reduce the lagtime for contemporary Hispanics and their political participation.

Another contextual issue has to do with the role of the urban political "machines" and the way in which they politically socialized earlier immigrant populations. Although the machines no longer exist in the same form, there are lessons about forming local organizations and effectively using a group's vote that can be learned from those experiences. However, if there is no effort to point out the commonality between immigrant groups' experiences, it is unlikely that such lessons will be learned, and valuable organizing skills and principles will be wasted.

The central policy issue for Hispanics in a political sense is the issue of participation. Information needs to be gathered and disseminated in order for the lagtime to be reduced and for groups to begin to exert influence more in accord with their numbers. Ours is a political system which stresses representation based on levels of participation. An increase in the participation level of the Hispanic population is a vitally important element in all the other policy issues mentioned in this book.

References

Abramowitz, Alan I. 1980. "The United States: Political Culture under Stress." In *The Civic Culture Revisited*, ed. C. Almond and S. Verba. Boston: Little, Brown.

Almond, Gabriel, and Sidney Verba. 1963. *The Civic Culture*. Boston: Little, Brown.

Antunes, George, and Charles M. Gaitz. 1975. "Ethnicity and Participation: A Study of Mexican-Americans, Blacks, and Whites." *American Journal of Sociology* 80: 1192-1221.

Bonilla, Frank, and Ricardo Campos. 1981. "A Wealth of Poor: Puerto Ricans in the New Economic Order." *Daedalus* 110:103-31.

Castro, Tony. 1974. *Chicano Power: The Emergence of Mexican America*. New York: Saturday Review Press.

Chicago Tribune. 8 April 1981, part 2, p. 3.

Cornelius, Wayne A. 1981. "Mexican Migration to the United States." In Susan K. Purcell, ed., *Mexican-United States Relations*. Academy of Political Science 34:67-77.

Cornwell, Elmer E. 1968. "Bosses, Machines and Ethnic Groups." In *American Ethnic Politics*, ed. Lawrence H. Fuchs. New York: Harper Row.

de la Garza, Rudolph. 1977. "Mexican-American Voters: A Responsible Electorate." In *Graduate Studies Texas Technical University* 14:63-76, ed. Frank L. Baird.

del Olmo, Frank. 1981a. *Los Angeles Times*. 19 January 1981.

_____. 1981b. *Los Angeles Times*. 21 May, 1981.

Dinnerstein, Leonard, and David M. Reimers. 1975. *A History of Immigration and Assimilation*. New York: Dodd, Mead.

Estrada, Leobardo F., Chris García, Reynaldo Macías, and Lionel Maldonado. 1981. "Chicanos in the United States: A History of Exploitation and Resistance." *Daedalus* 110:151-76.

Falcón, Angelo. 1980. "Puerto Rican Political Participation: New York City and Puerto Rico." A revised version of a paper presented to the 1980 Annual Meeting of the American Political Science Association, Washington (August).

Felice, Lawrence G. 1973. "Mexican-American Self-Concept and Educational Achievement: The Effects of Ethnic Isolation and Socio-Economic Deprivation." *Social Science Quarterly* 53:716-26.

García, F. Chris. 1973. *Political Socialization of Chicano Children: A Comparative Study with Anglos in California Schools*. New York: Praeger.

García, F. Chris, and Rudolph O. de la Garza. 1977. *The Chicano Political Experience*. North Scituate, Mass.: Duxbury.

García, John. 1980. "Politcal Integration of Mexican Immigrants: Explorations into the Naturalization Process." Paper presented at the Annual Meeting of the American Political Science Association, Washington.

General Social Survey. 1983. The Roper Center, Office of Archival Development and User Services. Box U-164R. Storrs: University of Connecticut. (Cumulative Codebook: ISBN 0-932132-28-6.)

Gersham, Carl. 1980. "Race vs. Class." *New York Times Magazine*.

Glazer, Nathan, and Daniel P. Moynihan. 1970. *Beyong the Melting Pot*. Cambridge: Harvard University Press.

Graeber, Lillian. 1938. *A Study of Attendance at Thomas Jefferson High School, Los Angeles, California*. Master's thesis, University of Southern California.

Greeley, Andrew. 1971. *Why Can't They Be Like Us*. New York: Institute of Human Relations.

Greeley, Andrew, and William C. McCready. 1974. *Ethnicity in the United States*. New York : Wiley.

Handlin, Oscar. 1959a. *Immigration as a Factor in American History*. Englewood Cliffs, N.J.: Prentice-Hall.

———. 1959b. *The Newcomers*. Cambridge: Harvard University Press.

Jennings, James. 1977. *Puerto Rican Politics in New York City*. Washington: University Press of America.

Lamberty, Gerald. 1978. "The Growing Political Strength of America's Latinos: A Case Study." 20th Sess., Executive Seminar in National and International Affairs, U.S. Department of State (mimeo).

Levy, Mark R., and Michael S. Kramer. 1973. *The Ethnic Factor*. New York: Simon Schuster.

McClesky, Clifton, and Bruce Merrill. 1973. "Mexican-American Political Behavior in Texas." *Social Science Quarterly* 53:785-98.

McNamara, Patrick H. 1972. "Catholicism, Assimilation, and the Chicano Movement: Los Angeles as a Case Study." In *Chicanos and Native Americans*, ed. R. de La Garza, Z. W. Kruszewski, and T. Arciniega, Englewood Cliffs, N.J.: Prentice-Hall.

McWilliams, Carey. 1949. *North from Mexico*. Philadelphia: Lippincott.

Milbrath, Lester W., and M. L. Goel. 1977. *Political Participation*. Chicago: Rand McNally.

Moore, Joan W. 1981. "Minorities in the American Class System." *Daedalus* 110:275-97.

Nie, Norman H., G. Bingham Powell, Jr., and Kenneth Prewitt. 1969. "Social Structure and Political Participation: Developmental Relationships, Part I." *American Political Science Review* 63:361-78.

Nie, Norman, Sidney Verba, and John R. Petrocik. 1976. *The Changing American Voter*. Cambridge: Harvard University Press.

Novak, Michael. 1972. *The Rise of the Unmeltable Ethnics*. New York: Macmillan.

Olsen, Marvin E. 1970. "Social and Political Participation of Blacks." *American Sociological Review* 35:682-97.

Pachon, Harry. 1976. "Politics in the Mexican American Community." In *Mexican Americans*, 2nd ed., ed. Joan Moore with Harry Pachon. Englewood Cliffs, N.J.: Prentice-Hall.

Pettigrew, Thomas F. 1981. "Race and Class in the 1980s: An Interactive View." *Daedalus* 110:233-53.

Pierce, Neal R., and Jerry Hagstron. 1979. "The Hispanic Community: A Growing Force to Be Reckoned with." *National Journal* (April 7):548-55.

Steiner, Stan. 1970. *La Raza: The Mexican Americans*. New York: Harper & Row.

U.S. Bureau of the Census. 1980b. *Advanced Report*, p. 25, no. 929. Washington: U.S. Government Printing Office.

U.S. Department of Commerce. 1974. "Population Profile of the United States." *Current Population Reports*, series P-20, no. 322.

_____. 1978a. "Voting and Registration in the Election of November 1974." *Current Population Reports*, series P-20, no. 293.

_____. 1978b. "Voting and Registration in the Election of November 1976." *Current Population Reports*, series P-20, no. 322.

_____. 1979. "Voting and Registration in the Election of November 1978." *Current Population Reports*, series P-20, no. 344.

_____. 1980. "Persons of Spanish Origin in the United States: March 1979." *Current Population Reports*, series P-20, no. 354.

_____. 1981. *Statistical Abstract of the United States, 1980.*

Verba, Sidney, and Norman Nie. 1972. *Participation in America: Political Democracy and Social Equality.* New York: Harper & Row.

Walker, Helen. 1929. "Mexican Immigrants and American Citizenship." *Sociology and Social Research* (May-June):465-71.

Welch, Susan, John Comer, and Michael Steinman. 1973. "Political Participation among Mexican-Americans: An Exploratory Examination." *Social Science Quarterly* 53 (March):799-813.

Wilson, James Q. 1960. *Negro Politics.* New York: Free Press.

Wilson, William J. 1980. *The Declining Significance of Race.* Chicago: University of Chicago Press.

Wolfinger, Raymond E., and Steven Rosenstone. 1980. *Who Votes?* New Haven: Yale University Press.

Conclusion

Pastora San Juan Cafferty and *William C. McCready*

One of the central themes of this book has been the diversity that exists among groups of people we refer to as "Hispanic" in the United States. They come from different cultures and places and have different social histories within both their country of origin and their new home. Some come here to stay, some come and return several times, some do not know what their future holds, only that it ought to be brighter than their past. In this way, these new immigrants are no different than the millions who have preceded them to this country.

Many of the authors in this volume have pointed out that this diversity has influenced the way in which people are perceived and treated by the larger society. Policies are created for Hispanics which help some and harm others because there are, in one sense, no "generic" Hispanics. It would be as though the country, in the early part of this century, had tried to create a policy to deal with the new "Euro-ethnics" without realizing that there were differences among the groups that were greater and of more significance than the differences between the groups and the host society. It is likely that such a policy would have done more harm than good.

One of the questions that comes to mind when we consider the historical point of view is why our society is now so concerned with creating policies which respond to the needs of various immigrant groups and why the concern for policy is so great with regard to Hispanics. One possible, though untestable reason, might be that we are now a nation of immigrants and, social cynicism to the contrary, we may have learned something. Perhaps those who have their roots in the immigrant experience are just a bit more likely to understand that certain assistances are appropriate for those who come to a new land.

Another, more documentable, answer is also possible, and that is that there is now in place a large public and a publicly funded bureaucracy, which has as its task supplying social services and aid to those in need. When immigrants arrived here in the early part of this century there was no public consensus that they should be helped. Private agencies, individuals, and community groups and organizations were available or were started to serve the needs of the immigrants. Churches and settlement houses took on the responsibility and developed programs that helped immigrants acclimate to their new surroundings, find jobs, gain an education, and make their way in this society.

The consensus changed and developed during the pre- and post-Depression era until it was generally accepted that it was appropriate for the government to step in and provide services and funds to those who were unable to care for themselves. This was begun as a stop-gap measure and was based on the idea that eventually the people who were so helped would be able to support themselves and begin their own independent contribution to society.

Now the public consensus, albeit somewhat shaky, is still that it is appropriate to use public funds to aid those in need, including newcomers to the country, and this has cast the national government as the arbiter of such aid. If there is one type of problem that has been most difficult for a large centralized bureaucracy to respond to, it is a problem involving diversity of culture and the need to tailor policy to individual, small communities. The theme of many of the chapters in this book is exactly that—that "Hispanics" is much too generic a term for policymakers and that much greater information and insight must be generated in order to enable our contemporary system to make intelligent and productive responses to the needs of these citizens and newcomers to the country.

Another theme that appears in several places is the critical role played by education in the process of economic assimilation and cultural adaptation. The school system is the one central agency that offers the opportunity to learn the skills required for a stable economic life in the society. Enabling young people of Hispanic heritage to stay in school and to learn is one of the challenges facing us in the present situation. Once through school, they appear to do as well as if not better than their contemporaries, but the obstacles to staying in a program appear to be formidable.

Some may ask, "How is this different from the situation that faced the Euro-ethnic immigrants in the early 1900s?" Two things have changed dramatically since that time. First, the school system was more equipped to teach what was useful to the immigrants of that time, and second, the Euro-ethnic immigrants were not trying to compete in an information-communication based economy that values articulation and reasoning powers rather than muscle and physical labor.

In the earlier part of our century schools concentrated on teaching basic skills, including English, which enabled the students to know enough to be able to get jobs in manufacturing and heavy industry, where their work education was completed on the job. They learned what they needed to know by working with others and emulating them.

Today, emulation of the articulation and communication processes required to function in our language-oriented economy is not as simple a task. The population with which the newcomer is competing is much farther ahead of them today than it was eighty years ago. The perceived gap may well work to the detriment of ambition by being too great a gap to cross. If students see entry into a profession as a goal, but recognize a great distance between where they are and where they may wish to be, ambition may suffer. Part of the role of education is to show students what is possible in their lives. For all too many students today, education simply shows them what is irrelevant and unreachable.

What is the future likely to bring for the diversity of groups living on this North American continent? As mobility and information technology become more prevalent, is it not likely that we will see the emergence of a North American culture? The Hispanic influence on the United States has been in process for some time and will most likely keep growing. The influence of the United States on Canada has also been increasing. Canadian natural resources have yet to be developed and the same may be true for those in Mexico. One of the scenarios for the future brings together the capabilities of all the various groups on the continent and blends them into a new macro-society. One of the greatest obstacles facing this sort of communal effort, however, is the polarization of groups that will be the result of the continuation of vastly unequal statuses. As long as the gaps between groups increase rather than decrease, development and prosperity for all are endangered.

Several policy themes emerge from reading the various contributions to this volume. First, there are many calls for more and better research concerning the needs and strengths of Hispanics and Hispanic communities. Much of this needs to be done by professionals with roots in those communities who are trained in the methods of social, political, and economic research. Additionally, more attention needs to be paid to the Hispanic potential in existing research projects.

Second, there needs to be developed and nurtured a Hispanic point of view with regard to the development of social policies. The future of this society is going to involve many more and varied Hispanic people than we ever dreamed in the past. They are citizens and they are going to become citizens, and policies must always keep their cultural diversity in mind. This may mean decentralizing many policies. It may mean additional technical assistance to community groups so that they can do their own information gathering and analysis. It may mean the development of multidisciplinary research and training centers for dealing with complex social and economic issues. It will probably mean devoting much more of our resources to the schools in our society, which is rapidly becoming a major agenda item for all groups. *Resources* in this case means much more than funding. The creation of human capital by those groups that are now without it would seem to be both necessary and very complicated. Yet it seems that accomplishing that would be the best legacy this generation could leave for those that follow it.

Third, social policies should be able to plan for cultural changes and diversity. This is not the same as planning the direction of change. By planning for change we mean creating flexible plans that can take into account the changes that cultures bring to a society. This entails creating policies that do not constrain every group to be the same, but which combine the need for standardization with the need to preserve the autonomy and individuality of the diverse groups themselves. For example, it is clear that in treating alcohol problems, the methods used by non-Hispanic agencies have not worked very well for Hispanics who come for treatment. On the other hand, Hispanic agencies, most of which employ staff trained in non-Hispanic centers, have been having a great deal of success in helping people overcome problems. This is most likely not just a matter of language or "like-to-like" treatment. There is an understanding of how to work within the culture that exists within the Hispanic agencies that makes the skills learned from the more general treatment model applicable and useful in this specific setting. A great deal of planning for cultural change can be done simply by incorporating Hispanics into the development and decision-making aspects of policy formulation.

Finally, much of this book speaks to our learning to ask the right questions. By this we mean learning to be aware, in the creation of social policies, that we need to think about the way we frame questions and how that tends to guide the way we derive answers. For example, take the issue of whether a Hispanic baby should be adopted out to a non-Hispanic family. The question has often been framed in terms of the dichotomy between having the child reared in a compatible cultural setting, but possibly one that is disadvantaged, or having the child reared with advantages, but with no cultural support. Why not spend some resources to encourage advantaged Hispanic families to adopt Hispanic children. Why not have some programs and informal networks whereby non-Hispanic families could learn the language and something of the culture so they could provide the cultural supports necessary to enable the child to develop roots and wings? (Perhaps they could form a "twining" relationship with some Hispanic families as part of their commitment to raise the child in a culturally compatible manner). Perhaps there are other ways in which the question could be framed, but the point is that in creating policies, all such ways of framing a question ought to be explored.

The overall theme we have tried to suggest is that the policy discussions of how to respond to the needs and strengths of the rapidly increasing Hispanic portion of our citizenry need to be expanded and opened up beyond those issues which have been relevant up until now. If we are to have growth rather than confrontation between groups, we need to develop policies which combine the strengths of the various peoples of our country, rather than separate them. We need to be able not only to account for Hispanic diversity in policy formulation but also to use it, support it, and enable it to combine with the other kinds of cultural diversities which have contributed to the richness of our society. We hope that this book has been part of a beginning toward such conversations.